'Think of children and the Second World War, and evacuation comes immediately to mind. Berry Mayall and Virginia Morrow have a different story to tell, one in which all the children of the nation were encouraged to contribute to the war effort. Many responded enthusiastically. Evidence from school magazines and oral testimony shows children digging for victory, working on farms, knitting comforts for the troops, collecting waste for recycling, running households. What lessons, the authors ask, does this wartime participation by children have for our own time? The answers are challenging.'

Hugh Cunningham, Emeritus Professor of Social History at the University of Kent and author of *The Invention of Childhood*

'Hitherto, the dominant image of British children in wartime has been that of the evacuee, now something of a historical cliché, and about whom there are numerous studies of variable quality. This informative, imaginative and sociologically aware study of children's work, however, presents an alternative and more challenging set of images. Mayall and Morrow have performed an enormous service, not only in broadening our perspective of children to include their economic and social contributions to the war effort, showing them to be, in many respects, participatory agents, but also in exploring both the nature of "childhood" and the ambiguity surrounding adult–child relations at a time of national crisis (and beyond). Where the evacuee was confined to a specific social (children's) space, the child worker, in vacating the classroom, implicitly frequents "adulthood". In raising questions about the nature of children/childhood, this is a timely, relevant and accessibly written book, and is an ideal text for students in education, history and sociology.'

Professor Harry Hendrick, Associate Fellow, University of Warwick

'The work of children during wartime and the service to the community that some of them gave, on both an organised and *ad hoc* basis, is an important part of the social history of the time which has often been overlooked. This book is therefore unique within the area of war-child studies in that it covers, in depth, a topic that is usually commented on, at best, in a superficial way and often lost within the overarching and perhaps more emotive topic of evacuation. As the authors admit, the book should only be seen as the tip of a very large iceberg, but what it will do is hopefully ignite an interest in other researchers, in both war-child and childhood studies, who wish to pursue the plethora of other tangential and complementary areas. I will certainly add it to my student reading list.'

Dr Martin Parsons, Director of the Research Centre for Evacuee and War Child Studies, University of Reading, UK

D1089475

'As the historiography of childhood turns decisively to an examination of children's experiences and definitions of "the child" since World War Two, Berry Mayall and Virginia Morrow have given us an astute, exhaustively researched book that establishes the "starting line" for work on post-war childhood in Western societies. The resonance of the issues they explore – children's work in all its forms, the role of schooling, the juxtaposition of parental authority with that of the state, and the decline of the household economy in the industrial era – will have a familiar ring to historians on both sides of the Atlantic. And importantly it comes at a time when the field itself is increasingly concerned with the similarities and differences that have characterized growing up in a global context during the second half of the twentieth century.'

Professor Stephen Lassonde, author of _Learning to Forget: Schooling and family life in working-class New Haven, 1870–1940_ (Yale, 2005), and Deputy Dean of the College, Brown University, USA

'In this book, Mayall and Morrow have collaborated to continue their already individually substantive contributions to childhood studies. They vividly show how history, derived from English children's accounts of their contributions to war-work during the years of the Second World War, can inform current rethinking on what children's lives have been and can be about. Their discussion has resonance beyond the specific example of England during a certain time in history. The links drawn between work and schooling in the war years have relevance for contemporary policy debates on the nexus between schooling and child work/labour, in both Western and Eastern countries and on issues of children as participants and citizens, able to make valuable contributions to their communities.'

Jan Mason, Emeritus Professor, Social Justice and Social Change Research Group, University of Western Sydney, Australia

'Another major contribution to the sociology of childhood by two pioneers in the field. Drawing from a rich variety of previously untapped resources, including children's own accounts of their lives during the Second World War, Mayall and Morrow document the extensive labour and other contributions to the war effort made by English children. Though focusing on a particular period of crisis, when traditional views about children were undermined by pressing national needs, comparisons with earlier and later periods show that the debate on children's place in society is a continuing one, pitting those who view children as passive recipients of education and adult protection against those who would accord them greater autonomy and agency. The authors also identify social, economic and political considerations that have shaped definitions of childhood and child–adult relations. _You Can Help Your Country_ makes a strong case for enabling children to speak for themselves, and to participate more fully in socially useful activities.'

Sarane Spence Boocock, Emeritus Professor of Sociology, Rutgers University, USA Co-author, _Kids in Context: The sociological study of children and childhoods_ (Rowman & Littlefield, 2006); co-editor, _Minorities and Education in Multicultural Japan: An interactive perspective_ (Routledge, 2011)

You Can Help Your Country

You Can Help Your Country

English children's work during the Second World War

Berry Mayall and Virginia Morrow

Institute of Education, University of London

First published in 2011 by the Institute of Education,
University of London, 20 Bedford Way, London WC1H 0AL

www.ioe.ac.uk/publications

British Library Cataloguing in Publication Data:
A catalogue record for this publication is available from the British
Library

ISBN 978 0 85473 889 2

Typeset by Quadrant Infotech (India) Pvt Ltd
Printed by Cats Solutions

Contents

Illustrations

Chapter 6

Chapter 7

Chapter 8

Abbreviations

ACF	Army Cadet Force
ARP	Air Raid Precautions (Department)
ATC	Air Training Corps
BBC	British Broadcasting Corporation
CCSB	Central Council for School Broadcasting
CORB	Children's Overseas Reception Board
DES	Department for Education and Science
FBI	Federation of British Industries
GGA	Girl Guides Association
HMSO	Her Majesty's Stationery Office
IOE	Institute of Education, University of London
IQ	Intelligence Quotient
JTSs	junior technical schools
LEA	local education authority
MERL	Museum of English Rural Life, Reading University
NEF	New Education Fellowship
NUT	National Union of Teachers
PP	Parliamentary Papers
SCF	Save the Children Fund
SHCAC	Schoolboy Harvest Camps Advisory Committee
SLA	School-leaving age
TES	*Times Educational Supplement*
TUC	Trades Union Congress
UNCRC	United Nations Convention on the Rights of the Child

USSR	Union of Soviet Socialist Republics
VE Day	Victory in Europe Day
WAAF	Women's Auxiliary Air Force
WAEC	War Agricultural Executive Committee
WEA	Workers' Educational Association
WI	Women's Institute
WVS	Women's Voluntary Service
YAC	Youth Advisory Council

Acknowledgements

First and foremost, we thank the people who were children during the Second World War who we interviewed or who provided us with written accounts of their experiences (and those who introduced us to them): John and Audrey Balsdon (and Claire Cameron), Joan Barraclough, Joyce Bateman (and Anne Wright), Christine Bondi, John Chambers (who showed us numerous Scouts badges, photographed by Ella Towers), Frank Chappell (and Kathy Hilton), Colin Dibbs, Joy Ewer (and Teresa Ewer), Stella and Derek Fairbairn (and Sandy Oliver), Tony Giles (who sent us his privately published book *Not Evacuated*), June McMahon (and Katherine Tyler), Patrick Morrow, Tony Rees (and Rebecca Rees), Gillian Sjödahl, Teresa Letts (and Sheila Triggs), Hayley Davies for interviewing her grandmother (who wished to remain anonymous), Rose Pockney, Peter Rivière, Susan and Roger Sawtell (and Mary Sawtell) and Roy Lowe (and Angela Hobsbaum). We also drew on interviews carried out for an earlier study with grandmothers about three generations of childhoods (funded by the Nuffield Foundation) and we are grateful to them, and to Sue Sharpe and Abiola Ogunsola who interviewed them.

Secondly, we thank the following people: staff at the IOE – Jane Martin for reading our first draft and making innumerable helpful suggestions; our editors Jim Collins and Nicole Edmondson for their unfailing enthusiasm and support for the book, and especially Nicole for searching out and clearing copyright for photographs; Gary McCulloch and David Crook for helpful comments; and Institute of Education library staff. We also thank Cambridge University Library staff for their help; Museum of English Rural Life archivists and Oliver Douglas, Assistant Curator at MERL, who invited us to present a seminar at MERL in March 2009; archivists at the BBC Written Archive Collection at Reading; archivists who helped us locate material at the headquarters of youth organisations: Karen Shapley at the Guides Association (now known as Girlguiding UK), Pat Styles and Daniel Scott-Davies at the Scouts, and Emily Oldfield at the British Red Cross.

We thank Mrs C. Brown, for the loan of her marvellous collection of wartime children's fiction, and Min Cornelius at the Bletchley Park 'Toys and Memorabilia Collection', for sending us a newscutting about conkers and their uses during the First World War.

We are grateful to Louis Mayall, who nobly formatted the reference lists according to IOE conventions and cross-checked references in the text against the reference lists; anonymous reviewers of our book proposal for their many helpful suggestions; audiences at conferences and seminar presentations; and Professor Moore-Colyer for early encouragement.

We thank Anne-Marie Markström, Maria Simonson, Ingird Söderlind and Eva Änggärd, editors of a book compiled for Gunilla Halldèn's retirement, who kindly included our early chapter: Mayall, B. and Morrow, V. (2009) 'Children's contributions to the war effort (1939–45)'. In *Barn, Barndom och föräldrarsskap*. Stockholm: Carlssons Bokforlag.

We have thus received help from many people, but all the errors and omissions are our own.

The authors and publisher gratefully acknowledge the permission granted to reproduce copyright material in this book:

The image of a feeding clock, originally published in Truby King, F. (1913) *Feeding and Care of Baby* (Wellington, NZ: Plunket), p. 74, was reproduced by kind permission of the Royal New Zealand Plunket Society Inc.

The image of Eglantyne Jebb was graciously provided by Save the Children UK.

The images of Sir Percy Nunn and a 1930s classroom were graciously provided by the Library and Archives at the IOE.

The image of Sir Fred Clarke, which also appeared in Aldrich, R. (2002) *The Institute of Education 1902–2002: A centenary history* (Institute of Education, University of London), was reproduced by kind permission of Claudia Clarke.

The portrait of R.H. Tawney was graciously provided by the Archives at The London School of Economics and Political Science (LSE).

The image of mothers watching their children exercise in the gymnasium at the Pioneer Health Centre, originally published in Pearse, I. and Crocker, L. (1943) *The Peckham Experiment: A study of the living structure of society* (London: George Allen & Unwin), was reproduced by kind permission of the Pioneer Health Foundation.

The Home Office poster, Ministry of Health Evacuation Scheme poster, 'Knitting for the RAF' book cover and excerpt from the King's Christmas Day Speech (1941) are Crown Copyright material, which is reproduced with the permission of the Controller of HMSO and the Queen's Printer for Scotland.

The illustrations from *The Beano* comic, which appeared in the same format in Heggie, M. and Riches, C. (2008) *The History of* The Beano: *The story so far* (Waverley Books Ltd), were reproduced by kind permission of D.C. Thomson & Co., Ltd.

The posters by Fougasse (Cyril Kenneth Bird) were reproduced by kind permission of the family and estate of C.K. Bird.

The advertisement for Mars® bars was reproduced by kind permission of Mars, Inc.

The woodcuts, originally published in *St Mary and St Giles Church of England Middle School: Golden jubilee 1937–1987*, pp. 13 and 15, were reproduced by kind permission of the school.

The excerpt from a poem about potatoes (page 157), originally published in a school magazine and reprinted in Morley, J. and Monk-Jones, N. (1969) *Bishop's Stortford College 1868–1968* (London: J.M. Dent), was reproduced by kind permission of the school.

The drawing of a farm by John Waters, originally published in Evans, G. (1999) *A Century in the Life of Merton Court School, Sidcup, 1899–*

1999 (Stafford: Stowefields Publications), p. 104, was reproduced by kind permission of the school.

The image of children pea-picking, originally published in Grammer, D. (1999) *Trinity: A school with a past*, p. 45, was reproduced by kind permission of Don Grammer and the Trinity Old Scholars Association.

The image of Lord Wandsworth College boys pulling a haywagon, originally published in Stranack, D. (2005) *Schools at War: A story of education, evacuation and endurance in the Second World War* (Andover: Phillimore & Co. Ltd), Plate 8, was reproduced by kind permission of Lord Wandsworth College.

The images of Tommy Bridger on a tractor, girls gathering cattle beans and children catching butterflies are all courtesy of the Museum of English Rural Life, University of Reading.

The image of children harvesting carrots at Cheltenham College, Gloucestershire, was graciously provided by Cheltenham College Archives.

The image of children sorting the post was graciously provided by The British Postal Museum & Archive.

The image of children completing metalwork at Oundle School was graciously provided by Oundle School Archive and reproduced with kind permission of Wolf Suschitzky.

The image of a fire-fighting party, originally published in Weatherley, P. (1982) *A History of St Georges School, Harpenden*, p. 40, was reproduced by kind permission of Pam Weatherley and St George's VA School.

The image of children feeding hens, originally published in Osborne, C.H.C. (1976) *A History of Rendcomb College*, p. 88, was reproduced by kind permission of the Old Rendcombian Society.

The Girl Guides Association logo from wartime and the image of a Girl Guide packing Red Cross parcels were graciously provided by Girlguiding UK.

The Boy Scouts logo from wartime and the image of Scouts

collecting waste paper were reproduced by kind permission of The Scout Association Trustees. The copyright of images used is held by The Scout Association as defined in the Copyright, Designs and Patents Act 1988.

The illustrations of Scouts acting as messengers, fire-fighters and rescue-workers were originally published in the booklet, *They Were Prepared* (1941), relating to the Boy Scouts National Service during the Second World War, which was published by Bedfordshire Scouts and is now held in Bedfordshire and Luton archives (National Archives ref: X619/142/42 [1941]). They were reproduced by kind permission of the Bedfordshire County Scout Executive Committee.

Every effort has been made to trace copyright holders and to obtain their permission for the use of copyright material. The publisher apologises for any errors or omissions in the above list and would be grateful if notified of any corrections that should be incorporated in future reprints or editions of this book.

About the authors

Berry Mayall is Professor of Childhood Studies at the Institute of Education, University of London (IOE). She has worked for many years on research projects studying the daily lives of children and their parents. In the last 25 years she has participated in the development of the sociology of childhood, contributing many books and papers to this process, including _Towards a Sociology for Childhood_ (Open University Press, 2002). This book – on children's work in wartime – is based on a sociological approach to history, and in particular explores ideas and practices about children and childhood at a time when children were not yet understood mainly as schoolchildren, but as contributors to the division of labour.

Virginia Morrow was Reader in Childhood Studies at the IOE until 2010. She is currently Senior Research Officer in the Department of International Development, University of Oxford. Her main research interests are sociology and history of childhood; child labour and children's work; children's rights; methods and ethics of social research with children; and children's understandings of family and other social environments. She is the author of numerous papers and reports and co-edits _Childhood: A journal of global child research_.

Chapter 1

Starting points

The difference between this war and previous wars is that now we are all in the front line in a struggle for the principles of freedom and justice and respect for the laws of God and honour amongst men. Whether we are in uniform or not, we are in the war. And no matter how young we are or how old we are there are jobs we can do for our country.

One of the many exhortations to children to help with the war effort was issued by the Ministry of Information in 1941; its opening paragraph is our opening quotation and its title, which we have borrowed for this book, is *You Can Help Your Country*. In the book we address a neglected topic, which is, nevertheless, a part of the history of childhood in twentieth-century England. We focus on children's work during the Second World War, and in particular the contributions children made to the war effort. The topic may have been neglected because another topic has – perhaps understandably – dominated discourse on children in the war years: evacuation. Indeed, when we have mentioned the words 'children' and 'the war' to people as an introduction to explaining what our book is about, they immediately assume that we are interested in 'evacuation'. Many people have stories to tell about evacuation and it was indeed a huge social upheaval, with about 1.5 million children evacuated in September 1939. Further movements of children, parents and teachers took place during periods of intensive enemy action (autumn 1940, summer 1944). But the story we shall tell in this book is of a parallel set of events, whereby children of all ages, whether evacuated or not, were encouraged to take part in the war effort, and we shall also detail what work they did.

Before proceeding, we note that, in recent years, a number of books have appeared that document children's lives during the Second World War, at a purely descriptive level. These are books which draw on memories, on records in the Imperial War Museum, on photos and letters. In describing children's lives they identify topics such as daily life, evacuation, leisure activities, schools in wartime and contributions to the war effort; so the authors have briefly identified a parallel story to that of evacuation and trauma.[1] However, none of these authors have offered analysis or contextualisation in social policy, history or sociology for these descriptions. Some of the many books about evacuation (see Chapter 4, page 86) also refer to children's contributions in the households where they were billeted, but do not focus on this work in a consolidated way.

Key themes

The fact that English children were encouraged, and indeed urged, to help suggests a different set of ideas about what childhood should consist of and did consist of, in contrast to ideas and practices fashionable nowadays. This set of ideas is sharply divided into two by social class. Drawing on the history of childhood, with a principal focus on the inter-war years (1918–39) we present evidence which strongly supports the view that at the time it was considered normal for the majority of children to take part in immediately useful activities, and indeed to do paid work. Poor families needed and asked for the contributions children could make. These could include doing paid work, and foraging for and stealing food, coal and wood.[2] Children were expected to do housework, though girls more than boys, and they were also expected to run errands and mind the baby. Children did casual work, as shop assistants, as messengers, on paper rounds and on grocery and milk delivery. However, during this period there were also moves and pressures to consolidate children within the category 'schoolchild', as we shall discuss in later chapters. Thus one major theme of the book is to consider the tension between children as earners and children as learners. For by the start of the Second World War, childhood had not yet been firmly defined as a period in which children are first and foremost learners, in schools, though some processes were in train to reformulate childhood thus. We are referring here to the majority of children (nine in ten) who attended state schools up to the age of 13 or 14 and thereafter went into paid work. But under-14s also worked, as already noted, and their work had been endorsed from the start of the state education service, through the half-time system. This meant that many children, especially in the textile areas of Lancashire and Yorkshire, worked for half the day and attended school for the other half; and it originated in factory acts dating back to 1802. It persisted into the twentieth century and legislation failed to halt it (see Chapter 3 for more detail).

In these inter-war years, a small minority of children attended private schools and grammar schools; their principal activity was learning, up to the age of 18 or 21. It was learning based on the rationale of service – for boys in professional jobs and in the legislature, for girls, principally, in marriage and motherhood. As we shall see in later discussion of these children's contributions to the war effort, the appeal to service – to the country, to the King and to God was powerfully made (Chapter 7). Encouraging the mass of children, too, to understand themselves as members of the religious community and of their country was an important theme in elementary schooling, where school assemblies and remembrance days promoted Christianity, and patriotic loyalty to King, Country and Empire. These values were key to youth work, where workers aimed to guide young people into respecting moral values based on Christianity, and to enable them to prepare for citizenship through practising democracy:

> *In the club committee young people learn the power of the vote and in practising democracy in a miniature society they fit themselves to become intelligent members of a democratically governed society.*[3]

But in the inter-war years there was also increasing pressure for change, for offering more schooling to the nation's children. We consider some of the thinking that led to such pressure in Chapters 2 and 3. Themes include harnessing the talents of all the children, and the needs of the nation for a better educated workforce. Another strand in thinking was the importance of improving the health of the nation – partly in the name of eugenics, and the idea that such improvement could be made through offering better physical education to children at school. An important theme was the desirability of maintaining adult control over young people, whether at school or via youth clubs.

So a key debating point, from the start of state schooling, has been the division of responsibility between parents and the state for the welfare and education of children. The twentieth century saw tensions between parental and state interests, as to children as earners or learners; and between the liberties of the people and social justice.

Educational opportunity and social control go hand in hand. However parental rights and duties are understood at any time, there has always been room for state agencies to blame parents. And within the dual control by two sets of adults, children themselves have often been understood as objects rather than as subjects. This makes their emergence as active participants in the war effort of particular interest.

For, one question we address in our book is why children were asked to participate. One view is that enlisting children was merely a morale-boosting exercise, a government move to prevent panic and despair.[4] Indeed, Titmuss (1976: ch. II) describes how psychologists and psychiatrists in the 1930s anticipated an increased demand for their services during any forthcoming war (in fact, he notes, demand did not increase). Certainly, keeping people's spirits positive, and helping them to 'keep calm and carry on' was one motive for government to ask people to help. But, equally certainly, help was needed; perhaps the three main problems faced by government on the domestic front, problems with which the people could help, were: (1) the reduction in goods obtainable from abroad; (2) the reductions in available manpower as adults were called up to various kinds of direct war service; and (3) the huge financial costs of running the war. Children, alongside women and men, did indeed help, as we show in later chapters – with food production and with salvage, by substituting for the work of adults – especially at home, and in raising money. As we suggest, the idea that children should not be encouraged to help – if it is current nowadays – is a vision rooted in more recent conceptualisations of childhood; for English children's principal activity is now thought to be learning, and children are to be protected from social and political worlds, not engaged with them. At the time, and in the face of war, it was acceptable to call on children, and if some had to endure hard childhoods, they could be thought of as participants in a social crisis, in which many adults endured hard adulthoods. It is noteworthy, too, as Tawney wrote in 1940, that the Labour members in the National Government quickly implemented plans to use existing resources more fairly, and to try to ensure that people were cared for by the state to an extent never before attempted (Tawney, 1981). The hardships of war went hand in hand with increased respect for the people, and this may have been a factor that made demands on the people acceptable.

Who is a child?

In this book, though as already indicated there were widely diverging childhoods, we include under the notion of 'child' all people under the age of 18. There are a number of reasons for this. First, there is a good historical basis for so doing. In the inter-war years, an important strand in educational thought was that, one way or another, under-18s should come under the umbrella of education. Although only a tiny minority attended school full-time to 18, educationalists and psychologists were concerned that young people should come under the tutelage of adults, partly to restrain young people from morally dubious activities by inculcating democratic principles, partly to offer some educational opportunities to more children and partly to alleviate the youth unemployment problem (see Chapter 2). Various ideas were proposed: part-time education alongside paid work; raising the school-leaving age; and encouraging young people to join youth organisations, such as Scouts. Some radical observers argued for equality of educational opportunity for all children. Within welfarist thinking about children in need of care other than parental care, those under 18 years were the target group. Thus the 1889 Prevention of Cruelty to and Protection of Children Act, and the 1899 Poor Law Act gave boards of guardians authority to take parental rights over children up to age 18. The later Children and Young Persons Act (1933) defined a 'child' as aged 1–14 (that is, a definition linked to school age) and a 'young person' as aged 14–17; it also raised powers of protection from 16 to 17 (Heywood, 1965: 93). Furthermore, under the Act, the duties of protection were removed from boards of guardians and given to counties and county boroughs (Heywood, 1959: 126). Similarly in the health field, a measure was introduced to include 14–18s who were in paid work in a health insurance scheme.[5] So in at least three arenas of social policy – education, welfare and health – policy-makers shared some common ideas and were implementing policies or moving towards measures based on the notion of some state responsibility for children's well-being up to the age of 18.

A second allied reason for settling on under-18s is that on a number of counts they were not considered adults. Firstly, in paid work: while at 18 a boy or girl could expect an adult wage, before that their work tended to be in lower paid casual and dead-end jobs (boys) and 'in service', shop work and office work (girls). And secondly the formal age of conscription into the armed forces during the Second World War was 18 (though pre-military training schemes included younger children). Studying this period from the standpoint of the present day, we also find it interesting that how the under-18s should spend their time was then, as it is today, a matter for adult concern. (We return to that theme in Chapter 9.) From a pragmatic point of view it is also important to include the upper end of childhood, since it allows us to consider the contributions to the war effort of older children, including the minority who went to private schools (Chapters 7 and 8).

A sociological approach to the history of childhood

In this book, we bring a sociological approach to considering childhood in the past. Our understanding of a sociological approach has several components. Firstly, we aim to consider the social status of children: how far children were taken seriously as members of society, both as individuals and as members of the social group 'children'. We promote the view that children should be regarded as experts in their own lives, in the sense that they can provide unique accounts of their experiences and understandings; so we aim to give space to children's views: what they said at the time. In our topic we are fortunate since some of their descriptions of their experiences do survive (whereas children's own accounts are generally not accessible to those researching earlier periods).[6]

Secondly, we recognise that adult social constructions of children and of childhood will not be the same at all periods of history and, in particular, that many adult assumptions about childhood nowadays (2011) will probably not hold for assumptions in the 1930s and 1940s. So one task is to explore how adults conceptualised childhood; what was the range of conceptualisations (stratified by social class and gender); and how far such conceptualisations structured policies and practices. This involves considering the adults who wrote policy documents, the journalists, teachers who worked with children, and the teachers who wrote school histories. Clearly, there was a mass of sometimes conflicting ideas at large and it is hard both to tap into them and to describe them. But one question we ask is whether assumptions held in the 1930s continued into the 1940s or whether they were modified by the socio-political circumstances of the time. We note too that while children are constrained to live childhoods as defined by adults, they may at times step out of those constraints and challenge these social constructions; wartime could, perhaps, offer such opportunities.

Thirdly, and most importantly, we aim to consider how far, in the inter-war and war years, children were recognised as participants in the division of labour. Was it regarded by adults as appropriate to ask children to work? We have already suggested that for poor families it certainly was; children were expected to work, and family members were interdependent. Children in all social classes were trained in loyalty to God, King and Country, and the minority of children were educated towards gendered careers in the service of society. Under war conditions, however, as we shall show, adults from government to parents urged all children to contribute to the war effort.

We also note that, when thinking about how far children contributed to the division of labour, we must pay attention to the generational order whereby relational processes work their way through. Children live in socio-political worlds where adults hold the power both to construct childhood and to shape children's experiences of childhood. The generational order also gives precedence to adult participation and to adult views. Children may have been asked to do work that they were unwilling to do. Or they may have wished to do more than they were allowed. It will also be important to note that children's contributions may be disregarded or underplayed or interpreted as other than contribution. In some respects and at some times, to take a Marxist view, we may want to say that adults – both parents and the state (as representative of adults) have exploited children's work (Oldman, 1994). Parents sent young children out to work; the state asked children to work. Yet children's work was a contested area, though as we seek to demonstrate, the contest was not always about children's interests as conceived by adults; it was often based on attempts to promote and protect adult interests (for instance, trades unions objected to children's work partly because it might jeopardise adults' work, and adult rates of pay). And the question of how children should spend their time runs like a thread through this book. During the war, some teachers thought children should be engaged in school-based learning, not in 'war-work'. But both school and other work can be construed as the exploitation of children by adults for their own interests. On the other hand, some children noted that they were glad to serve their country; and this view was promoted by government.[7]

The central topic of the book is what children did for the war effort and how their work was understood by them, by their teachers, by parents and by government. We consider the varying adult discourses (those that were work-related and those in health, education and welfare) on children's work. We also consider what children said at the time, and what adults looking back said. Some of this work was directly related to what the war required, such as savings schemes and salvage-collection. Some was work that children did anyway, but which contributed to the work of keeping the country going; included here might be running errands, childcare, housework and foraging for fruit and vegetables. Some children, living on farms and smallholdings, were expected, by tradition, to contribute to the work of the farm, alongside schooling. So for some children, according to their later accounts, what they did was a continuation of typical childhood activity; others explained that under war conditions they and other children took on a greater share of the tasks children normally did. Older children embarked during the war years on war-related activities, for instance, helping evacuees, serving tea to the army or manning air raid warning posts. We are also concerned with how social commentators understood children's war efforts and we have drawn largely on the comments made at the time. These give a flavour of contemporary thinking that cannot be matched by later histories.

So we are interested in both children and childhood. That is, we aim to consider how children experienced childhood and how childhood was structured or defined. We try also to show how, to some extent, childhoods (that is understandings of childhood, or the limits of childhood) were stretched or widened to meet what children were asked to do during the war, and whether children responded positively or negatively, or both, to these demands.

As sociologists dealing with history, we note the critical stance advocated by historians, so we try to respect the necessity of maintaining scepticism about the views proposed in documents; this has been characterised as a necessary 'attentive disbelief' by E.P. Thompson.[8] In writing this history, we started from what we perceived to be the fact that children were asked to help out; we then, bearing in mind the necessary scepticism, sought explanations in social history for this phenomenon. But we were interested in the topic not only on the levels of description and of explanation, but also with a view to thinking about today's English children; and our principal theoretical tool was, as outlined above, the sociology of childhood. Were there some positive values in the idea that children could and should be called upon to work, in some cases to work beyond their strength and for long hours? Are there perhaps some suggestions from the past about desirable modifications today to our ideas about children and about childhood?[9]

We note therefore that as sociologists – like feminists writing about and especially *for* women in order to contest dominant male discourses – we are writing *for* children and we challenge some adult discourses; we want to promote a better discourse about children and about childhood. This we hope will be a more inclusive discourse. This discourse entails, among other enterprises, trying to think about the events touched on from the perspectives of children, as well as those of adults. It means taking account not only of what adults said, but of what children said; indeed, we aim to make a start on constructing a child standpoint on the war years and what they were asked to do.[10] We know that there is no truth out there; so we cannot get at the 'truth' of what actually happened (see, for example, Smith, 1998: 14) but can only investigate and report on varying accounts of what happened. But we want to put the record a bit straighter than it has been to date.

Childhood through the eyes of health, welfare and education thinking

A distinctive feature of this book is looking for ideas and changes in ideas across the domains of developmental psychology, health, welfare and education thinking. We are interested in ideas within each domain and in how ideas in one domain may feed into ideas in another. As we note in Chapter 2, individual domains have been the topic of sustained and comprehensive analysis, for instance by Rose (1985) on the 'psychological complex' (see also Donzelot, 1980) and by Hendrick on child welfare (2003). Our aim (though it may lead to relatively superficial work) is first to start, as far as possible, from children's lives and to consider what childhood experience was like; secondly, it is to look across the range of ideas and services (health, welfare and education) in order to consider what constructions of childhood were being worked through (and implemented). As noted above, it is always important to recognise that ideas about childhood at the time may differ from children's own experiences of childhood at the time. We should also note that while we are interested in ideas about childhood, these are not always made explicit in writing at the time, and many social and political histories then and now omit children and themes relating to childhood. This point has of course been made about other social groups, such as women – their invisibility in histories.[11]

Children as earners and/or children as learners

What is work?

Definitions of work in relation to children are contested. Some 'Western' ideas about 'work' and 'labour' equate work with paid employment in the formal labour market, so the assumption is that children do not work. But 'work' has many meanings, and can be broadly understood as the performance of necessary tasks and the production of necessary values (Wallman, 1979). Many children are 'economically active', and accordingly, there are many definitions of child labour and children's work.

Jens Qvortrup's pioneering paper, 'Placing children in the division of labour' (1985) underpins his construction of the sociology of childhood. He describes how 'Western' children, who traditionally worked in fields and in factories, were gradually excluded from this productive work for their family and for the economy, and were sited in schools. This led to a change in ideas about what the tasks or contributions of childhood are. Nowadays, he argues, children's principal work – their economic contribution to the division of labour – is in school work, though this contribution is not generally recognised by adults, who regard it as preparation. However, he also notes four categories of work engaged in by children, and these provide a useful summary for our purposes. Within their families or households they may do paid work for family businesses – for instance, in the corner shop or smallholding (Chandra, 2001; Song, 2001) or unpaid work – housework and childcare (Morrow, 1996, 2008). Outside the family, they may engage in paid work – paper rounds, shop work, cleaning cars, baby-sitting, and they also engage, unpaid, in school work, both at school and at home (Qvortrup, 1991: 20). In this book, we are particularly interested in children's active contributions to the war effort, that is, what can be counted as 'war-work'.

In a study of the status of childhood in 16 industrialised countries, led by Qvortrup, researchers found that while detailed statistics were kept of children's school-related activities, their other kinds of work were not documented (Qvortrup, 1991). Their contributions had, in a sense, been written out of history. For it is substantially the case that during the later twentieth century models of childhood changed in these societies. Children were to be valued for their school work, and not for their other kinds of socially useful activity; they have come to be regarded as adults in preparation, rather than as contributing members of society.[12] But it took a long time for systematic study of the transformation in

British childhood in relation to children's work during the twentieth century to be carried out. The eminent educational historian Gillian Sutherland called this a 'puzzling gap':

> For many of us working in the general field there has seemed a puzzling gap between Edwardian enquiries and the re-discovery of child labour in the Emrys Davis report of 1972. Yet the extent of child labour in both World Wars made it impossible to believe that work had ceased to figure in the peace-time lives of British children.[13]

She was reviewing a book edited by Lavalette (1999), which does include detailed studies of children's work from 1918 to 1970 (Cunningham, 1999) and from 1970 to 1998 (Leonard, 1999). These studies, mainly via surveys, of children as economic actors have been followed by more detailed studies of children's own accounts of the experiences of work. This work includes taking part in the work generally ascribed to women, that of maintaining the physical, emotional and moral health of family members.[14] Furthermore, empirical studies with children have found that a majority of English children do some paid work at some point in their childhoods.[15] Researchers have found that children value paid work: it gives them funds for their own use and in some cases for contributing to household finances; it provides them with experience of the world of work.

However, many English studies of children's work and child labour have emphasised the negative. This emphasis may derive from a conceptualisation, developed in the wake of developmental views of childhood, that childhood is to be viewed as a vulnerable period, that trauma is just around the corner and that child protection is to be the dominant duty of adults towards children. The issues surrounding the exploitation of child labour in Britain during the Industrial Revolution have been comprehensively examined and are well documented.[16] As to the history of the war years, the two eminent social historians of British childhood, Hugh Cunningham and Harry Hendrick, are each preoccupied with evacuation. Hendrick, in his book *Child Welfare: Historical Dimensions, Contemporary Debate* (2003), discusses child welfare in the period up to the war, particularly concerning juvenile delinquency, but does not discuss children's work or child labour at all; he focuses (necessarily) on 'children's problems and problem children' (Qvortrup, 1987: 3). Hendrick does note of evacuation that when children were being selected by host families: 'Older boys usually went quickly in rural areas, since they could help around the farm' (2003: 125). Hugh Cunningham (1991, 2006) also focuses on child poverty and children's welfare, and argues that in many respects the Second World War was good for childhood:

> *children, quite as much as, if not more than, any other group in society, could be seen to emerge from the war with their status and prospects significantly enhanced. As Lady Astor put it in March 1945, 'The country has become child conscious'.*
>
> (Cunningham, 1991: 224)

And Cunningham draws attention to the salience of developmental psychology in shaping people's ideas about childhood, when he argues:

> *The first half of the 20th century can be seen as a terrain on which a battle was fought between behaviourist and psychologically informed views of childhood. The victory went to the latter. Its impact was to place the spotlight on the family, not so much for its adherence or otherwise to the gospel of hygiene, but for its ability to mould the character and personality of the children who were by now so firmly placed in its care. Children showed little awareness of the debates that raged around them. Their memories of childhood, unless they were living in institutions, were taken up more with the way they spent their time outside school and beyond the remit of the state.*
>
> (Cunningham, 2006: 202)

And indeed, we emphasise that most childhoods were also constructed by forces other than those battling for supremacy within psychology. Childhoods – as already suggested – were structured by poverty, by social class distinctions and by parental demands that children work.

However, the question how far childhood was becoming scholarised during the inter-war years and war years is of central interest in this book. By 'scholarisation' we mean the tendency to value childhoods only in so far as they are specifically childhoods spent under adult tutelage in schools. What is clear is that childhoods differed by social class, with the vast majority going into paid work at 14 or at younger ages, with girls also expected to do domestic work, while the minority of children were already scholarised, as pupils in private schools. However, we must immediately note that the story is cross-cut with gendered assumptions. While wealthy boys may have travelled on well-marked paths through school and university towards high-status careers, girls' paths were less clear-cut. Though some girls attending private and grammar schools may have been urged to do well academically and to proceed to university (Tizard, 2010: 115), other such girls were deflected into preparation for marriage and motherhood and into low-status occupations. Some of our interviewees still resented these barriers, years later. But even if girls got to university, their career paths were not simple and linear; as a study of girls who went to Girton College, Cambridge shows, in the inter-war years and at least until the 1970s they found themselves limited to teaching jobs with intervening periods of domestic and voluntary work as they juggled motherhood and paid work (Thane, 2004).

But as we track through the slow developments towards more school-based opportunities for the majority in the 1930s, we are continually faced with debates at the time about how far children should be considered as earners primarily and how far as learners. These debates, as we shall try to show, are rooted in ideas about suiting schooling to the future lives mapped out for two broad classes of children, and in the vexed question whether intelligence was class-related. We suggest that justifications for government encouragement to children to participate in the war effort were based on the position that the parameters of childhood included work. However, we also stress that the social and political conditions of war constituted a crisis in face of which everyone had to be asked to help, even if that meant stepping out of normal behaviour. The appeal, based on notions of patriotism and of service, allowed for recruiting not only the majority of children, but also those at grammar and private schools, where the concept of education for service was well established.

It will indeed be important to trace how ideas rooted in social class pervaded policies and practices. Many commentators about education simply assumed that the working classes were less intelligent than their betters, that they should have less opportunity than the rich and should be trained for their station in life. A crucial example in the history of education policy is opposition views on the Fisher Bill (1917) – there were dangers in educating the working classes, for 'if you make the cattle think, they will become dangerous' (Chapter 2, pages 33–4). Later, during the 1940s, government and civil service, staffed by ex-public school boys, ensured that their schools were not touched by proposed educational reforms (see page 98). These same people chaired enquiries into perceived social problems (such as the Youth Advisory Committee – see pages 92–3). Women who had good class-based connections, such as Jebb (see Chapter 2) could work for social improvement. Specifically, as women operating outside masculine 'relations of ruling' (Smith, 1987), they could identify the problems faced by women and children and propose initiatives to mitigate them. But social work also involved the well-to-do 'doing good' to the poorer classes. For instance Jane Martin (2005) tells the stories of four Victorian women who used their social and cultural capital to shape their society and to enjoy power and prestige in poor communities.[17] A later example is Peggy Jay, brought up in a wealthy family with servants, who did voluntary work in the slums of King's Cross between the wars (Williams *et al.*, 2001: 71).

As noted above, deep-rooted gendered assumptions, linked with social class, but in some cases cutting across social class, shaped girlhoods. Working-class girls were expected to do housework as soon as they physically could, but middle-class girls shared perceived working-class destinies as wives and mothers. The educational curriculum for girls was to be different from that for boys, for this was girls' main mission in life. This posed a problem for those thinking about school curricula, for schools must play their part in providing appropriate training; since housewifery and motherhood skills, as well as more academic subjects, must be taught to girls, perhaps they should take public examinations a year later than boys (see page 65). And since, during the war, it was obvious that older girls and women could provide only auxiliary war service, training for it would differ from that for boys (see page 225). The war years provided opportunities for girls to help out in ways that fitted gendered role models, for they could be asked to take on even more domestic work; within the main organisation for girls, the Guides, suggestions given to them by their leaders and by the guiding magazine could also be along traditional gendered lines. But as with women's contributions to the war effort, so with girls; some of their work challenged traditional assumptions, for instance in agriculture, as land girls and in fire watching.

So far we have outlined the theoretical basis for our book, in the sociology of childhood. Also, we have indicated along the way how the status of children, the social construction of childhood and the contributions of children to the division of labour are structured through the intersections of social class, poverty and gender. These will help us work our way through considerations of children as earners and/or as learners, especially in the inter-war years and in the war years.

Our study

Our interest in English children's contributions to the war effort was re-ignited as we reconsidered work done by one of us (Morrow, 1992, 1994), which explored what children in two areas of England did outside school hours and revealed that most of them did some economically significant work. Morrow carried out, as historical context for her study, documentary analysis of the status of work, including paid work, and of schooling in the lives of children from the 1870s onwards (when state schooling began in England). The study noted children's participation in work during both world wars, particularly in agricultural production. As sociologists of childhood we are interested in children's status as contributors to the division of labour in society, whether through work or school work. And we are dissatisfied with what seem to us partial accounts of childhood during the Second World War, which stem mainly from adult concern for the possible psychological damage done to children as victims of evacuation and bombing. These studies began in 1940 with Susan

Isaacs' evacuation study (1941) and have continued ever since. We knew that government and many other agencies and voluntary bodies urged everyone to contribute what they could to the war effort, as famously symbolised, for instance, in the Dig for Victory campaign. At a simple level, we wanted to describe and consider the efforts of the majority of children – including those not evacuated or bombed, but who were perhaps affected by the war in a variety of ways.

We decided therefore to carry out a study, though we knew that this was a large field and that we could only start the process of considering the phenomenon of children's work in the Second World War. In order to keep the study manageable, we have limited our focus to English childhoods. There are very many further, more detailed studies that could be carried out (we make some suggestions in Chapter 9).

We describe here the sources of our information. In the first place we have considered the history – mainly in the inter-war years – of ideas about childhood: the debates that were held and the legislation. In considering this history, we have focused on writings contemporary with the social problems of the time; we have also looked across writings on social welfare, health and education. This was a period when many debates were held about what were the proper activities of children, and people's views were of course heavily influenced by their social class and gendered prejudices and assumptions.

Secondly we have given considerable attention to children's own commentaries on their childhoods. For this we have been able to draw on 700 or so histories of schools held in the IOE library.[18] These include histories of a range of types of school in existence at the time: state elementary schools (5–14), state secondary schools (called senior elementary, central or modern) (11–14/15), state grammar schools (11–18) and private schools, which varied in age-range; some had preparatory sections for children under the age of 13 and many catered for 13–18s; some were boarding, others day schools. Some of the histories draw on school magazines – and these are especially valuable, because they give contemporary students' accounts of what mattered to them and, therefore, insights into the character of childhood and the social construction of childhood at the time. They give vivid accounts of experiences and feelings, some expressed in poems. The authors of some of the histories called on former students to send in their memories and these are valuable not least because some were submitted not long after the war; they include evacuees' and refugees' memories. Some of the histories consist largely or in part of reprints of logs kept (presumably) by the headteacher ('two chicken coops delivered today'; '£25.4s.6d raised for Salute the Soldier week'), and these also point to the activities of children at the time. Of the 700 histories, about two-thirds offer descriptions and commentary on children's war-related activities, with the rest focusing on student and staff achievements, disruption, evacuation, and resource and staffing problems. In the 'School histories' section at the end of the book, we give a list of the histories from which we have quoted, with information about the author, date, title and publisher of the book (page references are in the text). A further source of information about schools comes from a survey of schools' activities during the war years carried out by the Association of Representatives of Old Pupils Societies. Stranack (2005) summarised the information and wrote it up, under each school. He notes in his introduction (2005: xiv) that for some children wartime was miserable, for others an idyllic time. We add that while it may be alleged that no adverse comments or stories of hard times will be documented in school histories (since the authors will want to project good aspects of their school), in fact we found negative stories and memories alongside positive ones, including stories of endurance, fear, resentment and irritation and we have given due reference to these. Other sets of information gathered in the 1940s are three surveys of children's views, the Cambridge and Oxford evacuation surveys and a survey of children's leisure activities (see Appendix). These provide some accounts written by children, and detail, based on children's answers, of their activities and views.

A further way of exploring children's experiences is more indirect. We have collected memories of childhood from adults. Such memories of the past take place through the lens of the present. They elicit people's ideas now about what they thought then and about how they think and feel now about the past, and the interviews explore intersections between public and private memories. In one study we carried out interviews with 24 grandmothers, asking them to reflect on their own childhood, their daughters' childhoods and their granddaughters' childhoods, in order to explore changes in ideas and practices. These women ranged in age, were from a range of backgrounds and were recruited through personal contacts. They included 12 who were schoolchildren in England at some point between 1939 and 1945 (Mayall, 2005).[19] A second empirical study was of 23 men and women, again recruited through personal contacts; we interviewed 16 of them and seven sent in written accounts about their wartime experiences.[20] These 35 adults, between them, lived in cities and villages, in many parts of England and had varying school experiences, in elementary schools, grammar and other secondary schools and private schools. Some stayed put, some moved about the country. While all these people gave permission for their words to be quoted, we have given the interviewee's name if they gave permission for that, or simply referred to them as 'our interviewee', if not. In carrying out these interviews we adhered to the principles of oral history and simply asked people to tell us their story, with prompts and further suggestions (Bertaux and Thompson, 1993; Popular Memory Group, 1982/1998). We have also referred to some autobiographies about the war years. In some the author chooses to focus on family life, schooling, games and sport; terrifying experiences during the bombing also featured in some accounts.[21] Some describe war-work as a minor or unremarkable part of their wartime lives; for others, work, including war-work, was simply an expected part of childhood.

These three kinds of data therefore provide two kinds of information – one is the voices of children speaking to us from the past, and the other is the memories of adults looking back to their childhoods. In both cases, the accounts will reflect the times at which they were given. People then may have assumed that everyone should work for the common good and in the face of crisis; they may also or instead have been wearied and irritated by demands on their time. People nowadays may assume that protection, rather than participation, should be the guiding principle for how childhood was and is to be lived. They will emphasise some points over others and in some cases their stories themselves give a flavour of what mattered at the time. In quoting from these accounts we have tried to maintain a balance between the two kinds of information, accounts emanating from the past and memories of the past.

In addition, as already suggested, we have studied social histories and commentaries written at the time in the fields of welfare, health and education. These include comments and analyses in newspapers, such as *The Times*, and the *Times Educational Supplement*, reports of TUC conferences (especially those reflecting on children as agricultural workers), and statements from the National Union of Agricultural Workers. We have collected data about the BBC's wartime broadcasts for schoolchildren, drawing both on an archive of schools broadcasting programmes and leaflets held at the IOE, and on material kept in the BBC's written archives at Reading. We have also consulted documents held at the Museum of English Rural Life (MERL) at Reading, in particular letters sent in response to a radio broadcast in 2004 by the agricultural historian Moore-Colyer on children's agricultural work (see Chapter 6, page 147). As part of our study of organisations to which children belonged we have consulted the national archives of the Scouts, Guides and Junior Red Cross. These varied documents 'provide potent evidence of continuity and change in ideals and in practices, in private and in the public arena' (McCulloch, 2004: 6–7).

Clearly all of this is a considerable mass of material, and our presentation of some of it will owe much to our particular interests and to our limitations as amateur historians. We also note a particular problem with our topic, which is that children are often written out of history by adults or, when written in, are presented through the lens of unproblematised assumptions. In seeking to recover, in some sense, childhoods of the 1940s, we are moving on to the territory ably investigated by Harry Hendrick (2008), as noted earlier. The advantages of our approach are as follows. First, our theoretical frameworks in the sociology of childhood allow us to reflect on conceptualisations of childhood in the past: (1) children as social actors; (2) childhood as a social construction; and (3) childhood as a constituent part of the social order. We have tried to recognise and pay tribute to interrelations between these three positions. Secondly, we have moved beyond description of children's war-related activities to consideration of how these were valued (or not) during the war and in the context of social policies and social practices in the years leading up to the war. And thirdly, at the level of documenting what children did we have given more detail, from a wider range of sources, than any earlier account.

The organisation of the book

Following this introductory chapter, we consider in Chapter 2 English children in social thought between the wars (1918–39), in order to investigate the ideas that may have underpinned how children were conceptualised during the war. We start by referring to some general points about the social scene as presented by commentators at the time, and later. We consider whether ideas were changing about the extent of state responsibility for welfare and for employment. We then discuss how far it is fair to say that commentators saw commonalities in childhood, and how far stratification by social class and gender were both assumed and valued. We consider developments in psychological thinking and in measuring intelligence, notably in the context of current education policies and practices, and the importance of childcare manuals in shaping people's ideas. An important theme is the debates about improving the nation's health, including that of children, and the linkages in people's minds between health-promotion strategies and the role of education. And we note that child protection – a principal theme in the children's rights movement nowadays – was emerging through the work of pioneers, including Eglantyne Jebb.

In Chapter 3 we go back in time to the beginning of the twentieth century, in order to consider how historical and legislative changes both reflected and shaped the character and status of English childhoods. We take account of the intertwined forces of welfare, education and employment policies and of how concern for the physical, moral and mental welfare of children focused on the employment of children, in the context of worries about the nation's prosperity. Children's employment during the First World War both in agriculture and in factory work is discussed, as well as the two rather differently conceived social problems of boys' labour and girls' labour. We note that 'young people as a social problem' refers to working-class children and that the 'problem' was further stratified by gender, since girls were thought to be especially at risk of physical and moral deterioration. These reflections form the backdrop for considering an important education bill – the 1917 Fisher Bill which aimed to raise the school-leaving age to 15 and introduce compulsory part-time education for school leavers to age 18. The Bill's failure had many causes, and not least the economic downturn in the early 1920s, but ideas about the character of working-class children, as Tawney brilliantly describes (see Chapter 3, page 74), provide some explanations. We go on to consider the division of children's lives between education and employment, noting that improvements to the education system were slow to take place and that working-class children's employment – both under-14s and over-14s – was widely accepted. However, we also note that pressure to improve the education system and to regulate child labour continued through the 1930s.

We start Chapter 4 with some notes on the lead-up to war, as far as children were concerned. We then add a brief section on evacuation and the broader welfare initiatives during the war years, designed to maintain the health and well-being of children. The next section is about wartime work in the lives of children and contemporary views on the merits and demerits of children's work, including those of children. We document the discussions leading to the 1944 Education Act. We go on to consider the moves made to encourage children's participation in the war effort, notably government action in partnership with the BBC, through which schools could be targeted, and we note the importance of films and children's fiction in promoting patriotism and willingness to help.

Chapter 5 continues with discussion of how far children were aware of the war and through what means, drawing on our interviews and on school histories. We then go on to consider younger children's contributions to the war effort, through four main kinds of activity: (1) gardening and food production; (2) household and domestic work; (3) savings schemes; and (4) salvage collection. Again we draw on interviews and on school histories, especially those of elementary schools (attended at ages 5–14).

Chapter 6 is about the best-documented kind of work – in agriculture, for children worked both to plant and to harvest, and spent time away from home and school, in camps at harvest time. They also worked to help local farmers as required throughout the year. This chapter considers the views of adult commentators, including government, education and union representatives, and farmers, and how these views changed during the war years.

Chapter 7 focuses on the contributions of older children. We note that the majority were in full-time paid work by the age of 14 and thus contributing directly to the national economy. An important kind of work was in technical training and in munitions. Older children still at school – at grammar and private schools – worked to produce food, both at school and at home, and they made contributions appropriate to their older age: preparing their schools for bomb attacks; reorganising them to receive evacuees; and carrying out domestic duties when servants were called up to war service. They also worked for the community, for instance in schools, canteens and hospitals and in some cases had direct contact with the armed forces.

Chapter 8 concerns the war-related activities of children who belonged to youth organisations. Among the many organisations in existence at the time, we provide sections on only five: the Boys' Brigade, the Junior Red Cross, the Scouts, the Guides and Woodcraft Folk. These draw – for the first four – on archive material, and on books detailing the histories of the organisations. We include a section on pre-military training for boys and for girls. This chapter highlights the concept of service promoted in many of these organisations, within a framework of patriotism and Christianity.

In Chapter 9 we summarise the main points made in the book, with emphasis on themes that run through it: (1) the importance of social class and gender in shaping childhoods; (2) the status of work as an accepted part of most childhoods; (3) the concept of service; and (4) the rationales for asking children to help in the war effort. We revisit the concept of work and consider tensions between 'education' and 'work'. We go on to consider the place of work in children's lives today and the character of schooling today. We discuss aspects of child–adult relations in the years leading to the Second World War and during it; we also consider changes in the relative responsibilities of parents and the state for children, both then and now. We revisit the notion of children preparing to be citizens and discuss recent work on the concept of children as citizens. We then note how the sociology of childhood has helped us understand the character of childhood during the war, with its emphasis on children as social agents contributing to the division of labour. Finally, we point to further studies which would help elucidate the history of childhood in the war years, and argue that our work to date does present a revised version of childhood then, to complement the dominant evacuation story. We wonder whether English children today can be thought of as a reserve army of labour, who can contribute to social welfare, and we point to some examples where children do indeed do just that.

Notes

1 Gardiner, 2005: ch. 5; Smith, 2008: ch. 9; Anderson, 2008: ch. 6; Harvey, 2009; Brown, 2009: ch. 5.

2 Humphries, 1981: ch. 6 gives many examples of this work by children, some of which was done by absenting themselves from school. He calls this 'subsistency truancy'.

3 Macalister Brew, 1943: 13. She discusses Christianity in relation to youth club work in ch. X.

4 Morale-boosting initiatives are discussed by McLaine, 1979 and Mackay, 2002, but neither focuses on initiatives directed at children.

5 This measure was introduced under the 1937 National Health Insurance Act.

6 A good source of autobiographical accounts was edited by Burnett, 1994. Most are of nineteenth-century childhoods, but a few are of early twentieth-century childhoods, and reveal in detail how poverty structured children's lives.

7 The Ministry of Information leaflet (1941) is addressed mainly to children aged 14–18; its title is *You Can Help Your Country*. It lists useful jobs children could do; these include knowing your way about locally, doing jobs at home and lending a hand outside – helping others, collecting salvage, working for farmers, learning first aid.

8 E.P. Thompson's words are quoted by Hendrick, 2008: 46, who discusses the problems of doing research on childhood in the past, given that children have no 'authorial voice'.

9 In Chapter 9 we consider whether the history of the war years has comments to make on today's adults' constructions of childhood.

10 Alanen, 1992; Mayall, 2002: ch. 7.

11 For instance, Asa Briggs, 1955, in his history of 'people' who made a difference to English socio-political life in Victorian England, omits women. He says in his introduction that he wishes he could have included a chapter on an important woman, but that only one, Florence Nightingale, fitted the bill.

12 It has also been argued that over the twentieth century children have come to be valued by adults for their emotional worth, rather than for their contributions to the division of labour (Zelizer, 1985, 2005).

13 Gillian Sutherland's (2000) comments come in a review of a book on child labour edited by Lavalette, 1999.

14 Stacey, 1981; Mayall, 2002: ch. 5.

15 For instance, Morrow, 1992; Hobbs and McKechnie, 1997; Mizen et al., 2001.

16 See, for example, Cunningham, 1990, 1991, 1995, 2006; Hendrick,1990, 1994, 2003; Horrell and Humphries, 1999; Humphries, 2010; Jordanova, 1987, 1989; Pinchbeck and Hewitt, 1969, 1973; Rose, 1989; Walvin, 1982.

17 See also Lewis, 1991.

18 The IOE library holds about 7,000 school histories, but we were able to access only those 700 or so which had been catalogued.

19 The interviews were carried out by Sue Sharpe, Berry Mayall and Abiola Ogunsola.

20 The authors carried out the interviews.

21 Autobiographies we have consulted include those by Hattersley, 1983; Oakes, 1983; Bakewell, 2004; Tizard, 2010; and Giles, 2002.

Chapter 2

Children in social thought between the wars

Our purpose in this chapter is to consider ideas about children and childhood during this period; by so doing we aim to provide a sociological context for our consideration of children's activities in education and in 'work' in Chapter 3. This purpose presents a difficult task since both children and childhood are commonly written out of 'mainstream' historical and social studies, or at best surface from time to time, but without a sustained focus on them. However, ideas about childhood and social policy towards children have been the central topic of excellent studies (notably Rose, 1985; Cunningham, 1991; Hendrick, 2003) and we draw on them, though it is not appropriate or possible for us to summarise them. Rose's work on the rise of intelligence testing and of the 'psychological complex' as it led on to and comprised attempts to raise the quality of children through neo-hygienic services is exemplary. Cunningham (1991) provides a wide-ranging and sensitive account of representations of childhood since the seventeenth century, with especially useful discussions (for us) in his last three chapters. Hendrick's study of child welfare in the period between the wars is comprehensive, and, like Cunningham, he encompasses a clear set of understandings about how sociological approaches to childhood help us come to terms with the complex history, with its paradoxes and twists and turns (Hendrick, 2003: ch. 3). We also draw on debates in the education field, since these are not only of fundamental importance to concepts of childhood, but they interlink with debates on children as workers.

The social scene in the inter-war years

Since the inter-war years provide a mixed picture of childhood, it is appropriate, just briefly, to point to some histories, descriptions and events that may have been influential. The inter-war history of the UK has attracted many studies; one bibliography of important publications includes over 40 books and papers (Smith, 1998).[1] Apart from political and military history, scholars have studied, notably: (1) the significance of the social aims and failures of the Labour Party; (2) social policies on intervention to combat unemployment and how far these heralded, or did not, the welfare state settlements of 1945; and, perhaps most intriguingly for scholars, (3) what kind of a story is adequate to describe and account for the extraordinary paradoxes of the time – high unemployment contrasted with a general rise in living standards.

Thus we are told of the rise of the Labour Party, mainly on votes from the old industrial areas (e.g. Barker, 1972; Thorpe, 2008), and of its inability to move forward substantially on its commitments to nursery education (Penn, 2004) and to secondary education for all (Richmond, 1945). Labour was 'in power' for only short periods (1924 and 1929–31); both these were dire times economically and the party did not have adequate majorities. Furthermore, it moved to the centre-ground in order to attract a wider voting base. It did, however, put in place a house-building policy, which meant that by 1939 one-third of all families in Britain were living in houses built since 1918, and these were built to higher standards than those typically built in the nineteenth century (Smith, 1998: 34–5). About half were built by private enterprise, and with house-purchase loans more readily available, 31 per cent of families owned their dwelling, compared to 10 per cent in 1911. Commitment to council housing by governments between the wars also meant that whereas almost no family had council tenancy before the First World War, by 1939, 14 per cent of all families lived in council accommodation.[2]

This picture of improved living standards has to be balanced with accounts of the conditions in which many families lived. An enquiry carried out in the late 1930s with 1,250 wives across the country, aimed to include women across the social classes and unmarried women too. But it failed to get cooperation from the better-off and unmarried. However, while not claiming to be representative of all wives and families, it gives a harrowing account of appalling housing, extreme poverty, poor diet and poor health among the women, and also of linkages between these factors, through the women's stories and also through some tables showing associations (Spring Rice, 1939). About a third of the families lived in housing that was overcrowded, decrepit, lacking services, sharing facilities and verminous. The author focuses on the women, but notes that though the schoolchildren escaped the home each day, their chances of thriving were poor.

And a study of the nation's nutritional status, published in 1936, found that half the population was in some respects poorly nourished, with a third of the population having diets severely lacking in essential ingredients.[3]

An important topic in the inter-war years was the perceived conflict between libertarianism/freedom and interventionist measures to promote social justice. A key question for debate was the half-time system; under this, children aged 12 and over could attend school for half the day and do paid work for the other half. Pressures from, notably, the Labour Party and educationalists to abolish this scheme ran up against parental rights to decide their children's activities, supported by some trades unions.[4] Another noteworthy example was government reaction to the very high unemployment levels in some areas, notably those with one main – and collapsing – industry: South Wales, the North East of England and Scotland. Influential in provoking a government response were three articles in *The Times* about the dire effects of long-term unemployment in Durham (21, 22, 23 March 1934). The government responded with the Special Areas Act (1934); this aimed at interventions to mitigate some of the effects of unemployment – for instance by encouraging initiatives to improve health and nutrition, but did not legislate to intervene to generate employment or to promote the development of industries. However, further legislation in 1936 and 1937 augmented the commissioners' powers towards introducing new industries in the depressed areas. These new measures can be seen as the start of regional policy-making, bringing work to the people, rather than expecting the people to move to the work; though government was unwilling to intervene in economic matters, it did in the end intervene to support industry (Thomas, 2005: 34). One reason for intervention was that senior men in the National (coalition) Government thought (from 1934) that failure to act might lead to Labour winning more seats. A further relevant reason is that because local services were provided to some extent out of local rates, poor areas would have poorer services, and this regional inequality was becoming unacceptable to the public (Thomas, 2005: 260). This conclusion is supported by Harris (1995a: 92–8) in relation to the school medical service: it tended to be more poorly funded in poor areas (as it was dependent on local rates), although need for services was almost certainly greater. Massive campaigns, for instance by the NUT, for better services, were supported by surveys of the extent of the problems.[5]

Social observers at the time provide useful descriptions and analyses of one of the great paradoxes or contradictions of the 1920s and 1930s: that high unemployment, dreadful housing, poor provision of health services and high rates of infant mortality and especially of maternal mortality persisted alongside the prosperity of a new class of people. Thus J.B. Priestley, after touring the country in 1933, and describing the striking divide between the old rural, traditional hat-doffing society of southern England and the deprived lives of those living in the industrialised areas, concludes his book with a chapter discussing these two Englands and a third new class of people (Priestley, 1933). These were people living (mainly in the suburbs of the southern cities and towns) in the newly built semi-detacheds, employed in newer 'light' industries and having a newly acquired good standard of living, and, he argues, having access to much the same goods as the more traditional wealthy or upper-class people. Thus they could own the same lampshades, wear the same dresses (or mass-produced equivalents) and eat the same foods. He also points to their access to information and entertainment, via books, radio, mass newspapers and films.[6] For instance, Penguin Books started publication in 1936 (at 6d) and included modern classics, such as *A Passage to India,* and earlier classics such as Shakespeare and Jane Austen; there were also Pelicans on science, the arts, history and sociology (Graves and Hodge, 1985: 426). And *Picture Post*, a weekly journal started in 1938, documented and discussed daily life, enlivened by photos (ibid.: 421).

We could add that while the formal school system made little progress between the wars,[7] many children and adults now had much better access to education – in the sense of widened horizons – acquired through these media. Somewhat similar points were made by George Orwell in his 1941 paper 'The lion and the unicorn'.[8] For instance: 'The modern council house, with its bathroom and electric light, is smaller than the stock-broker's villa, but it is recognisably the same kind of house, which the farm labourer's cottage is not.' He notes too that, willy-nilly, some middle-class ideas and practices were spreading into the lives of the working class, because some measures taken would affect everyone irrespective of why they were implemented. 'A millionaire cannot, for example light the streets for himself while darkening them for other people.' The same is true of 'good roads, germ-free water, police protection, free libraries and probably free education of a kind'.

Of particular interest here are the experiences of girls, leaving school at 14 and entering the labour market. Though domestic service was still their main source of employment in the 1930s, other opportunities were opening up, in clerical work, shop work and light industry. So girls could remain in the parental home, and earn enough both to contribute to the household economy and to spend on entertainment – magazines, cinema, dancing (Todd, 2005: 23–32). However, because girls as well as boys earned less than adults they often lost their jobs when they turned 18; the next generation of school leavers then took on these dead-end jobs (Todd, 2005: 46).[9]

Changing ideas about state responsibility for welfare?

The brief notes and examples above point to some social trends observable during the inter-war years. Debates about freedom and liberty versus social intervention continued, as they do to this day.

Some improvements, or at any rate changes, were taking place in the social composition of the country and people's opportunities for learning and for entertainment were increased. It can be argued that the huge gulf between rising prosperity and the condition of the unemployed and poverty-stricken was becoming unacceptable to some of the people.

On this last topic, Harris (1995b) argues that many historians writing since the establishment of the post-war welfare state have accepted the concept of state responsibility and so have looked for evidence of progress towards the welfare state, and have played down the role of voluntary organisations, including charities. For instance, David Owen (1964: 525) suggests that from the start of the twentieth century there was increasingly strong support for state intervention to tackle poverty. But more recently historians have studied the part played by voluntary organisations: for instance, Prochaska (1988) argues that governments were timid in the inter-war years and relied on voluntary work, and he shows that these organisations played a big part in improving people's lives. It was in voluntary organisations, as members of political parties and on local authority committees, that women could have most influence; and it was here that, as Koven and Michel (1993: 2) put it, 'they transformed motherhood from women's primary *private* responsibility into *public* policy'.[10]

Debates about responsibility for child welfare have always raised the question of parental responsibility – and, in particular, maternal responsibility. One theme discussed in reports on child health from the start of the state education service in 1870, is how far poverty and how far mothers' poor practices were responsible for poor child health. Through the years up to the Second World War, the question who should take responsibility for feeding children during their school day pinpointed divisions of opinion. State feeding might diminish mothers' sense of responsibility, but not feeding might mean children could not learn, and perhaps taking children into state-run institutions during the day implied that the state (*in loco parentis*) should feed the children.[11]

We note here other policy initiatives that may be thought to have made an impact on children's lives. It can probably be safely noted that the 1920s and 1930s were a time of great interest in planning. Among the many initiatives were the New Fabian Research Bureau and surveys commissioned by universities, which documented social problems and suggested ways forward. For instance Political and Economic Planning (PEP) published a report on the nation's health and argued for health promotion measures to improve it (Graves and Hodge, 1985: 400). Examples of apparently successful centralised planning of services and industry came from the USSR (First Five-Year Plan, 1928–32) and later from Sweden and New Zealand (Thorpe, 2008: 90). There was huge interest in debates on the value of socialism and communism, with intellectuals and other socialists signing up for the war against Franco, and visiting Russia (before news of the show trials and mass murders came through). Orwell describes (in 1945) how belief in communism was a popular response to the perceived collapse of capitalism and to social disarray (Orwell, 1965). In the later 1930s and onwards, the German sociologist Karl Mannheim produced a thorough analysis of the problems faced by democracies.[12] He argued in 1943 that just as totalitarianism planned in order to get what it wanted, so democracies must plan, in the spirit of freedom and variety (Mannheim, 1954).

Ideas about childhood in the inter-war years

In this section, we consider ideas current in the 1920s and 1930s about childhood. We look across commentaries and proposals in the fields of physical health, psychological health, welfare and education. Though this is risky, for it encompasses a very wide range of ideas and attitudes, it may serve to identify some understandings of childhood and how these were shaped during these years. In Chapter 3 we consider intersections of work and schooling in more detail, and the ideas underpinning them.

We suggest three important kinds of discourse during these years. Firstly, there was debate about how far there were commonalities between children, and how far there were differences. Secondly, and arising out of the first concern, there was much emphasis on monitoring children, and on dividing them up according to certain criteria, particularly as regards the provision of services. And thirdly, there was a growing sense that children – as compared to adults – were in special need of protection and had a special right to protection.

Commonalities versus differences

There are any number of ways into this topic. One dramatic instance of the debate about childhood – about children as earners or as learners – took place in August 1917, when Herbert Fisher, President of the Board of Education, presented his Education Bill to the House of Commons and met with furious opposition. The Bill proposed: (1) that all children should have compulsory full-time schooling until age 14; (2) that therefore the half-time system in operation in some areas should be abolished;[13] (3) that from 14 to 18 if they were not in full-time school they should have part-time schooling in 'day continuation schools'; (4) that any paid or unpaid 'work' they engaged in should be more restricted than before; and (5) that local education authorities be required to plan for adequate services in their area. In presenting his Bill, he argued forcibly that current opinion was moving towards social solidarity, created by the current war. When 'the poor are asked to pour out their blood. . .then every just mind begins to realise that the boundaries of citizenship are not determined by wealth, and that the same logic which leads us to desire an extension of the franchise points also to an extension of education.' The industrial workers of the country 'are entitled to be considered primarily as citizens and as fit subjects for any form of education from which they are capable of profiting'. He observed too that the people 'of our industrial army' were demanding education, not in order to rise out of their own class but because they valued education for its own sake, for 'in the treasures of the mind they can find an aid to good citizenship, a source of pure enjoyment and a refuge from the necessary hardships of a life spent in the midst of clanging machinery in our hideous cities of toil.'

Lieutenant-Commander J.C. Wedgwood replied to Fisher's proposals. He argued that Fisher was completely out of touch with parents, for, he claimed, they wished to decide and had the right to decide whether to send their children out to work or to school. We MPs, he said, should be especially careful about intervening in parental rights, because 'it is not our children we are legislating for, but other people's children'. And 'every penny that goes into the working-class home at the present is of vital importance. If you curtail the wage-earning power of those children, you are doing a serious injury to the working-classes as a whole.' Compulsion would take away working-class parents' pride in sending their children to elementary education, a pride comparable to ours 'in sending our children to the best public school to get as good an education as we got in our time'. He argued therefore that the Bill, and notably its proposals on part-time schooling for 14–18 year olds, was a 'very serious danger to the liberties of England'. He then identified a threat to social stability, for the masses, if educated, might turn to violence. His clinching argument was that underpinning the Bill was not the welfare of the working classes but a desire to promote efficient 'producers of wealth', and thereby to strengthen the nation against the Germans, both now and in the future. So working-class children were to be controlled from the age of 4–18 in order to promote the nation's power and security.

These two statements say much about assumptions and perspectives at the time. First we note the assumption by both speakers that paid work was a component of most children's childhoods. But Fisher's appeal to common citizenship was met by Wedgwood's recognition of huge class differences in perspectives. He countered the argument favouring the value of education for its own sake with reference to the economic problems that poorer parents faced. He opposed plans for a better education service by appealing to freedom to determine how one lived. Wedgwood's argument rested on the assumption that parents should decide how their children spent their time, and on the assumption that the earning power of working-class children should not be challenged by the state.[14] Both speakers accepted that well-to-do people, including legislators, would not be affected by the proposed Act since their own children attended well beyond the age of 14 and, for as long as parents chose, private schools, and then, in some cases, university.

A thoughtful account of the rock-solid character of class differences in how people lived is given by Virginia Woolf, writing in 1930. This was her introduction to a collection of memories about working-class women's lives, edited by Margaret Llewelyn Davies (Woolf, 1982). Writing as a well-to-do 'middle-class' woman, she reflects on her experiences at a national conference of the Women's Co-operative Guild in 1913, when working-class women gave five-minute speeches about their lives. They wanted better education, better sanitation, better working conditions and more money. But she already had all these things. So: 'If every reform they demand was granted this very instant, it would not touch one hair of my comfortable capitalistic head' (1982: xxi). And later she notes that her middle-class sympathy for these women, for their lives and their wishes 'was aesthetic sympathy, the sympathy of the eye and the imagination, not of the heart and of the nerves; and such sympathy is always physically uncomfortable' (1982: xxviii).

In the context of wide and seemingly uncrossable gulfs between people's lives, is it possible to argue that between the wars some solid ground was being constructed, which emphasised commonalities between children, as well as differences? We may turn to linked ideas within education and developmental psychology to consider the argument that education should be responsive to children's interests and abilities, and not dictated by social class. Influential in the 1920s and 1930s were scholars working at the IOE. Percy Nunn, Director of the Institute, rejected the notion that an education service existed to promote the interests of the state; rather it should promote individual talents. In his best-selling book on education[15] he argued in favour of maximising children's individual potential; thus he overrode social class, and proposed that educators consider each child on his or her merits, and offer an education appropriate to those merits. This point was also made by Fisher (Van der Eyken, 1973: 224). Nunn was a leading light in the New Education Fellowship, which promoted such 'progressive' ideas through international conferences, where examples of children's active engagement with learning in child-centred schools were discussed. In a report of its 1929 conference he says: 'The new education. . .insists upon thinking of the pupil as a whole. . .It regards the young human being as a "body-mind", which grows as a whole and is to be educated as a whole.'

Photo of Sir Percy Nunn (left) courtesy of the IOE Archives. Photo of Sir Fred Clarke (right) courtesy of Claudia Clarke.

Two previous directors of the IOE, who wrote best-selling books. Nunn was the author of Education: Its data and first principles *(1920). Clarke was director during the Second World War and was the author of* Education and Social Change *(1940).*

He calls this the 'activity school' of thought:

> *the vital interpenetration of physical, intellectual and moral activities and growth. . .The new education thinks of a child's life dynamically as a process of give and take between him and his environment, and consequently of the work of the school as primarily to supply an environment containing the elements deemed necessary for the best types of human growth.*[16]

Thus the newly fashionable developmental psychology drew attention to commonalities. The theoretical study of childhood rested on universalising underpinnings. All children go through the same stages of development, and so all children will benefit from approaches to teaching and learning based on this knowledge. Susan

Isaacs (recruited by Nunn to the Institute, and the first head of the department of developmental psychology) sets out her views in further best-sellers – *The Nursery Years*[17] and *The Children We Teach*[18]. In *The Nursery Years*, she details how children develop and the implications of these developments for how mothers and nursery staff should care for and nurture children. This was to be responsive, child-sensitive care. In the second book, aimed at teachers, she deals with 'individual differences' (ch. 2). First and foremost is difference in inborn ability – the child's 'original mental equipment' (p. 25). A second difference is in qualities of character – perseverance, stability or steadiness in aims and wishes (p. 25). And a third difference is the nurturing children get at home: the home with books and talk, excursions and holidays, where parents take an interest in the child's friendships and progress, versus a home lacking these. Worst of all is the slum home where nearly every need of childhood is neglected. Children from these worst homes will need more 'spoon-feeding' and 'prodding' in order to get on (Isaacs 1961: 28).

We flag up here a further universalising idea current at the time, which was that children were the hope for the nation's future.[19] This was a key theme for Margaret McMillan, who campaigned through the Labour movement, from the mid-1890s until her death in 1931, for improvements to working-class children's lives and for the value of nursery education for all children.[20] As she said, in one of her many publications, she aimed to send the nursery children back to their homes with messages of how life could be lived better; all children could benefit from the social and physical environment of the nursery (McMillan, 1930). The notion of the next generation as the hope for society also features largely in the work of Mannheim, who had proposed young people as constructing and carrying forward new ideas and new cultures – in his 1928 paper 'The Problem of Generations' (Mannheim, 1952). In the war years he vigorously promoted the idea that young people, far from being a social problem as was commonly conceptualised, would carry forward democratic ideas.[21]

Indeed it has been argued that war promotes revulsion against its folly and waste and leads to conceptualising the next generation as the hope for the future; as one writer said, 'it is not without significance that the Education Acts of 1870, 1902, 1918 and 1944 were passed in times of war'.[22] In 1917, a paper printed in *The Times* (19 February) gave a stirring vision of how England could and should provide a better education service for all children.[23] The paper concludes:

> *If, as we claim, the cause of England is the cause of all the higher possibilities of the human spirit, then we ought to perpetuate that cause in our social institutions, the character of which must depend on the character of the education we give to all our sons and daughters.*

The same point was made repeatedly during the Second World War: that the English deserved better education, and not least because, as things stood, they were ill-equipped to face the stresses of war (Dent, 1944a : ch. 2).

However, the question whether the working classes were intellectually able to profit by secondary education was at the heart of objections to Fisher's 1918 Education Act, as, for instance, set out by the Federation of British Industries (FBI). As Tawney comments – with satiric fury (in 1918), the FBI's first objection is 'that unlimited supplies of juvenile labour are indispensable to industry and that the proposals of that arch-Bolshevik, Mr Fisher, will shake to its foundations the fragile fabric of British industrial prosperity'. But the FBI's fundamental objection is that working-class children are less intelligent than middle-class children, and further, that since they are destined for certain kinds of employment, there is no point in educating them towards higher expectations (Tawney, 1973).

Image courtesy of LSE Archives.
Influential social critic, R.H. Tawney.

The idea that intelligence is inborn and fixed was the product of many years' research, initially undertaken in order to identify subnormal – or 'feeble-minded' – children for exclusion from elementary schools. Ideas about social-class differences in intelligence built on the eugenics movement early in the twentieth century. As Rose documents and discusses (1985: ch. 3), Galton, a leading eugenicist, argued that the lowest strata of society were there because they lacked adequate intelligence to function well in society; they had sunk to the bottom, and worse, they passed on their defective intelligence to the next generation. Proposed eugenicist actions to deal with the perceived threatened degeneration of the race included permanent segregation, sterilisation and murder. Given the huge disparities in how people lived, these ideas found some acceptance among the middle classes, though little practical action along these lines was envisaged. Indeed, during the 1920s the rise of national socialism in Germany put paid to the notion of drastic action. But eugenics did form a convenient basis for the developing 'science' of intelligence testing, and the idea that children should be sorted for schooling by intelligence was widely accepted. Important here was Cyril Burt, the first psychologist to be attached to the Board of Education in 1913. Burt propagated the idea that intelligence was linked to social class. As Rose says: he postulated 'a unitary function of intelligence, biologically based and innate, eminently inheritable, a common basis to all the attributes and qualities of the individual, manifested in social rank' (Rose, 1985: 122).

These propositions within psychological thinking can be contrasted with the arguments set out in the Hadow Report on 'The Education of the Adolescent' (Board of Education, 1926), commissioned by the 1924 Labour government, and influenced by 'progressive' ideas. The report argues that schools have a central civilising mission and the authors thus emphasise respect for each individual child as a future citizen. Schools are to be understood as 'ordered societies' which will carry out two kinds of activities. One kind are the intellectual activities, such as languages, history and science. But these are only the second kind. First and foremost are:

> *the moral and physical activities necessary to a proper social and individual life. . .The curriculum will accordingly comprise suitable moral and religious instruction and general physical training, including the acquisition of habits of graceful movement by means of physical exercises and dancing and the development of the spirit of team work and co-operation by means of corporate games.*
>
> (Board of Education, 1926: 188)

Clearly, debates held in the inter-war years about schooling for the majority of children were based on class-ridden assumptions; it was not yet time for middle- and upper-class policy-makers to reject the notion of children as earners, in favour of children as learners.[24] And it was certainly not time for these powerful people to challenge assumptions about the wealthy – their intelligence, schooling and future careers. Proposals for the extension of compulsory schooling rested somewhat on a universalising concept – all children had a right to education – but an important theme was also the needs of the state for a better educated population. On the other hand, an instrumental view of schooling dominated many accounts: school should fit children for the kind of work they would later do.

Planning, guiding and dividing
Children of the state

The ideas promoted within the education arena were certainly not matched by concerted action during the inter-war years (see Chapter 3, pages 73–9), and if we turn to the welfare arena, we find supporting evidence for the contention that children had low status as candidates for the right to state interventions to improve their health; instead, social class assumptions ensured that grudging help was offered to the poor (Hendrick, 2003: 15).

However, the concept of state responsibility for children was well underway by the late nineteenth century, at least at a rhetorical level – to judge from titles such as *Children of the State, The State and its Children* or *Children of the Nation*.[25] At the level of policy formation, a key piece of legislation is the 1889 Prevention of Cruelty to Children Act. This reconsidered parental rights and proposed that children had rights to protection from parental cruelty. Fifty-two Acts related to child welfare were passed between 1885 and 1913

(Hendrick, 2003: 33), some of which, such as the 1908 Children Act, attempted to regulate specific forms of child labour.

PUBLIC WARNING.

CHILDREN ACT, 1908.

Among other provisions of the Children Act, Parents or other persons having the charge of Children are made liable to fines or other penalties for

(1) Leaving a child under the age of 7 in a room with a fire without a fireguard, or without taking other precautions, if the child is burned to death or seriously injured.

(2) Taking or sending a child under the age of 14 into the drinking bar of a public-house, or any part of the premises exclusively or mainly used for the sale and consumption of intoxicating liquor.

(3) Giving to a child under the age of 5 any intoxicating liquor (except in cases of illness, &c.)

Persons, other than relatives, undertaking for payment, and for more than 48 hours, the care of one or more infants under the age of 7 away from their parents, must send notice of the fact to the Clerk to the Board of Guardians (in London to the Clerk to the London County Council, Spring Gardens, S.W.; in Scotland, to the Clerk to the Parish Council).

Exceptions may be made where the infants have been boarded out by a charitable society.

PAWNBROKERS must not accept goods from children under 14 (in London and Liverpool, under 16).

DEALERS IN OLD METAL must not buy from children under 16.

TOBACCONISTS must not sell to persons under 16 cigarettes or cigarette papers (nor any other tobacco if there is reason to believe it is for the use of the person under 16).

This does not apply to boys employed in the trade or to boy messengers in uniform employed by messenger companies.

Persons giving entertainments to children, where there are more than a hundred children and any of them go up a staircase to their seats, must have a sufficient number of grown-up attendants to secure the safety of the children in case of fire, &c.

This does not apply to entertainments in private houses.

The Act is in force from April 1st, 1909.

Home Office, 24th March, 1909.

Copies of the Children Act, price 9½d., or 11¼d. post free, may be ordered at certain Post Offices, or may be obtained from Wyman and Sons, Ltd., Fetter Lane, London, E.C.; Oliver and Boyd, Tweeddale Court, Edinburgh; or E. Ponsonby, 116, Grafton Street, Dublin.

(7148). Wt. 34532—113. 10,000. 3/09. A. & E. W.
(2903). G. 124. 10,000. 4/09.

Poster issued by the Home Office, setting out some of the provisions of the Children Act, 1908, including restrictions on pawnbrokers accepting goods from children under 14, and under 16 in specific localities. Note that the age of children barred from certain dangers is judged to vary according to the danger.

From our point of view, an important feature in these developments is their intersection with activities within the child study movement. This movement, pioneered, as far as England is concerned, by Darwin, who conducted a detailed study of his own infant son (published in the 1870s), was strengthened by the presence of children in the elementary schools, from the 1870s onwards. Medical doctors, psychologists and educationalists could now study the growth and development of the nation's children. This new public presence of the nation's children led to changes in thought. Tanner, the historian of human growth, observed:

> *When children were regarded as small adults it was natural for them to be worked not reared. . .But when children's growth began to be studied, that forced a different view on the organism, the view of a developing organism.*
>
> (Tanner, 1981: 402)

When services were provided by the state, this also had implications for making those services appropriate, as well as cost-effective, and both educational planning and health service planning have been bitterly contested domains ever since. As we shall see (Chapter 4), the state found itself taking on more responsibility for child welfare and education during the 1930s and 1940s. An important constituency working for change was women (see page 15).

However, while state responsibility increased in the early twentieth century with the advent of the elementary school, there were always opportunities for insisting on individual responsibility, by noting difference and identifying offenders. The idea that there was a normal path of development comprised the complementary idea that childhood carried risks, for children could be defined as deviating from these norms, as nervous, delicate, enuretic, neuropathic, maladjusted, unstable or solitary – classifications described by one medical sociologist as the 'problematisation of normality'.[26] So while the idea of normalcy offered hope for all children, the perceived difficulties of maintaining and fostering normalcy allowed 'experts' not just to educate mothers but to blame them when they deviated from expert advice.

For the experts (mainly male), the concept of the normal child implied that mothers should bow to experts about how best to raise the children. The 1920s was the era of prescriptive childcare books. The field was dominated by Truby King and Watson, who respectively prescribed good physical and good psychological care.

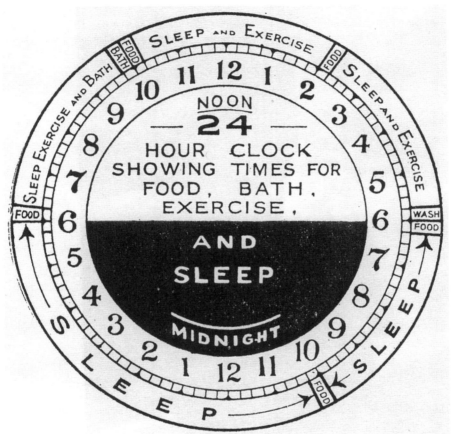

Reprinted with kind permission from the Royal New Zealand Plunket Society Inc. Originally published in Truby King, F. (1913) *Feeding and Care of Baby* (Wellington, NZ: Plunket), p. 74.

Truby King's guidelines for infant welfare included this clock face prescribing exact times for food, bath, sleep and exercise.

These were popular books (at least many were bought!). Truby King first published his *Feeding and Care of Baby* in 1913.[27] On the same lines, slightly less rigorous and also a bestseller, was Mabel Liddiard's *The Mothercraft Manual*.[28] These books made it clear that it was experts who knew how to raise children, and that children should be reared on scientific principles, with what to modern eyes looks like an intensely rigid regime. In Truby King the main emphasis is on physical care, the inculcation of regular habits. The ideal mother is like a disinterested, quiet, sensible, trained baby nurse. Mothers should not regard children as playthings; they should not over-stimulate the child – which will lead to irritability and lack of moral control in later life (Truby King, 1942: 43–5). And Liddiard notes:

> Today as a result of much study by experts not only does a woman undertake a far less hazardous task in becoming a mother, but her offspring will have a greatly increased prospect of coming into the world a perfect child and of growing up with an abundance of health and vigour.[29]

In *The Psychological Care of the Infant and Child*, Watson (1928) argued as follows:

> The sensible way to bring up children is to treat them as young adults. Dress them, bathe them with care and circumspection. Let your behaviour always be objective and kindly firm. Never hug and kiss them. Never let them sit on your lap. If you must, kiss them once on the forehead when they say goodnight. Shake hands with them in the morning. Give them a pat on the head if they have made an extremely good job of a difficult task. Try it out. In a week's time you will find how easy it is to be perfectly objective with your child and at the same time kindly. You will be ashamed of the mawkish, sentimental way you have been handling it.[30]

However, an alternative vision of the child and especially of the child's relations with his (*sic*) mother is presented in Susan Isaacs' *The Nursery Years*, mentioned earlier. Her vision of children, through psychoanalytical spectacles, emphasised the baby's close relation with his mother, his primitive urges of love and rage, the blend of physical and emotional learning babies go through and the consequent need for mothers to interact with protective and responsive love and understanding. Isaacs specifically rejects 'the strict tenets of modern hygiene' promoted by 'medical opinion' which emphasised sleep and quiet and long hours alone (Isaacs,

1965: 40). And other women, drawing on their own experience of child-rearing, attracted a following for their practical, responsive, experientially based advice (Hardyment, 1984: 164).

Health services for children?

In her study of childcare advice to mothers over the centuries, Christina Hardyment describes the particular character of these childcare books between the wars as comprehensible in the context of state arrogance and individual defeatism (1984: 164). She sees women as demoralised by the rise of experts, and by the growth of services which claimed to know best about the emotional and physical care of children. Books offering guidance on child-rearing were complemented during the 1930s by the gradual development of child guidance clinics.[31] These again asserted the authority of experts, the importance of mother–child relations, and the risks of abnormality even for the 'normal' child. Dissemination of this psychiatric work was through radio talks and also through books for the general reader, such as *The Growing Child and its Problems* (Miller, 1937).

The state had already taken some limited responsibility for children's physical health during the first years of the century. The school medical service started by defect-spotting, with parental responsibility for paying for treatment. Gradually over the inter-war years, clinics were established for the treatment of school-age children and, though parents were asked to pay if they could, treatment was not dependent on parental payment. What was provided varied by local authority but by 1939 virtually all were providing these clinics (Harris, 1995a: ch. 6).

However, George Newman, Medical Officer to the Board of Education, pointed out that the physical health of children had very low priority in education spending: for instance, expenditure in 1923 on the school medical service was 2.2 per cent of overall education spending.[32] Furthermore, the service could do very little, for it did not cover pre-school children; Newman, in his annual reports to the Board of Education, repeatedly quoted percentages of children (e.g. 35 per cent in 1922) who started school at five with a defect that could have been prevented or cured.[33] And the school medical service had no powers to treat children of any age who became ill at home. It was a parental responsibility to ensure that children received medical care – and for this they had to pay. However, Newman claimed that the school medical service had improved children's health, a claim disputed by other observers, who point to a complex set of factors. The social historian of health and health services, Charles Webster, notes that the service did develop in the inter-war years, in terms of numbers of staff, clinics and special schools, and so contacts with children must have increased. But child health among poor people, especially in the 'depressed areas', remained very poor and any improvements in child health could be assigned to a range of factors, such as rising affluence, better standards of public health and some improved housing (Webster, 1983). However, it is clear that the annual publication of these reports drew attention to state responsibility and to health care as an integral component of an education service. Government action also initiated health care for young workers: the 1937 National Health Insurance Act established that young people from age 14 in paid work should contribute to health insurance, thus giving them access to medical services (Morgan, 1943: 80).

Health promotion

While much service provision was geared to identifying, monitoring and curing health problems, there were also important initiatives aimed at health promotion. Via the eugenics movement, many suggestions were made for providing healthy, including outdoor, environments for schoolchildren – to some extent as a remedial measure for children living in poor home environments. This open-air movement led to the establishment of some schools based on these ideas (Bryder, 1992). The three Hadow reports on secondary, primary and nursery education endorsed physical activity as a key part of the curriculum.[34] In its *Handbook of Suggestions for Teachers*, the Board of Education (1937: 162–3), building on the 1933 edition, gave physical exercise and training first place in its list of curricula. Schools should provide opportunities for children's 'bodily activity' because educating the body as well as the mind leads to 'self-control, self-respect, courage, decision, good temper and a sense of well-being':

For them, as for any other young animals, free and active movement is as necessary for health and development as are fresh air, sunshine, pure water, suitable food and sleep. Games and other physical activities provide a necessary outlet for the natural impulses of children and the real but easy discipline associated with them is one of the best means of training in self-management. Physical training helps children build up strong, beautiful and graceful bodies and to keep them fit. It is probable, too, that the development of the brain itself is to a considerable extent connected with bodily activity.

The ideals of the nursery school movement chimed in with this health promotion emphasis and the Nursery Schools Association (founded in 1923) emphasised the importance of free activity: 'spontaneous and purposeful activity in spacious open-air conditions' (Penn, 2004: 84). Again, Susan Isaacs was influential. In her emphasis on free play, freedom to explore, and the acquisition of responsibility through taking responsibility for one's actions for oneself, she provided guidance for both parents and nursery staff (Isaacs, 1965). The expansion of nursery school places was promoted by the Labour Party, with Margaret McMillan as a key player[35] and by permissive powers to local authorities in the 1918 Education Act. The Hadow Report on infant and nursery schools (Board of Education, 1933) also endorsed their expansion, though, recognising hard economic times, it suggested poor industrial areas as a priority. In 1933 there were only 55 nursery schools, of which 30 were state-provided; by 1939 there were 118 nursery schools, fewer than half state-provided.

A more radical move, in practice, was the 'Peckham Experiment', developed as a model of how intervention could improve health (Pearse and Crocker, 1943). After a start in a house in Peckham in 1926, a purpose-built centre – the Pioneer Health Centre – was opened in 1935. The Centre aimed to improve people's health through positive action; this was social eugenics in practice. Influential in planning, especially for the youngest, was Maria Montessori, on the basis of her concept of an 'inherent sequence of development of the faculties' (ibid.: 182, 317).[36] Members of families living locally were offered a regular 'health overhaul', leading to treatment as required. Most importantly they were offered a wide range of activities, based on the principle of free choice. A swimming pool, gym, nursery, outdoor playspace, dance hall, books and board games were provided and from the central cafeteria, parents could see their children actively engaged in their chosen activities and could themselves begin to participate. The Centre also had access to a 'home farm' and holiday camp in Kent.

This was health promotion in practice: it focused on both individuals and the family – on children's active engagement in physical and mental learning and on parents' engagement with their children's activities. This focus contrasts with the defect-spotting approach of many welfare initiatives, and with children as objects of narrow, mainly sedentary schooling, where parents played virtually no part. Of interest too is the Centre's focus on the value of countryside experience for children. Another voluntary initiative, on the same principles, was the Children's Country Holiday Fund, dating back to the 1880s. And we shall see later that in wartime observers found plenty to praise in children's experience of country life.[37]

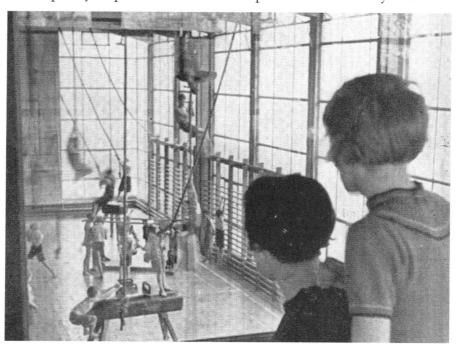

Reproduced by kind permission of the Pioneer Health Foundation.
Mothers watching their children exercise in the gymnasium at the Pioneer Health Centre.

Contrasting ideas

We can see in these developments contrasting sets of ideas about childhood and how it was best shaped. On the one hand, ideas about norms, and best maternal behaviour suggested that all children had much the same needs and that prospects were bright for good childhoods (and thereafter good adulthoods), provided experts and mothers under their guidance worked towards these goals. On the other hand it can be argued that the way services were provided sharpened class divisions and exacerbated the idea that some mothers and some children were better than others.[38] Thus on physical care, infant welfare clinics and school medical services were aimed largely at the working classes; middle-class mothers would pay for medical monitoring and care. As to emotional, psychological nurturing in nursery schools, few of these were provided in the state system and so it was the well-to-do who would pay to get these advantages. And it would be mainly these mothers who would buy baby books and try (perhaps) to implement their programmes. Perhaps these differences helped to demonise working-class mothers, who would not have these books and who were the object of interventions by health visitors.

Furthermore, while in the 1930s a story was told with 'relentless optimism'[39] of a brave new world where childhoods had been seriously improved by psychological and health interventions, another story, based on observation, challenged this vision, for it described the poverty in which many children lived – and which the evacuation scheme of 1939 revealed to the nation.

Child protection and children's rights

The moves outlined above to provide for children, to some extent as investments in the future of the state, based in some cases on the principle that all children had the right to health-promoting conditions of life, are complemented by further movements that emphasised child protection. An important strand of work arose from the point that while working men had some health insurance, women and children did not. And while some health services for pregnant and nursing mothers and their babies had been put in place, working-class women in general endured appalling ill-health, and the poverty of many women and children in working-class families was dire (Spring Rice,

1939). Women were key in the pressure for change and improvement. They worked, hands-on, as social workers, health visitors and teachers; perhaps most importantly they took advantage of the right to join political movements and voluntary organisations and to work on local education committees. It has been argued that through their 'maternalist' promotion of motherhood and the need for better health and welfare services for mothers and children, women paved the way in the inter-war years for the post-war policies which confirmed women as mothers and returned them to the home (Thane, 1993).

We note that the 'maternalist' movement tended towards conflating 'mothers-and-children'. Children were not here conceptualised as a separate constituency. So among the many women who worked for social improvements, we give space here to Eglantyne Jebb, for she was perhaps unique at the time in providing a theoretical basis for children's right to protection. After the First World War, she travelled widely in Europe and started the Save the Children Fund (SCF) in 1919, in order to help relieve children's distress consequent on the war. From the beginning, the SCF worked internationally, across Europe and later in Africa. The fact that in the first four years large sums were donated to finance the

Courtesy of Save the Children UK.
Eglantyne Jebb worked for children's welfare and human rights.

work – over £4 million (for instance from the Labour movement, the Miners' Federation of Great Britain and from many individuals, such as Nancy Astor) – indicates that there was a climate of ready-made support for this initiative; indeed, it spread rapidly to other countries – Rädda Barnen started in Sweden a year later. During the 1920s and again during the Great Depression in the early 1930s, SCF used some of its funds to improve the health and welfare of English children; the organisation provided funds to help with infant welfare clinics, and to support the work of the Salvation Army, the Invalid Children's Association, and the National Council for the Unmarried Mother and her Children. In 1926, SCF opened an open-air school for London children at Broadstairs. During the General Strike of 1926 and onwards the organisation provided emergency aid to children and established nursery schools (on the open-air principle established by the McMillan sisters), especially in the North East and Wales. They initiated a sponsorship scheme whereby children in prosperous areas became 'godmothers' to classes of schoolchildren in the depressed areas (Freeman, 1965).

Through this work, Jebb and her colleagues were drawing attention to an important theme, which she considers in her final essay: there were commonalities among children, across nations; notably, what adults did (including violence) impacted particularly harshly on children, so adults had a duty to redress the wrongs done to children. The starving children in Europe and the poorly nourished children in England suffered in common from social policies that did not take their interests into account. In effect, she is characterising children as a social group whose welfare depends on adult action; in this sense it is a minority social group. In her last years, Jebb worked with a committee of people experienced in social work and consulted with the National Council of Women of Great Britain, whose thoughts had been moving along similar lines, towards a charter of children's rights.[40]

Jebb's essay (1929) begins with the Declaration of the Rights of the Child (endorsed by the League of Nations in Geneva in 1924). Its five main points are:

The child must be given the means requisite for its normal development, both materially and spiritually.
The child that is hungry must be fed, the child that is sick must be

nursed, the child that is backward must be helped, the delinquent child must be reclaimed and the orphan and the waif must be sheltered and succoured.

The child must be the first to receive relief in times of distress.

The child must be put in a position to earn a livelihood and must be protected against every form of exploitation.

The child must be brought up in the consciousness that its talents must be devoted to the service of its fellow men.

The

Declaration of Geneva

PAR la présente Déclaration des Droits de l'Enfant, dite Déclaration de Genève, les hommes et les femmes de toutes les nations, reconnaissant que l'Humanité doit donner à l'Enfant ce qu'elle a de meilleur, affirment leurs devoirs, en dehors de toute consideration de race, de nationalité et de croyance :

I. L'ENFANT doit être mis en mesure de se développer d'une façon normale, matérielle-ment et spirituellement.

II. L'ENFANT qui a faim doit être nourri ; l'enfant malade doit être soigné ; l'enfant arriéré doit être encouragé ; l'enfant dévoyé doit être ramené ; l'orphelin et l'abandonné doivent être recueillis et secourus.

III. L'ENFANT doit être la premier à recevoir des secours en temps de détresse.

IV. L'ENFANT doit être mis en mesure de gagner sa vie, et doit être protégé contre toute exploitation.

V. L'ENFANT doit être élévé dans le sentiment que ses meilleures qualités doivent être mises au service de ses frères.

This typographical layout was inspired by that which appears in Jebb, Eglantyne (1929) *Save the Child! A posthumous essay* (Weardale Press).[41]

The Declaration of the Rights of the Child in its original French.

The charter is notable in placing duties of protection on adults, but also in proposing children's rights to priority care and protection. Notably, too, it stresses children's responsibilities to their society; the concept of service makes its appearance – a theme emphasised in many twentieth-century discourses about children, for instance by leaders of Scouts and Guides and by heads of private and grammar schools.[42] This seems to be the first time children's rights had been set out formally in England. But pioneers across Europe were arguing that children deserved respect as persons, rather than as 'becomings'. For instance, Maria Montessori aimed to free children from adult oppression, and devised methods whereby children could educate themselves, rather than be schooled.[43] Her work was known by Korczak, who observed the children's activities at a newly opened Montessori nursery in Kiev in 1917, and he ran his orphanages on the basis of respecting children, and promoting their rights.[44] The international New Education Fellowship held regular conferences to discuss such ideas, and in 1942 the conference produced a charter of children's rights.[45]

While some moves were thus being made, by people outside the mainstream of politics, to raise the status of children and of childhood and to alter ideas and practices, there were also moves afoot in the mainstream. The Children and Young Persons Act 1933, which legislated for people under the age of 18, was described by a social historian of welfare reforms as ground-breaking in its stated aim of moving away from blame and stigma towards the welfare of the child. For, within the terms of the Act, both delinquent and neglected children were regarded as having commonalities: they were in need of care and protection. 'The welfare of the child, and not the judgment of society, was now paramount' (Heywood, 1959: 130). The Act emerged from a growing set of beliefs that young people who 'offended' were psychologically disturbed and had also suffered poor social and physical environments; a viewpoint developed in the 1920s, notably in Cyril Burt's influential book *The Young Delinquent* (1927) (Hendrick, 2003: 115–19). Bailey documents resistance to the spirit and terms of the Act, among those who thought punishment, including physical punishment, was appropriate for offenders. A speaker in the House of Lords describes the proposed abolition of whipping as 'this effeminate, over-humanitarian, ultra-sentimental view' (Bailey, 1987: 108). As both Bailey and Hendrick note,[46] however, the 'treatment' young delinquents received continued to be harsh, including a strict regimen of hard work, tough living conditions, poor diet and physical punishment. One factor encouraging harsh response was the continued rise in juvenile crime in the 1930s.

Discussion

A general point about the inter-war years is that there was a ferment of ideas about childhood. The social construction of childhood was in the process of change. Traditionally there were thought to be unbridgeable spaces between childhoods: (1) with some children worth more than others; (2) with high intelligence concentrated in the upper classes; (3) with deficient childcare practices among working-class women; (4) with schooling to fit children for the station in life to which they belonged; and (5) with some children, such as those 'in care' regarded as worthless – fit for nothing but domestic service and menial labour. Just as today, the social evils perceived as attached to poverty allowed for deeply entrenched social assumptions about working-class people to flourish – their low intelligence, deviance from social norms, and their role as workers in the state machine.

But in the inter-war years ideas originating in earlier times gained new strength and cohesion. These include the following: (1) All children go through a developmental trajectory and require life conditions that promote healthy development. (2) All children have a right to a decent education service, including nursery and secondary education. (3) Childhood is a period of vulnerability – physically, emotionally and mentally – and therefore adults have responsibility to protect children. Even children who transgress should be protected and enabled. (4) Children are people with rights. (5) The nation needs to develop and harness the abilities of all its children, in the interests of efficiency and prosperity. (6) The state has a responsibility to ensure a decent standard of living for all children.

The pioneers focused on particularly dire aspects of policies and services for children and demanded that they be improved (such as child health and welfare, women's and children's poverty and education practices). Some models of practice based on new ideas showed what could be done. There was, however, a huge gap between pioneering ideas and practices, structured by the low status of children (and their mothers), the insistence on parental responsibility, and the class-based blame and stigma attached to poor parents' behaviour. The division of responsibility for children and for childhood continued to favour parental over state responsibility.

This chapter provides a context for Chapter 3: the more detailed consideration of education policy and practice, and the lives of children, split between schooling and work. It also looks forward to Chapter 4, which considers the exigencies of war as they began to affect children's lives: (1) the demands for manpower in the armed forces and factories; (2) the need to grow as much food as possible; (3) the need to procure from the people as much financial help for the war effort as possible; and (4) the need to replace, through children's efforts, the work of adults called up to the armed services and factories. We shall document how children were therefore enlisted over the course of the war years.

Notes

1   A more recent edited collection of papers on the political and social history of Britain in the early twentieth century gives, apart from primary sources, 35 pages of secondary sources, with about 30 per page, or over 1,000 references (Wisley, 2009).

2   Smith, 1998: 35.

3   J.B. Orr, 1936: 49, *Food, Health and Income*, quoted in Morgan, 1943: 70.

4   See page 73 for debates on the 1917 Education Bill.

5   Hendrick, 2003: 96; Harris, 1995a: ch. 6.

6   See also Chapter 4, pages 103–6.

7   The slow progress towards improvement in the education service is described in Chapter 3.

8   Reprinted in Van der Eyken, 1973. See also Taylor, 1965: ch. IX.

9   See Chapter 3, pages 67–9.

10   For discussions on women as social reformers, see Williams, 2000; Martin and Goodman, 2004; Martin, 2010.

11   Hendrick, 2003: 87–94; Hurt, 1979: chs V and VII.

12   Karl Mannheim (1894–1947) was the first professor of sociology at the University of Frankfurt, Germany. He was removed from his post in 1933 and came to England, where he taught at the London School of Economics and at the Institute of Education, University of London (Whitty, 1997).

13   Parts of Fisher's and Wedgwood's speeches to the House of Commons in 1917 are reprinted in Van der Eyken, 1973.

14   Indeed, some trades unionists opposed the halting of child labour (Barker, 1972: 31).

15   Nunn's *Education: Its data and first principles,* first published in 1920, was reprinted 23 times up to 1961.

16   This speech is set out in a report on the conference held in Elsinore, Denmark in 1929 (Boyd, 1930: 454–6). See also, in similar vein, Dora Russell, *In Defence of Children* (1932); she argued that schools should engage children with the natural world and should stimulate in children the power of independent judgement.

17   *The Nursery Years,* first published in 1929, was reprinted 18 times up to 1965.

18   *The Children We Teach,* first published in 1932, was reprinted 15 times up to 1961.

19   Children as hope for the future will be considered in more detail in Chapter 3.

20   Margaret McMillan's life and work (1860–1931) is analysed in Carolyn Steedman's 1990 biography.

21   Karl Mannheim's *Diagnosis of our Time*, 1954, first published 1943.

22   Barnard, 1968, first published 1947, p. 293.

23   This paper, on 'A national college of all souls: The true war memorial' is reprinted in Van der Eyken, 1973: 201–6.

24   Children as earners or as learners in the inter-war years is the main focus of Chapter 3.

25   By, respectively, Florence Davenport, 1868; Gertrude Tuckwell, 1894; and John Gorst, 1906. See Hendrick, 2003: ch. 2 for a comprehensive account of late nineteenth-century work on the condition of childhood and state responsibility.

26   David Armstrong, 1983: ch. 6 analyses the development of child surveillance from a Foucauldian perspective.

27   Truby King's book was published in 1913 and reprinted 22 times up to 1932. The 1942 edition has been used here.

28   Mabel Liddiard's book was published in 1923 and reprinted 17 times up to 1944. The 1954 edition has been used here.

29   Mabel Liddiard, Preface to the 12th edition.

30   Quoted in Hardyment, 1984: 175.

31   Fourteen child guidance clinics were established by 1932, and 54 by 1938 (Hendrick 2003: 104–8).

32   This is noted in Harris, 1995a: 115.

33   This figure is quoted by Jebb (1929: 18) in her argument in favour of better child protection.

34   The report on secondary education (Board of Education, 1926); the report on primary education (Board of Education, 1931); the report on nursery education (Board of Education, 1933).

35 Margaret McMillan worked for the expansion of nursery education and, with her patron, Lady Astor, was instrumental in establishing the Rachel McMillan Training College, for the training of nursery workers (Steedman, 1990: 186).

36 See note 43 for a summary of Maria Montessori's career.

37 See Chapter 4, page 84.

38 See, for discussion, Jane Lewis, 1986.

39 Cunningham, 1991: 220 provides detail on this story.

40 Jebb's life is described by Oldfield, 2006: 118–20 and by Buxton and Fuller, 1931.

41 It was impossible to obtain the original image because copying or scanning may have damaged the document. This image is an imitation but not an exact replica.

42 For discussion of the concept of service, see the sections on organisations such as Scouts and Guides in Chapter 8. The concept of children's responsibilities to their society and their family appears in the African Charter of Children's Rights (in line with local traditions), but not in the UN Convention on the Rights of the Child.

43 Maria Montessori (1869–1952) was a trained doctor and pioneer in freeing children and their education from the domination of parents and teachers. She founded the Children's House in Rome, equipped with tools, toys and self-correcting devices to allow children to manage and educate themselves, as far as possible (Boyd and Rawson, 1965: 21–3).

44 Janusz Korczak (1878–1942) was a Polish medical doctor who devoted much of his life to caring for orphans and to promoting their rights. During the Second World War, he continued with this work, finally in the Warsaw ghetto, and died with the children at Treblinka (Lifton, 1988). Lifton draws on his written works to summarise his ideas for a declaration of children's rights (1988: 355–6).

45 See Chapter 4, pages 110–11.

46 Bailey, 1987: ch. 7; Hendrick, 2003: 120–1.

Chapter 3

Earners or learners? Work and school 1900–1939

In this chapter we discuss how historical and legislative changes in the early twentieth century reflected and shaped the character and status of English childhoods, in considering the question of how far children were sited as earners or learners. The chapter provides a historical context for understanding children's work during the war years, as detailed in later chapters. The argument is that an adequate understanding of children's work during the war requires consideration of the contradictions, conflicts and changes over time in the social construction of childhood through this early part of the century.

Background: 1870–1918

Despite a growing awareness of the exploitative nature of child labour during the nineteenth century, there never was a clearly identifiable national policy towards child labour, and it declined only gradually through a combination of employment legislation, in the form of factory and workshop controls, and educational policy towards the development of a national education system with compulsory attendance. The Factory Acts[1] of the nineteenth century initially regulated the employment of children in the textile industries, and were gradually extended to other industries. As Cunningham suggests, the earliest attempts to control child labour effectively only 'set up a minimum age for work in certain trades' (Cunningham, 1991: 164), and controlled the hours and conditions of work for children in those trades. Local variations in the legislation have always been possible through additional local bye-laws, but enforcement has always been patchy.

The gradual introduction of compulsory schooling and concomitant increases in the school-leaving age effectively removed large numbers of children from the labour market. The Elementary Education Act 1870 was intended to set up a system of elementary schools for working-class children, with publicly provided schools filling the gaps where there was no existing church-administered school.[2] The education historian Brian Simon notes that the schools were to provide 'strictly circumscribed teaching up to the school-leaving age which, under certain bye-laws, could be as early as ten' (Simon, 1965: 112). The importance of the Act was, Simon suggests, to 'lay essential foundations on which could be built a highly organised and strictly segmented system of schooling designed specifically for the working class' (ibid.: 112). The 1874 Factory Act raised the half-time age to ten years old,[3] and the 1880 Education Act made school attendance compulsory for all children between the ages of five and ten, with exemptions for employment based on proficiency and attendance obtainable up to the age of 14 years. The school-leaving age was raised to 11 years in 1893, and to 12 years in 1899. However, the introduction of compulsory schooling by no means nullified the demand for cheap child labour and effectively pushed children into various 'unregulated' forms of employment, such as outwork, street selling, and particularly the informal labour market for casual juvenile workers.

The development of welfare policy to 'protect' children

As we noted in Chapter 2, the last two decades of the nineteenth century saw rising concern for children's welfare, and the development of ideas about welfare in general. The social historian Rubenstein suggests that 'the establishment of the National Society for the Prevention of Cruelty to Children, rate-provided school meals for needy children and legislation for the protection of children were among the products of this newly expressed concern' (Rubenstein, 1969: 70). Recruitment for the Boer War focused political and public concern on the well-being of the nation, and this concern was to have important implications for child welfare and children's moral, spiritual and physical health. Alongside this concern, there was increasing anxiety over Britain's declining trade position, the widespread poverty, poor physical health and diet of the mass of the population, inadequate housing, poor industrial conditions and high infant mortality rates.[4]

The 'Child Study' movement, which sought to identify and explain the 'problems' of youth and childhood in scientific terms (Chapter 2, page 42), focused somewhat on the employment of children, because working children were likely to be unhealthy children, who would become unhealthy adults and hence endanger the future of the nation. Indeed, there had been renewed concern about child labour towards the end of the nineteenth century (Cunningham, 1991: 174–89). For example, a 1904 volume of essays on the 'town boy' edited by Urwick, a sociologist and Toynbee Hall settlement resident, drew attention to the chronic physical unfitness of army recruits. Only 1,200 out of 11,000 volunteers in Manchester had been judged to be fit enough, and:

> *The examination of school children does not give a more reassuring result. In the industrial and reformatory schools, we are told that the boys at the age of 13 average 4 inches less in height and a stone less in weight than the ordinary public school boy at that age.*
>
> (Urwick, 1904: 259)

Another concern was about the moral character of boys and girls: children engaging in paid work, out and about on the streets, could rapidly be drawn into crime and prostitution. One important kind of welfare reform was to organise young people – to keep them off the streets, to engage them with character-building activities, including militaristic ones, to teach them Christian virtues and ideas about service and citizenship.[5]

'Boy labour' and the related 'problem' of children's employment

At the turn of the century there were separate labour markets in many large cities, but particularly London, for juvenile and for adult unskilled labour, and many occupations were solely 'boy's work': messengers, van boys, as well as unskilled factory labour.

During the first half of the twentieth century, apprenticeships declined in numbers; one reason was that mechanisation broke down skills into small component tasks, which could be quickly learned (Morgan, 1943: 20). Apprenticeships also fell into disrepute among boys, because they offered only limited practical training, hard labour and poor pay (Ryan, 1999; see also Humphries, 1981: 10). So working-class boys were trapped in a downward spiral because those who found unskilled work on leaving school tended to lose their jobs at 16 or 18 to the next generation (since boys could be paid less than an adult wage). But because they had no formal training, they were unsuited for anything but casual work (Stedman Jones, 1971). This phenomenon became known at the time as 'the boy labour problem', and the economic conditions that encouraged it persisted until the late 1930s.

In the early twentieth century many publications by predominantly upper- and middle-class social reformers drew attention to the 'boy labour problem'.[6] A smaller body of research described the less visible but related topic of children who worked part-time while attending school.[7] This research reflects a growing awareness of the possible disadvantages of paid work, consequent on the introduction of state schooling, which, in modern terms, 'problematised' wage-earning schoolchildren, part-timers and partial-exemption schoolchildren or half-timers, by establishing a norm for childhood and adolescence different from anything that had previously existed. 'In this historical context, working children began to be seen as deviating from the norm' (Springhall, 1986: 96). Among commentators, a tentative norm for childhood was beginning to be outlined: the child was to be a schoolchild. Working-class childhoods persisted, however, as working childhoods.

Thus, in 1901, a report of the Interdepartmental Committee on the Employment of School Children had recognised that so long as children attended school regularly, the hours they worked outside school were completely unregulated. It also drew attention to street trading by children, because those children were seen as at moral as well as physical risk. But the report concluded that employment would not be harmful if it were restricted to 20–25 hours a week: 'What is required is not the total prohibition of school child labour but its regulation.'[8] Following the report, the Employment of Children Act 1903 forbade the employment of children between 9 p.m. and 6 a.m. and banned street selling by children under 11 years of age, but 'almost all of the effectiveness of the measure depended on the willingness of local authorities to enforce it'.[9] The working child posed a moral problem: 'it is part of the street-bred child's precocity that he acquires a too early acquaintance with matters which, as a child, he ought not to know at all'.[10] Yet, there was reluctance to ban child employment because of the economic hardship that would be caused to families. In 1913 the *TES* reported a survey on child employment carried out in Surrey, where the medical officer who had carried out the survey:

> *arrived reluctantly at the conclusion that in a large number of cases the wages of the father alone were not adequate to maintain the family at even the lowest efficiency for health, and that therefore the employment of from one-half to two-thirds of the boys who go out to work is a necessity in the present state of social conditions. It is estimated that the average wage earned by boys is 2s 3d a week, an amount just sufficient to keep one child in food for one week.*
>
> (*TES*, 2 September 1913)

Yet the relief of poverty in families could be achieved through other means, as Rathbone's campaign for family allowances argued.[11] Trades union pressure was also important in highlighting conflicts between their members, parents and, possibly, children. On the surface, much trades union campaigning on child labour was presented in terms of the working-class child's right to education, but underlying these demands was often concern for safeguarding the interests of their own adult members. During the early part of the century, children under 16 were not eligible to join trades unions and the fact that they were cheaper to employ meant that they frequently displaced adult workers; farmers, for instance, cut their costs by employing children (Griggs, 1983: 38). Trades unions often attempted to limit the numbers of children and juveniles employed in relation to the number of adult workers purely 'in the interest of their members' (Keeling, 1914: xxii). Unionists argued that where children were only half-time at school, they should be kept at home, rather than sent into factories (Griggs, 1983: 38) – but parents needed the income their children could bring in.

The First World War

Concern over 'boy labour' appears to have diminished during the First World War, probably because war conditions substantially increased the demand for juvenile and child labour. Schoolchildren formed an important source of labour in agricultural production, and school leavers were employed in large numbers in factories. Objections to the war-time employment of schoolchildren were made by Labour and Liberal Members of Parliament,[12] and the employment of children in factories appears to have been resisted initially by the War Office, which early on stated that it 'deprecated the employment of boys. . .except as an extreme measure' (cited in the *TES*, 2 March 1915). However, there was a gradual realisation that children would have to work for the war effort, even though the effects were thought potentially deleterious to their health and education. The Board of Education issued various circulars which outlined the conditions to be satisfied before school exemptions could be granted. One condition was that 'the employment must be light in character', but 'light' was not defined (reported in the *TES*, 6 April 1915). Some school boards allowed 'holidays' for children over 12 so that they could work on the land during the hay, corn and potato harvests, and reports from local education authorities showed that ever-increasing numbers of children were being exempted from school for agricultural work, but that attempts to regulate child labour were inadequate.[13] The exemption from school of children for agricultural work during the First World War was opposed by the Secretary of the Agricultural Labourers' Union[14] who argued that 'farmers would find plenty of labour if they were prepared to pay an adequate wage' (*TES*, 2 February 1915). Annual statistics were collected by the Board of Education of the numbers of children exempted from school attendance for employment in agriculture. In October 1916, for example, 13,823 boys and 1,092 girls under the age of 14 were absent from school so that they could work on farms.[15] In some counties, children as young as 11 were exempted from school.[16] Bringing in the harvest was an established tradition for working-class families, who would, for instance, trek off from the East End of London to Kent, for the hop picking (McGrath, 2009).

Official statistics were not collected of the numbers of children involved in other forms of war-work. However, in his introduction of the Education Bill in the House of Commons in August 1917, the President of the Board of Education, Fisher, stated that 'in the three years of War some 600,000 children have been withdrawn prematurely from school and become immersed in industry'.[17] Young workers in munitions factories were reportedly well paid by war standards, though this in itself gave rise to expressions of moral concern that 'the excessive amount of pocket money that is at the disposal both of boys and girls [is] leading to extravagant expenditure both in dress and amusements' (*TES*, 7 December 1915). However, juvenile workers were not paid adult wages, just as women were not paid men's wages. For example, girls employed in men's work in engineering and shipbuilding establishments had deductions made on piece-rates, ranging from 10 to 30 per cent, according to age (Drake, 1984).

Girls' labour

Girls' labour attracted a somewhat different set of concerns, as compared to boys', although girls too faced the same syndrome – poorly paid jobs from 14 to 18, followed by dismissal in favour of the next generation of school leavers (Todd, 2005: 46). But girls mattered less to commentators, on the grounds that they would soon leave paid employment for marriage, and were not responsible for the economic support of the family. Of course 'girls' labour' meant working-class girls' labour; middle-class girls lived within controlled environments – the home with its many comforts, and, for some, the school.[18] One theme in the debates was that girls – in adolescence – were 'liable to seasons of lowered vitality, in which nervous fatigue is serious', yet they were also required to undertake domestic work, including housework, childcare, and, in poorer households, home industries (such as making matchboxes and artificial flowers).[19] This work at home was not controlled in any way by law, unlike work in the public domain. A second theme was that girls and women should be protected from the dangers and vices of the public world: working-class girls, employed, for instance, in factories might quickly learn undesirable and immoral characteristics, for the 'average working girl is intensely individualistic, very excitable and pleasure-loving', and those working in street trading could be described as taking a first step towards a life of immorality.[20]

A third related theme was the natural destiny of women as homemakers and as mothers. This destiny implied that girls should learn homemaking skills at school.[21] The Hadow Committee, which reviewed masses of evidence, both written and oral, expressed the view that all children have to be educated with two ends in view: 'to earn their own living, and to be useful citizens; while girls also have to be prepared to be makers of homes' (Board of Education, 1923: 126). The Committee saw no way round the extra burden on girls (other than suggesting that boys might help out at home too) and they therefore endorsed the labour of school-age girls at home, and recommended that they take public examinations a year later than boys.[22] Pervasive in the literature through the inter-war years and beyond is the assumption that women are responsible for the home and for child-rearing. In its *Handbook of Suggestions for Teachers* (1937: ch. IX) the Board of Education said schools should teach housecraft to older girls; this should include cleaning, cooking, laundry and childcare, which together make up 'the combined work of the home'. A particularly interesting example is Margery Spring Rice's concluding comments to her harrowing report on the poor living conditions and poor health of working-class women (1939: 203–6); although she stresses the importance of welfare and health interventions to alleviate these problems, she ends with stirring exhortations to girls: they must educate and train themselves (with the help of courses at school) for the 'arduous and skilled job' of marriage and child-rearing.

A feature of debates, in the years after the First World War, can be seen as a response to the mass entry of girls and women into paid work during the war. Thus, for instance, whereas in 1911, 59 per cent of girls aged 14–18 were in paid work ('in service', textile trades, dress trades, clerical work), by 1917 proportions in industry increased by nearly a quarter and in professional and other such occupations, for instance transport, by four-fifths (Collier, 1918: xi). The entry of women into the professions, via colleges and universities, was another challenge to ideas about the proper activities of school-age girls. But old ideas persisted through the inter-war years: several of our interviewees, including some educated in grammar schools, reported being deflected from academic and professional ambitions towards early school-leaving and 'women's work'. Resentment was deep-seated; one of these women later won through to a PhD.[23]

More radically, Pearl Jephcott (1942: 56) tackled the gross social-class inequalities in access to education. She made a powerful plea for reform in the education of girls, based on her study of the long hours of tedious work done by 14 year olds and the lack of interesting outlets for their intelligence. This plea echoes the deeply held beliefs of a teacher in a secondary elementary school in London, who worked to secure grammar-school places for the girls at age 13, to widen their horizons and to save them from the drudgery of factory work, followed by domestic work, dependent on a man's wages (Tizard, 2010: 98).

Underpinning many of the concerns about girls – their schooling and their labour – was an intense outpouring of work on 'adolescence', boosted by Hall's 1904 tome,[24] and, for instance, by the establishment of a London Society of Psychoanalysts (1913) and of the British Paediatric Society (1926); this was eagerly pursued by psychologists in the following decades.[25] While the early twentieth century saw growing concern for the physical health of children who combined school work with manual labour, there was heightened emphasis on 'the effects of industrial work on the health and physique of adolescent girls' (Collier, 1918: 1). Furthermore, the new freedoms enjoyed by girls in the public worlds of education and work were understood to be leading to unnatural competition between girls and boys. So, for instance, psychologists such as Blanchard (1921) argued that the woman as individual is 'naturally' subordinate to the welfare of the society, for she is responsible for ensuring the continuation of the race; however, 'nowadays' girls during adolescence experience conflict between egoistic tendencies, the will to power and achievement, and the natural altruistic feelings of women. And Pailthorpe (1932), who studied the psychology of delinquency, thought adolescence a particularly dangerous time, because with the increase in sexual energy but no outlet for it, young people might turn to crime.

It seems then, in sum, that educationalists' and socialists' pressure to increase the years of schooling for all children drew attention to puberty as a factor to be taken into account when considering girls' paid and unpaid work. Middle-class lifestyles continued to provide the moral benchmark for girls. Debate continued about girls' and women's engagement with the public world of work, in the context of eugenic emphasis on the need for healthy new generations, and hence the need for competent mothers.

Children's work between the wars

Children under 14 continued to be legally employed half-time until 1 January 1921, when the Employment of Women, Young Persons and Children Act 1920 came into effect, prohibiting the employment of children under 14 in any industrial undertaking or on board ships, with the exception of children working for their parents or as apprentices (Simon, 1965). Wage-earning by schoolchildren continued during the inter-war period, especially where there was widespread poverty. The term 'subsistence truancy' has been used to describe non-attendance at school provoked essentially by poverty and social deprivation, when children took part-time or full-time employment to supplement household income. Humphries

(1981: 68) suggests that this form of truancy 'persisted. . .especially in country districts where attendance regulations were rarely reinforced'. One of our interviewees gives an example of what this poverty meant to children, as she looked back on her days at elementary school in the 1930s:

> *There was a lot of poverty. I remember one of the girls saying, 'It's alright for you, but when I go home my mother hires me out to scrub floors'. And she didn't have any shoes.*

Despite occasional reports about the deleterious effects of employment on schoolchildren, there was still confusion after the war as to which authority was responsible for administering the law relating to the employment of children. By 1920, it was the Home Office rather than the Board of Education which had responsibility for approving bye-laws on children's employment. The law itself was confusing, as illustrated by a prosecution case in 1920 under the Employment of Children Act 1903. The case raised questions over the exact meaning of the word 'employment', and concerned a newsagent supplying a child with newspapers, which the boy (aged between 10 and 11) then proceeded to sell. The boy made 3d profit and, in the initial case, the Magistrate had held that this was not a case of employing a child within the meaning of the Act, because 'the relationship of master and servant did not exist between the respondent and the boy, who merely took the newspapers on the usual trade terms'. The appeal court, however, took the view that 'the word "employ" was not limited to the relationship of master and servant. The term could be applied where the relationship of principal and agent existed. The respondent employed the boy as an agent, and an offence had been committed against the statute' (*TES*, 31 March 1921).

Successive governments during the inter-war period appear to have shown unquestioning acceptance of work by schoolchildren. We emphasise that legislation controlling children's employment usually falls under other legal instruments aimed at regulating children's activities and improving their welfare, and the main legislative control on children's employment today remains part of the 1933 Children and Young Persons Act. This prohibited the employment of children under 13 years of age, during school hours, before 6 a.m. and after 8 p.m., or for more than two hours on a school day or a Sunday. It also prohibited children from lifting or carrying anything potentially injurious and banned work in street trading under the age of 17. In a Memorandum on the Act, the Home Office stated that 'inquiries which have been made in recent years appear to indicate that the present system had worked well' and no important changes to the enforcement of legislation relating to the employment of schoolchildren by local education authorities were deemed to be necessary (Home Office, 1933: 1).

While some deplored child labour, others, such as employers, put a positive shine on it. Reportedly, a 1936 debate in Parliament on education and child labour included the comment from Lord Halifax that manufacturers in Lancashire had 'assured him there was work for nimble little fingers in the mills'. And an unctuous account of newspaper delivery for the WH Smith (WHS) business says:

> *As for the healthiness of the job – ask the parents of any WHS boy: the regular early hours, the fresh air, the exercise, have made it a perfect health cure to many a weakling, and there are plenty of men today who could tell you that they owe their vitality to their early days on 'rounds'.*[26]

The context in which these debates were taking place is important.[27] The Depression years saw escalating numbers of unemployed juveniles and adults, and schoolchildren's employment seems to have been regarded as particularly problematic only when and if it coincided with, or competed with, other forms of work, in other words, juvenile and adult labour markets (see Garside, 1977). Children's earnings from their part-time jobs were still an important source of income for families.

Trades unions

The subjects of working schoolchildren and juvenile labour were frequently raised at annual Trades Union Congresses in the inter-war period. In 1926, concern was expressed about the use of juvenile labour, particularly in unskilled work, which competed with adult labour: 'in the country areas there has been a tendency since the fixing of Trade Board rates to employ juveniles on milk rounds in place of adults who formerly worked at comparatively low wages' (TUC, 1926: 193). The TUC frequently urged its members to encourage their children to join the appropriate union as soon as they became eligible. Miss A. Loughlin of the Tailors and Garment Workers, in 1927, pointed out that 'children are being exploited by the employing classes, and in that way, directly or indirectly undercutting your own wages' (TUC, 1927: 429).

In 1932, the issue of wage-earning schoolchildren was raised in a resolution moved by Mr T. Scollan of the Distributive and Allied Workers, opposing the employment of children out of school hours or on non-school days, and calling upon Parliament to raise the minimum age for employment in non-industrial occupations to 14. Scollan criticised the loopholes in the 1918 Education Act and claimed that the exploitation of child labour:

> *has far-reaching effects in so far as it prevents children who leave school at 14 years of age from getting permanent employment. We have thousands of children who left school at 14 and who are now 18 or 20 years of age, who have never yet received a chance of one single job. We cannot expect that these young people will get jobs if we hand the work over to children who should be at school.*
> (TUC, 1932: 334–5)

Beneficial employment

Before the 1944 Education Act came into force, children could be exempted from school attendance in their final year on the grounds that they were undertaking 'beneficial employment'. The definition of 'beneficial employment' gave rise to debates which continued up to the outbreak of the Second World War, with questions in the House of Commons almost weekly (see, for example, Tawney, 1936). However, more often than not, the question of part-time work by schoolchildren was overshadowed by the ever-increasing problem of the unemployment of school leavers. Questions were frequently asked in the House of Commons concerning the possibility of raising the school-leaving age in view of the high levels of unemployed 14 year olds. By the early 1930s, the call to raise the school-leaving age became more frequent, and was increasingly justified in terms of its being a necessary part of the educational process (Finn, 1987: 29). However, as social historian W.R. Garside points out, 'the extent to which the raising of the school-leaving age was viewed in terms of its potential impact on unemployment' has received scant attention from historians and he suggests that:

> *it was against the background of turbulent economic fortunes between the wars that the manipulation of the school-leaving age for industrial rather than for educational purposes was raised as a serious policy option.*
>
> (Garside, 1981: 159)

Jewkes and Winterbottom (1933: 107), in a study of juvenile unemployment at the time, argued that the case for raising the school-leaving age should be decided on educational grounds and 'not by an appeal to the facts of juvenile unemployment'. However, the two issues became inextricably linked. R.H. Tawney, for example, argued that:

> *It is in our power to ensure, at no great cost, both that juvenile unemployment. . .is ended once for all, and that all children are secured the four years' secondary education which. . .all children should have.*
>
> (Tawney, 1934: 31)

One way of dealing with youth unemployment was to remove young people from sight, ostensibly to train them for work. In the early 1930s, labour camps were set up, mostly for young men, often in remote areas; their unemployment benefit was stopped to pay for their stay there and they were set to work in agriculture and road-building. But it is said that few, perhaps 20 per cent of those who went through the camps, then succeeded in getting jobs.[28]

Since the turn of the century, the TUC had repeatedly called for the school-leaving age to be raised to 16 (Griggs, 1983). In 1934 a resolution reiterating this also proposed adequate maintenance allowances and improved regulation of juvenile labour in non-industrial employment. The threat that young workers posed to adults was explicitly recognised: 'the child is [today] rival to the man. . .child labour is ousting adult labour' (TUC, 1934: 238). In

1936 the TUC again called for a school-leaving age of 16 as a means of alleviating juvenile unemployment (TUC, 1936). Nevertheless, despite a growing consensus that the school-leaving age should be raised, educational reform was hampered by continuous cutbacks in government spending and by conservative unwillingness to fund more schooling for the masses.

While in the inter-war years, children's earnings were still an important part of family income, Jewkes and Jewkes, in a discussion of the juvenile labour market in Lancashire, argued for the total abolition of the employment of children before school-leaving age:

> *At a time when it is customary to boast of the increasing power of production of the economic system and to express alarm at the frequency with which machines are displacing adult labour it is a grotesque anachronism that we should demand labour from children still at school between the ages of 12 and 14 years.*
>
> (Jewkes and Jewkes, 1938: 144)

They suggested that there were two obstacles to the total abolition of child work: first that children's earnings were an important part of the family income, particularly in poor areas; and second, the opposition of those who employed children. They saw this as a vicious circle, because children who worked could be prevented from taking full advantage of their education and 'this in turn tends to perpetuate poverty' (ibid.: 146).

Family poverty meant that in many cases children were forced to leave school at the earliest point possible, to forgo any educational ambitions, and to go straight into low-skilled work. For instance, one of our interviewees explained that family poverty meant that continuing in school after age 14 was impossible:

> *I went into the mill. . .I became a weaver and I hated it, loathed it, absolutely detested it because I wanted to do other things, but that's what I had. . .I wanted to be a primary school teacher, I knew I was capable, you just know — given the chance you would have been capable and it's been, I have to say, it's stayed with me, it's stayed with me, even now, it stayed with me — if only, I would have loved to have done it.*

Children's schooling between the wars

The Education Act 1918

As we described in Chapter 2 (page 33), the Education Bill was presented by Fisher to the House of Commons in 1917 on the basis of what was owed to the nation's children, many of whom were then engaged in war work. The Lewis Committee, established to consider educational provision after the war, had discussed child labour and argued for:

> a complete change of temper and outlook of the people of this country as to what they mean, through the forces of industry and society, to make of their boys and girls. . .Can the age of adolescence be brought out of the purview of economic exploitation and into that of the social conscience? Can the conception of the juvenile as primarily a little wage earner be replaced by the conception of the juvenile as primarily the workman and the citizen in training?[29]

The Education Bill proposed full-time schooling for all children to 14 years, and hence would have abolished the half-time system. Local education authorities would have the power to raise the school-leaving age (SLA) to 15, to provide nursery education for pre-schoolers and a compulsory part-time education for young people up to age 16, in day continuation schools. Commenting on the Bill, Richmond (1945: 103), an acerbic commentator on English education history, argued that it was almost 'pathetically wishful' and showed 'bland innocence', in the current political climate. However, another contemporary commentator, Barnard (1968 [1947]: ch. VIII) was more positive: he argued that the Fisher Act contained the seeds of reform – outlining plans for nursery education and for secondary education, proposing the day continuation school, and aiming to raise the SLA. In practice, these had to wait for partial implementation through the 1944 Education Act.

The Education Act 1918 was not implemented, and Richmond identified three reasons why not (1945: ch. VI).[30] First, it was permissive legislation, for although Fisher had wanted to give the Board of Education coercing powers, he had to abandon this plan in the face of parliamentary opposition. Secondly, the country – or Parliament – was debilitated after the war, not behind this revolutionary Act, and happy to slip back into pre-war habits and perspectives. Richmond identified the 'real culprits': the private-school-educated civil servants and MPs. For instance, he quoted a comment by the Select Committee on National Expenditure, deploring 'the alarming increase in the cost of education', and a vote by the Federation of British Industries against any extension of secondary education on the grounds that it would 'unfit the children for the employments they eventually enter' (Richmond, 1945: 107). And thirdly, there was the 'Geddes Axe'. In the face of the economic difficulties in 1921, Sir Eric Geddes, Chair of the Committee on National Expenditure, proposed massive cuts in services, with education as the major victim; Geddes recommended cuts of a third to grants for education (Barnard, 1968 [1947]: ch. XXVI). This focus on reducing education expenditure indicates the low priority assigned by powerful people to the education of the population.

The Labour Party, established in 1900, (one of whose founders, Keir Hardie, had worked from the age of 7)[31] had long campaigned for secondary education for all and for the expansion of nursery education. Tawney, a university economics teacher and a major spokesman for Labour, wrote a furious piece on the Geddes Axe.[32] He notes first that it was greeted 'amid paeans of applause from the greater part of the press', but:

> *The really tragic business is the menace to those who have no organisation and no votes, the children themselves. The result for millions of children will be a real catastrophe, which will leave its scar on our national life long after Geddes and Inchcape and [their critics] are mercifully forgotten. The schools, which in the seventies [the 1870s] were a kind of educational factory, were on the way to becoming places of natural and many-sided growth.*
>
> *All that movement, with its infinite possibilities for body and spirit, for the individual and society, is to stop. Geddes recommended the raising of the age of admission to six, the raising of class sizes*

from 32.4 per teacher to 50, and a big reduction in expenditure on special services such as medical provision.

Life in the twentieth century for the children of the poor is still a dangerous business: how dangerous the figures of child mortality and still more, of child sickness, reveal. Now, up to [the age of] six, in colliery villages and factory town, in overcrowded tenement and foetid slum, they are to scramble along unaided. All the delicate skill which was gradually laying the foundations of a new way of life for young children, is, so far as any but the rich are concerned, to be suddenly demobilised.

All the recent improvements in the primary schools – 'auto-education', freedom, responsibility, initiative for the individual child – are to be swept away. The abolition of all free places above 25 per cent [in secondary schools] will ruin the pioneer work of Durham and Bradford and a score of other enlightened authorities. That, with higher fees and fewer schools, will go far to make secondary education what it was before 1902 – the privilege of the rich.

The report does not actually state, in so many words, that the children of the workers, like anthropoid apes, have fewer convolutions in their brains than the children of the rich. It assumes it.

(Tawney, Manchester Guardian, 21 February 1922)

Education provision between the wars

We note here that state education was largely neglected in the inter-war years. For this is indicative of attitudes among those who distributed funds for education, and also suggests that for most children, schooldays were unlikely to be their most highly valued experiences, while some – and their parents – may have valued a daily life that comprised also some work, as Dent too suggests (1942: ch. 2).

The Geddes Axe put paid to expansion of services for the youngest and oldest children – nursery education and part-time schooling for 14 year olds.[33] In the 1920s, the elementary schools catered for children from 5 to 14, often in mixed-age classes. Few children – about 10 per cent – went to secondary schools (whether private or state), and while fees varied in differing education authorities, most parents had to pay. The Hadow Report (1926),[34] commissioned by the Labour Government in 1924, recommended a break at about 11 years, with everyone going on to a secondary school. These were to provide a range of types of education, to suit differing 'needs': grammar schooling for the academic; a practical, modern education for the practical; and technical education for the technically minded.

In 1936 an Education Act raised the school leaving age to 15 – from 1 September 1939, but retained exemptions for beneficial employment from age 14.[35] Effectively, 'this clause created so many loopholes in the law it was supposed to be promulgating that it would largely have negated its good intentions' (Van der Eyken, 1973: 366).[36] Opponents of the scheme complained in the debate on the second reading of the Bill that it 'is not really a bill for raising the school leaving age. It is a bill for regulating the entry of children into employment'.[37] Some local education authorities had begun to set rules as to forms of employment for which exemption would not be allowed. In contrast with pervasive views on domestic work as being natural for girls, helping mother at home was regarded as 'employment' in some of these discussions. As a result, some local education authorities apparently refused to release girls from attendance at school at 14 years of age to help at home, on the grounds that such work was not 'beneficial', though the 1936 Act contained a clause specifically allowing children to be exempted from their last year at school in order to help at home. However, it was noted that many older girls stayed at home to help mothers, especially those who were 'sick or ailing'.[38]

Perhaps the major provision of the 1936 Act was in offering increased grants for extending or building senior elementary schools. This 'gift from the gods' encouraged some local education authorities to improve facilities for 11–14s (Parker, 1996); these included assembly halls, gymnasiums, workshops and domestic science rooms.

Photo of children at Garlinge School, Margate, Kent, from the National Union of Women Teachers (NUWT) Archive, which is held at the IOE Archives.

One image of educational services in the 1930s.

Elementary schools were less fortunate. A survey of school buildings in 1935–6 concluded that four-fifths of elementary school premises were 'hopelessly out of date for the purposes of education as contemporarily conceived'.[39] And another survey by the DES in 1962 shows that of those primary schools built up to 1944, 71 per cent were built before 1902, whereas 45 per cent of secondary schools were built after the First World War.[40] Age of building is not a secure criterion for judging the quality of children's experiences of school, for they may be happy in both new and old buildings.[41] However, Dent (1942: 23) describes 'abominable physical conditions' in elementary schools, and notes that it was the schools run by religious organisations (mainly the Church of England) which were in the worst condition.[42]

An important topic is how far 'progressive' pedagogies, which emphasised child-centred education, and were widely accepted among educationalists and psychologists, filtered down to classrooms and affected children's experiences at school (Cunningham, 2002). Many teachers may have resisted changes to their professional identities, and to teacher–child relations. Even if they wanted to change their practices, perhaps three main types of barrier stood in their way: first, the legacies of decades of insufficient funding – inadequate space inside and outside the building, fixed heavy desks and poor learning resources; secondly, and perhaps even more critical, was the downwards pressure of the 'scholarship' exam at 11 which determined children's educational future (Selleck, 1972: ch. 5); and thirdly, large class sizes also affected teachers' ability to change their practices, as well as children's experiences of school.[43] Some of the school histories note improvements in the resources available for teaching and learning. Thus at Stoke Poges village school, radios and loudspeakers enabled children to hear BBC broadcasts from 1934, and the local education authority introduced a schools library service and circulated pictures to schools (p. 22).

For whatever reasons, however, in 1939 some 70 per cent of children left school immediately on reaching 14, about 12 or 13 per cent before they were 15, and another 6 per cent before they were 16. Of the 12 per cent or fewer continuing beyond 16, the overwhelming majority did so for a few months only. Fewer than five of every 1,000 elementary school children reached a university. Given the poverty of many families, almost all the 14 year olds went straight into full-time wage-earning jobs, and the 'criminal dilapidation of the nation's most valuable asset' was largely thereafter down to industry, for very few 14–18 year olds in full-time employment (2 per cent) were allowed time off during the day to continue with their education (Dent, 1942: ch. 2).

Meanwhile, private schools continued on their separate track, and while many offered poor quality services (Dent, 1942: 38),[44] the so-called 'public' schools continued to breed 'an exclusive social caste, which, in defiance of all the principles of democracy, has seized and holds fast the keys to political, diplomatic, religious, social and economic power; and has used and uses this power for its own benefit rather than for the common good.' (ibid.: 35). Some commentators thought that they provided good education and so should be linked into the state system but deprived of their exclusivity,[45] but others, more radically, argued for abolishing schools that gave such privilege to a 'governing class' (see Barber, 1994: 10–11).

Discussion

A combination of welfare, educational and industrial concerns shaped policies, practices and attitudes about 'childhood' and 'adolescence' during these years. Working-class children and adolescents were economic contributors, and their earnings were part of the family income. Thus working-class childhood was understood as a structural component of society, where children participated in the division of labour. In practical terms, working-class childhood was not a period of total dependence on adults, as it largely is nowadays; rather, children contributed to household welfare, both through paid work and through work for the household – such as domestic work and running errands, and through participating in the productive business of the family, such as helping in the corner shop, digging the garden, farm work.

It is very striking that whilst reformers and academics, including educationalists, were presenting strong arguments in favour of secondary education for all (see Chapter 2), progress was slow towards this goal. Just as we get the government we deserve, so our education system reflects current thinking, not least among those who run the country. As Raymond Williams (1961: 299) noted, 'The content of education, as a rule, is the content of our actual social relations, and will only change as part of wider change'.

At the turn of the twentieth century, the length of a school-based childhood for working-class children was not fixed and was still open to negotiation. This is reflected in persisting ambivalence over the school-leaving age, which varied from region to region under local bye-laws, presumably in relation to local labour requirements. This implies that children were an important source of labour, and is confirmed by the fact that the school-leaving age remained flexible during the Second World War. It was the 1944 Education Act that fixed it at national level, with no exemptions for 'beneficial' employment of any kind.

In the years leading up to the Second World War, it seems that the pressures towards a revised version of 'childhood' included the high rates of juvenile unemployment, which provided a motive for proposing a higher school-leaving age, but this proposal conflicted with continual lack of resources, and political unwillingness to make resources available with which to raise the leaving age. Throughout this period, the employment of schoolchildren appears to have been a 'problem' for the state, mainly when it interfered with their welfare and their development as healthy adults, or coincided and competed with other labour markets, particularly the juvenile labour market. The shifts in concern about issues surrounding the employment of children became linked to the argument that children's best contributions to societal welfare were through gaining an education, rather than through paid work. Outrage at the waste of the country's best hope – its children – through denial of their talents, was probably one factor, in pushing through changes in the education system. It may also be relevant that the changing social make-up of the country (see Chapter 2, page 29), with out-of-school education more widely available, through the media, led to the belief that casting working-class children out of school at 14 while continuing to endorse the education of the minority was simply inappropriate.

While changes to the education system took place only slowly in the inter-war years, it seems that emphasis on the quality of what was offered (and received) gradually became more prominent. In addition, new initiatives helped to widen the scope of what was offered. Development of curricula for older children, and provision of new premises for secondary education accompanied ideas about children as worthy of wider educational opportunities, and about children as learners rather than as empty vessels. For the two-thirds of older children (11 and up) who were attending the new secondary schools and classes by 1938, school may have offered a tantalising vision of possibilities for better education and for moving up the employment ladder. Yet assumptions about ability, and about natural destinies rooted in social status, stood in the way of many children. And many children continued to experience crowded elementary school classrooms, poor learning resources and overstretched teachers.

The universalising work of psychologists and mainstream sociologists (see Chapter 2, pages 35–7) during the inter-war years, did not serve to consolidate a vision of childhood as a special period of life, deserving of careful nurture and protection. Rather, the old class divisions, bolstered by the education system, continued to construct two widely differing kinds of childhood. Natural destinies, rooted in social status, constructed most children as workers in the present as well as the future; a minority of children experienced childhood as training for high-status lives.

Notes

1   The Factory Acts were a series of Acts intended to control the employment of children (and women) in specific industries, starting with the textile industry, regulated by the Factory Act 1802. Subsequent Acts include the Cotton Mills, etc. Act 1819, Labour in Cotton Mills Act 1831, Labour of Children, etc., in Factories Act 1833. Further Acts followed in 1844, 1847, 1850, 1874, 1878 and 1891. See Cunningham, 1991, 2006.

2   For a useful summary of the compromises reached in the 1870 Act, see Richmond (1945: 75–80).

3   The half-time system flourished in the textile areas of Lancashire and Yorkshire and meant that children attended school in the mornings and worked in textile factories in the afternoons or vice versa. By 1900 children aged 11 years and over were involved, and evidence from the 1911 Census indicates that children under 14 years provided one-sixth of the labour in the cotton industry. See Frow and Frow, 1970; Simon, 1965.

4   This information comes from Van der Eyken, 1973: 33–8, in quotations from the 1904 Committee on Physical Deterioration reports.

5   These organisations are discussed in Chapter 8.

6   See Bray, 1911; Freeman, 1914; and Springhall, 1986 for a useful review.

7   See for example, Sherard, 1905; Black, 1907; Adler, 1908.

8   Parliamentary Papers (PP) 1901 Vol. XXV Cmnd 849: 18 note 6.

9   PP 1901 Vol. XXV Cmnd 849: 74 note 7.

10 Urwick, 1904: 307; see also Cunningham, 1991: 174–89; Hendrick, 1990.

11 Eleanor Rathbone campaigned for money to be paid direct to mothers, so that they controlled it. She succeeded after 30 years of campaigning, in the post-war settlements of 1945.

12 The Government consisted of a Liberal/Conservative coalition between 1915 and 1922.

13 See Horn, 1983 for a thorough analysis.

14 This was gaining strength during the early part of the twentieth century. See Groves, 1949. The headteacher of the Burston Strike School in Norfolk

had lost her previous position as headteacher of Wood Dalling School in 1910 partly because she had objected to the practice by School Managers (i.e. school governors) who were local farmers removing children from school to work on farms when needed, claiming they were employing children illegally (Van der Eyken and Turner, 1969).

15 See 'Return of school attendance and employment of school children in agriculture', 16 October 1916, compiled by the Board of Education.

16 PP 1916 Vol. XXII Cmnd 8171.

17 Quoted in Van der Eyken, 1973: 222. For Fisher's speech see Chapter 2, page 33.

18 See Davin, 1990; and papers by Dyhouse and Ross in Lewis, 1986.

19 Discussed by Cloete, 1904: 133–6; see also the Board of Education 1923 report on the curriculum for boys and girls (Board of Education, 1923: xv).

20 Montagu (1904: 235) thought girls' work in the public domain was intrinsically wrong; they should work in the domestic domain.

21 Board of Education, 1923.

22 The Hadow Committee's 'Recommendation 12' (Board of Education, 1923: 139).

23 See also Celia Briar, 1997.

24 G. Stanley Hall (1920) was an American scholar whose famous book was first published in 1904. Its scope is indicated in its title: *Adolescence: Its psychology and its relations to physiology, anthropology, sociology, sex, crime, religion and education*.

25 Two psychologists in particular wrote about adolescent girls: Blanchard, an American, and Pailthorpe; later studies of adolescence include Musgrove, 1964 and Mayall, 1989.

26 The comment by Lord Halifax and the 1936 description of the newspaper round are both quoted in Colin Ward's book, *The Child in the City*, 1990: 120–1.

27 For discussion of debates and trends in the inter-war years, see Chapter 2, pages 33–40.

28 BBC Radio 4 programme (7 July 2009) between 9.00 and 9.45.

29 PP 1917 Vol. XI Cmnd. 8512: 5.

30 See also Finn, 1987: ch. 2.

31 Morgan, 1975.

32 Tawney's report appeared in the *Manchester Guardian* on 21 February 1922, and was reprinted by the *Guardian* on 21 February 2009. His book, *Secondary Education for All*, was printed in 1924 for the Labour Party.

33 Margaret McMillan had promoted nursery schools through the Labour Party and her presidency of the Nursery Schools Association from 1923 (see also her writings – for instance, McMillan, 1911). Day continuation schools had been only patchily established and only Rugby (the town) continued with this work (Kitchen, 1944).

34 The Hadow Report 1926: *Report of the Consultative Committee on the Education of the Adolescent;* Board of Education, 1926.

35 This exemption clause was supported by the agricultural lobby (Barber, 1994: 2).

36 Some 15 local authorities had already raised the SLA to 15, but, with exemptions for beneficial employment, over 80 per cent of children left school at 14 (Finn, 1987: 32).

37 Mr J.C. Ede, House of Commons 1936, Vol. 308 Col. 1231. See also, for a fiercely critical account of government refusal to move forward on educating the nation's children, Simon, 1974: ch. V.

38 M'Gonicle and Kirby in a 1936 paper on the physical condition of elementary school children. Quoted in Van der Eyken, 1973: 363–6.

39 H.C. Dent (1942: 22) quotes from this survey by F.H. Spencer, 1941.

40 The DES 1962 Survey is quoted in Central Advisory Council for Education (England), 1967: para. 1081. The Survey does not take account of the fact that by 1943 some 4,000 schools had been destroyed or severely damaged by bombs (Titmuss, 1976: 407).

41 Children's and teachers' views on new and old school buildings are discussed in Mayall et al., 1996: ch. 2.

42 Defects continued into the post-war era, as documented in Central Advisory Council for Education (England) 1967: para. 1088 and Table 30.

43 In 1922, there were 28,000 classes in England and Wales with between 50 and 60 children, and 5,000 with more than 60 children. By 1934 these numbers had reduced, with 6,194 classes having over 50 children; and Lowndes thought great pedagogic improvements took place during the 1930s (Lowndes, 1937: ch. VIII).

44 In 1932 a Committee on Private Schools reported that there were then about 10,000 private schools in the country, that fewer than a quarter of these were inspected by local education authorities or by the Board of Education and that many of the rest were 'a public danger' and 'ought to be closed forthwith'. Anyone could open and run a private school (Dent, 1942: 38–9).

45 Clarke, 1940: *passim*; Dent, 1942: 35–7; Richmond, 1945: 118.

Chapter 4

Children in wartime

In this chapter we continue into the war years with our exploration of tensions between children's work – notably work for the war effort – and children's schooling. We start with some reminders about the social conditions of childhood when the war began, and continue with a brief account of how the evacuation of children was understood at the time. This is followed by discussion of children as workers and as learners in debates at the time and a section on education policy developments during the war. We then outline the many routes through which children were urged to participate in the war effort. Finally we discuss some of the principal themes identified in the chapter.

The lead-up to war

From the point of view of English children's lives, we note here some movements (among many) that led up to the Second World War. Important were the plans to evacuate vulnerable people – especially children – from danger points. The country was divided into evacuation areas (the industrial cities), reception areas and neutral areas. As part of the scheme, 30 camp boarding schools were established in 1939 within the state system; the plan was that they would serve as schoolchildren's camps in peacetime – to give them a taste of country life, and as reception centres for some children in wartime.[1] Another innovatory set of schools was established in the 1930s in Cambridgeshire under the inspiration of Henry Morris, who wanted to educate boys and girls (11–14) for their lives 'as countrymen and countrywomen' (Dent, 1943: 11), and to provide a rural education for the whole community (ibid.: 32).

Planning for a possible war took place throughout the 1930s, including plans for dealing with physical injuries, material damage to homes and distress caused by traumatic events. Proposed measures included emergency medical services, rest centres and feeding centres for the homeless, and deployment of psychiatric services. From 1935 onwards the government organisation known as the ARP (Air Raid Precautions Department) worked on plans to relieve distress caused on the home front by enemy action, including injury, homelessness and loss of paid work.[2]

But while planners prepared for war, there was concurrently well-established anti-war feeling among people,[3] and in that context it is interesting that private schools and some grammar schools continued to train boys for military service, through Officer Training Corps. These built on traditions of service fostered in these schools, but were also preparation for war (Graves and Hodge, 1985: 212–15). Indeed, the concept of service was widespread among other organisations which many young people joined – such as Scouts and Guides. As we shall see in Chapter 8, such organisations exhorted their members to participate in the war effort.

As we have already noted, in 1939 the vast majority of children left school at 13 or 14 and went out to paid work. The legal position[4] was that no child under the age of 12 could be employed (i.e. paid for work); children over 12 could not work during school term before 6 a.m. or after 8 p.m. and not for more than two hours on a school day. But local authorities varied in their bye-laws about this – for instance they might permit under-12s to be employed by their parents in agricultural work. Furthermore, during their school years girls did unknown quantities of domestic work (cleaning, childcare, errands); and both boys and girls worked either for no pay in, for instance, household enterprises, or for pay in casual work, as messengers and errand boys and as shop assistants.

Over 90 per cent of children went to publicly funded schools; the rest to (mostly) fee-paying grammar schools and private schools, including the so-called 'public' schools.[5] In 1938, of two million young people aged 14–18 in paid work, only 42,000 were released for any school-based education during working hours (that is, one in 50) (Dent, 1944a: 130). According to the 1943 White Paper,[6] only

9.5 per cent of elementary schoolchildren went on at age 11, via an exam ('the scholarship'), to a grammar school; at age 11 onwards, just under half of elementary school children were in separate 'senior' classes or in 'senior elementary schools', or in central or senior schools. (The White Paper figures presumably mean that about 40 per cent of children aged 5–14 spent all their schooldays in elementary school, often grouped in only two or three classes.)[7] These figures reflect slow progress towards secondary schooling as advocated in the 1918 Education Act and the 1926 Hadow Report.

While the 1936 Education Act proposed raising the school-leaving age to 15 on 1 September 1939, this was postponed on the outbreak of war. But the Act's exemptions for 'beneficial employment' on attaining 14 years were no longer acceptable to the majority of commentators during the war years, according to Barber (1994: 9). Frustration among educationalists at the slow rate of change in the 1930s led to massive demands for free full-time education to 15 years for everyone (see the 'Education policy' section, below).

Welfare in wartime

As regards children's experiences during the war, the principal memory in the public mind nowadays is of evacuation. Indeed, to mark the 70th anniversary of the outbreak of the war (September 2009), a service was held in St Paul's Cathedral for evacuees, now in their 70s and 80s, and a BBC programme on evacuation was broadcast (BBC4, 2 September 2009). Evacuation, commonly regarded as children's central and traumatic experience during the war, has been the focus of many studies, including some at the time[8] and others, drawing on people's memories, in the succeeding years.[9] Studies describe difficulties of putting numbers on the scale of evacuation.[10] But out of a UK population of about 45 million people, about two million people evacuated themselves in 1939 (to stay with relatives and friends living in safer areas). The government scheme evacuated about 1.5 million people: expectant mothers, mothers of under-5s, school-age children and teachers. The scheme was voluntary and overall 47 per cent of those eligible took part, with variation across areas (Titmuss, 1976: 102–3). Margaret Cole (1940: 11), in one of the first accounts, says the scheme could have been proposed only by minds that were 'military, male and middle-class'. John Bowlby (1940) offered psychological justification and sympathy for mothers' unwillingness to let their children go. These movements at the start of the war were followed by returns home; for instance, by January 1940, 79,000 of 241,000 evacuated London children had returned. Later major evacuations took place during periods of intensive enemy action (autumn 1940, summer 1944).

In addition, some parents who could afford it sent their children overseas, to English-speaking countries which offered help; estimating numbers involved is difficult but perhaps 13,000 children left (Titmuss, 1976: 247–8). For a short time in 1940, the government also ran a scheme, the Children's Overseas Reception Board (CORB); under this scheme 2,664 children went abroad, most of them for the duration. The scheme was hastily stopped when a boat was torpedoed and 73 children drowned.[11] Some private schools, sited in dangerous areas (cities, coastal areas and southern counties), sent large groups abroad, Sherborne and Roedean girls' schools among them (Mann, 2005: 51); however, more common was the movement of whole schools out of danger areas, to share premises with schools in 'reception areas'.

The evacuation and planned evacuation of children from cities elicited interesting responses at the time. Policy-makers presumably thought parents and children would do as they were encouraged to do and leave the cities, for they closed not only the city schools, but also the school medical services (Hendrick, 2003: 125). Titmuss deals with revelations of class divisions in society: the shock to public opinion in the reception areas, when people met poorly clothed children, who were lice-infected and enuretic. He argues that indications of differing living standards and customs between city and country dwellers and government recognition that improved social services were necessary during the war provided an important impetus for the construction of the welfare state after the war.[12] Evacuation, in his view, put the children centre-stage as appropriate recipients of social services; it was only through national planning in the interests of social justice that the situation could be remedied.[13] A London organiser of evacuation services endorsed this view in 1940. The evacuation experience might be:

One of the things that will force us to accept a levelling up of the income of the insecure section of the community, even though we shall inevitably experience a levelling down of our comparative middle class ease.[14]

As to children who left Britain, some commentators saw them as rats deserting the ship. For instance, Churchill said in July 1940: 'I entirely deprecate any stampede from the island at the present time.' *The Lady* magazine promoted a patriotic view: children should be thought of, not as 'charming pets to be kept away from real life. . .They too are the British people and they may be better British people because of their patriotism being tested in their early years'. And the Headmaster of Winchester College put this point in overtly social class terms:

It cannot be right to encourage these [privately schooled] boys and girls to think first of their own safety and security. It may be possible for them to help here in many ways. How can we with any consistency continue to speak of training in citizenship and in leadership while at the same time we arrange for them against their will to leave the post of danger? I believe it is our duty to encourage those for whom we are responsible to stand fast and carry on.[15]

What did become clear during the war was that children in England, whether evacuated or not, of whatever class, participated in the war effort, in a wide range of ways – which we detail in later chapters. In these ways they promoted their own welfare, as well as that of the communities in which they lived. It is also clear that from the first days of the war, children became a prime focus for state intervention to ensure their health and welfare. As Butler, President of the Board of Education, put it in 1943: 'In the youth of the nation we have our greatest national asset.'[16] Previous stringent means-testing gave way somewhat to provision of school meals, milk at school and extra coupons for clothes and shoes. Though progress on these fronts was piecemeal and varied across local authorities, by 1945 more than a third of schoolchildren were having school meals and 70 per cent drank school milk (meals and milk were either means-tested or free). The official view was that the nutritional standard of elementary schoolchildren had 'almost certainly been improved during the war'.[17] The Board of Education's stated view in 1943 was that a national health service after the war would provide universalist medical treatment and so the school medical service would become merely an inspection and referral service.[18]

Work during the war – adults and children

Mobilisation of adults

Voluntary enlistment of adults early in the war gave way to conscription, and by 1943 Britain had over 4.5 million men in the armed forces. Of all women aged 18–40 (single, married, widowed), 55 per cent were in the armed services or employed in industry or employed as land girls in agriculture (Gardiner, 2005: ch. 18). Other women worked part-time or full-time in nurseries, canteens, hospitals, hostels, clubs and rest centres (Titmuss, 1976: 412); many other women worked voluntarily in organisations such as the Women's Voluntary Service (WVS), Red Cross and the Women's Institutes. For instance, the WVS, started in 1938, recruited women who were not mobilised – those with young children or other dependants, or who were too old for registration for war service. Women worked as unpaid volunteers in cooperation with local authorities all over Britain. By 1941 over one million women had joined, and not just well-to-do women, but women from all classes.[19] Their main activities were: (1) billeting, and arranging for feeding evacuees; (2) the Housewives Service – running canteens; (3) collecting salvage; (4) collecting for National Savings; (5) running rest centres; (6) keeping records of residents; and (7) training women in cookery.

Children as workers

Implications for children of the mobilisation of men and women aroused great interest at the time. Whether children should work was a debating point throughout the war. Some thought that if parents gave their children less attention this was bad for morale – neglected children ran wild (Titmuss, 1976: ch. XX). Others – such as teachers of evacuated children – thought that children who had previously been 'pampered and nervous kiddies' gained in self-reliance, learned to think and act for themselves and developed their own individuality.[20] Some evacuated children themselves – like their teachers and those who researched them – welcomed and enjoyed the changed character of school life, where community spirit was fostered and where activities had widened to include study of local life (natural and human).[21] Others endured hardships; one of our interviewees recalled that her childhood ended with evacuation, in the sense that she had to take responsibility, aged 5, for both herself and her younger sister.

Children who remained in the cities were less fully and extensively studied than evacuees, but two examples give contrasting accounts of life in London. An 11 year old attended one of the emergency secondary schools set up in 1940 when evacuated children drifted back to London. One day they were told that one of their classmates and her family had all been killed the night before:

> We did not cry, we seemed to freeze, but we did not talk about it. However, from then on, when one of us was away, we were anxious until we knew that all was well. . .The school grounds were dug up and we had little plots of land, 'digging for victory'. We knitted scarves for airmen, adopted a British prisoner of war in Germany and sent him Red Cross parcels and wrote to him. We collected waste paper and scrap metal. No one was fat, we were a lean lot. Every day we had gym or games. . .We were very well taught and cared for.[22]

Bombing, war-work and caring teachers contributed to her complex and memorable daily life. Another kind of experience of life in London is given by Benny Green. He recounts the bombing raids, the chaotic farce of 'education' offered by an assortment of teachers: dregs of the profession, dotards and young ladies 'with no suspicion of what they were letting themselves in for'; teenage years playing cricket and football, and exploring sexuality and music, importantly at the youth club where he developed his saxophone skills. Casually he refers to war-work:

> One morning in Goodge Street I spent an hour or two helping demolition men clear away the rubble and broken glass which were

the legacy earlier that morning of the descent of a doodlebug. There
was a girl living in the street whom I was anxious to impress.

(Green, 1994: 12–13)

Notably, however, many children had to do the jobs parents and other adults had done, especially at home. For instance, Tony Rees (aged 7 in 1939) took on domestic work when his mother went out to work. His contributions included raising soft fruit bushes from cuttings, bottling fruit and preserving eggs in waterglass solution. He quickly became:

> *a skilled food shopper, particularly for things that were unrationed,*
> *such as vegetables, or subject to the 'points' system which allowed a*
> *wide choice of tinned foods within a restricted allocation of points.*
> *The skill with points came in choosing things that were tasty or*
> *sustaining without costing too many points – spam cost a lot of*
> *points, for example, whereas the equally delicious army surplus*
> *tinned stew cost very few. South African jam, though disgusting,*
> *cost almost none. The skill with vegetables came in being there when*
> *the more desirable ones made their all too brief appearances.*

And Joan Barraclough (aged 6 in 1939) recalled gardening work, feeding the pigs and dealing with slaughtered animals:

> *I found the insides of animals very interesting and could clean and*
> *truss a chicken and skin a rabbit once they had been despatched.*
> *We were very disappointed when the war ended and my mother*
> *cancelled the cow she had on order.*

Children, both evacuees and those who stayed at home, had new opportunities to exercise their agency. And adults who observed them had new opportunities to recognise children as agents, who dealt with the exigencies of wartime as best they could. For instance, apart from domestic and household work, 30 per cent of the children evacuated to Oxford and 8 per cent of a comparison group living in London earned money.[23] But in addition, as we shall detail in later chapters, schoolchildren contributed directly to the war effort in a number of ways, in agriculture, and also in savings schemes, and in food production at school as part of the curriculum and outside school hours.

However, commentators were concerned with the possible health effects of hard physical labour. The Spens Report (1938), on secondary education in the state sector, echoed current sensibilities about children's developing bodies, but was not of course aware of the exigencies of war:

> *no adolescent. . .should be allowed to do heavy continuous muscular work either in or out of school, particularly if it involves postural fatigue. . .Great care should be taken to ensure that children do not overtax their strength in the garden, in digging and wheeling barrows, and at the bench in planing and sawing.*
>
> (Board of Education, 1938: 110)

And early on in the war the *TES* argued:

> *School children are losing health and strength for want of satisfying and wholesome meals; their hardworked parents, toiling all day, and it may be all night, are not at home to prepare them, and as yet the schools do not provide them.*
>
> (*TES*, 27 July 1940)

The General Council of the TUC was critical of government measures encouraging the employment of schoolchildren in the Second World War, but appeared to accept that in the emergency such employment was necessary and recognised that 'the exceptional economic circumstances of recent years have provided some justification for the employment of school children in agriculture' (TUC, 1949: 155). As we noted earlier (page 69), underlying the overt concern for children's childhoods was concern for union members' work and pay.

What young people thought about possible contributions to the war effort emerges through a government scheme established to deal with a perceived social problem – what working-class young people got up to in their leisure hours.[24] In November 1939 the Board of Education issued Circular 1486: 'The Service of Youth', with the aim of preventing physical, mental and moral deterioration among school leavers. Local education authorities were required to establish Youth Committees, which would work with voluntary organisations to provide young people (aged 14–20) with facilities to develop mind, body and spirit, notably in youth clubs and youth organisations. In June 1940 a further circular – 1516: 'The Challenge of Youth' was issued, offering guidance on 'this new national movement'. However, as this movement developed, it became clear that many young people did not prioritise being entertained; they wanted, not to be served, but to serve. Thus, when in January 1941, new pre-service training for young people was established for the air force, navy and army, the rush by boys to join these new organisations (Air Training Corps, the Sea Cadet Corps and the Army Cadet Force) far exceeded officials' expectations.[25] Similar organisations were started for girls, and from February 1942 these various ventures were grouped under the National Association of Girls' Training Corps.

The next stage in harnessing young people into the war effort was compulsory registration of all young people aged 16–18 (boys from January 1942; girls from March 1942); they would be invited to an interview to encourage them to carry out useful activities. The Prime Minister stressed that these interviews would help young people learn their responsibilities as future citizens: some might join pre-service training groups or work with the Home Guard – from age 16 (Dent, 1944a: 121). This measure had the unexpected effect of bringing to public and governmental notice just how hard and long many young people worked. Interviewers up and down the country sent in their reports; in many cases, they recorded young people working 50, 60 or even 70 hours a week. Given this, they felt unable to recommend that the young people should be asked to do extra voluntary work or training. The *TES* (27 June 1942) said: 'Apart from any other consideration, we cannot from the point of view of national safety afford to run any longer the risk of devitalising a whole generation.' The government reviewed these reports and came to the same conclusion: on average, 25–30 per cent of young people interviewed could not reasonably be asked to do more:

> *It was evident that some girls were tired out and unfit to undertake further activities, especially when they had to help at home after a day's work; a heavy burden rested on girls in large families.*
> (*TES*, 8 August 1942)

One father, thinking that registration implied compulsory war-work, wrote to the local education authority, asking for exemption:

> *Dear Sir, I wish to apply for exemption of my daughter as she is the one we depend on for our food here. There are five of us – all on war work, including my wife. We all work from 8 a.m. to 7.45 p.m. each day. We have no-one but my daughter to cook us a meal and to keep the house clean for when we come home; also she has to run the messages and is on war work herself from 8 a.m. to 5.30 p.m.*

One important effect of this registration of young people was that government, having read the reports from across the country, issued a White Paper, 'Youth Registration in 1942' (Cmd 6446), which proposed better regulation of hours of work for young people aged 14 and up (Dent, 1944a: 120–9).

During the war, when many schoolchildren were employed on the land,[26] the Home Office, under the Labour leadership of Herbert Morrison, was reported to be reviewing the law relating to the employment of schoolchildren, and the Education Committee of London County Council made a number of recommendations:

> *Firstly, there should be a general national standard laid down by statute for the hours of employment, both on school days and during school holidays, but that the LEA should retain the power of enforcements; secondly, that the employment of children on school days before the close of school hours should be prohibited by statute; thirdly, local authorities should keep children under close medical supervision by means of medical examinations before, and periodically during, employment. The licensing of children to perform in public houses shall be prohibited by statute.*
>
> (*TES*, 11 November 1944)

In presenting the report, the Vice-chairman commented that the committee 'would look forward to the time when the nation would prohibit all employment of children' (*TES*, 11 November 1944). But it seems that during the war there was conflict, or at any rate poor communication, between the Home Office and the Board of

Education and Ministry of Agriculture, and this disparity reflects the fact that there was still no coherent government policy concerning the employment of schoolchildren.

Education policy developments during the Second World War

The main policy development during the war was the passing of the 1944 Education Act, which is generally seen as shifting the emphasis decisively towards children as scholars rather than as workers. It heralded free education for all 5–15 year olds. There are any number of strands one could trace to explain why this measure, the principal domestic legislation passed during the war, did so. In brief, here are some of them, drawing on five main sources.[27]

Since the 1918 Education Act, the aim of providing secondary education for all had been supported by the Labour Party and by the 1926 Hadow Report. But government conservatism, class bias and economic bad times held up reform. As we have noted, up to 1939, gradual, piecemeal reorganisation took place and some 'secondary' education was provided in separate classes and schools.[28] These organisational changes, coupled with diffusion of educationalists' ideas on appropriate education for young and older children (as described in the three Hadow Reports of 1926, 1931 and 1933) began to seep into people's understandings and, furthermore, into practice (Richmond, 1945: ch. VI). Changes towards more 'progressive' methods may have been helped by the example of the privately run progressive day and boarding schools.[29] During the war, there was continued pressure from a range of educational and workers' organisations to implement radical reforms;[30] this was strengthened by the formation of a Campaign for Educational Advance (1942), bringing together the NUT, TUC, WEA and the Co-operative Union under the chairmanship of R.H. Tawney (Barber, 1994: 8). Groups of influential men, linked by their membership of 'public' schools, Oxbridge and London clubs, met to consider possibilities for change[31] and the National Government may have decided on modest reforms to placate the Labour vote, in order to defuse increased support for Labour.

In the lead-up to the 1944 Act, the Norwood Committee (1943) argued that there were three types of child: the academic, the technical- or arts-oriented, and the rest – practical people. Children could be sorted for secondary schooling into these three types.[32] This provoked an acerbic critique from Cyril Burt (1943: 131), who neatly encapsulated the Report's outdated and false assumptions, quoting 'a well-known political leader' whose view was that:

The child of the working man differs from the child of the professional classes, not by a lower intelligence, but a different intelligence, that is an intelligence directed towards technical skill or practical common sense rather than towards abstract work of a literary or scientific nature.

Such a notion, Burt adds, was not accepted by present-day psychologists. The crucial question was about the child's general intelligence, no matter to what it was applied:

In the interest of the nation as well as the child, the paramount need is to discover which are the ablest pupils, no matter to what school or social class they may belong, and generally to grade each child according to the relative degree of his ability, and give him the best education which his ability permits. . .The proposed allocation of all children to different types of school at the early age of eleven cannot provide a sound psychological solution.

(Burt, 1943: 140)

A further theme was what the war conditions revealed – the stark socio-economic inequalities. As a result, greater equality of opportunity was increasingly seen as just.[33] Measures introduced by government to ensure the welfare of children – school meals, milk, camp schools – suggested long-term implications for state intervention to improve the quality of the population. War was also revealing the gross inadequacies of the education system, in the light of war-time requirements. In 1939, 25 per cent of 16-year-old and 17-year-old recruits to the armed services were illiterate (Barber, 1994: 4) and there were not enough people skilled in making munitions.[34]

The reforms

The 1944 Education Act was an important step in consolidating the status of childhood as apprenticeship through schooling. Childhood as scholastic activity was to be lengthened, and sited under the control of a central government 'Ministry of Education', rather than under the varying policies of local education authorities.

The President of the Board of Education – R.A. Butler from July 1941[35] – went through a long, detailed consultation process, in order to ensure that a deal was done and that the Act went through. A 'Green Book' (a consultation paper) was issued to appropriate organisations in 1941, and over 100 organisations wrote in with their comments and suggestions. While there was basic disagreement between conservative and left-wing commentators,[36] there was almost universal agreement on some points. There should be a primary school stage, followed by a secondary stage for all. All forms of full-time secondary education should be equal in status. There should be a Code of Regulations applying to all types of secondary school. There should be a variety of courses in secondary schools to meet students' varied interests. The 'special place' exam ('the scholarship') should be abolished and children allocated to the type of secondary school 'judged most fitted for them'. The SLA should be raised to 15 at the end of the war and to 16 as soon as practicable. There should be compulsory part-time education for all from the age they left full-time education to age 18. The Service of Youth should be closely linked up with the education system and coordinated with arrangements for placing and training young people up to age 20 in industry and commerce (Dent, 1949b: 87).

The 1943 White Paper, 'Educational Reconstruction' (written by Butler) conceded most of these demands. The Bill was introduced in the House of Commons in December 1943 and passed in the summer of 1944. It laid down the principle of nursery, primary, secondary and further education, free to all. Children (assessed by teachers, supplemented perhaps by an IQ test) would go to the type of secondary school best suited to their talents and future lives: grammar, modern or technical. However, implementing these points would take time and would depend on finding the necessary resources (money, buildings, staff) and success would depend on the efforts of those implementing it, and on assessing the value of what was put in place. In practice, conservative forces slowed reform. An exam ('the 11+') determined children's fate. The SLA was not raised to 16 until 1972. Compulsory part-time education to age 18 for school leavers was not implemented. Nursery education continued to be low priority. In essence, the main achievement was free secondary education for all to age 15. The 'public' schools were not affected by these reforms.[37]

Encouraging children to participate in the war effort

Here we consider some of the main routes whereby children were encouraged to think they had a part to play in the war effort, and encouraged to do what they could. These include: (1) government action and BBC radio work with and for children; (2) messages beamed out at cinemas; (3) images of sturdy, active, competent children portrayed in children's storybooks; and (4) anti-enemy propaganda and heroic war exploits in comic magazines.

Government action and the BBC

Churchill had told Butler in 1941 that he did not want an Education Act (which would stir up domestic political battles, and might divert attention from the war effort) but that schools might be encouraged to be patriotic (Barber, 1994: 35). Indeed, the government made great efforts to encourage children to contribute to the war effort, particularly via the schools.

Thus, the Board of Education issued a series of memoranda entitled 'The Schools in Wartime', for instance on 'Schools and food production' (September 1939) and on 'Needle subjects' (November 1939).[38] Practical information about food production was issued by the Ministry of Agriculture and Fisheries, which also issued 'Dig for Victory' leaflets. The Ministry of Information supplemented this information with films on, for instance, making a compost heap, fruit tree pruning, sowing and planting.[39]

Ministry of Information poster, 1939–46.

These government departments worked closely with the BBC, whose school broadcasts would be a key means of contacting children. Thus, through the war years the Board of Education worked with the Central Council for School Broadcasting (CCSB), and early on, in December 1939, the Board's Memorandum No. 6: 'The use of school broadcasting' was sent to schools with a stamped addressed postcard asking them whether they listened to broadcasts, in which case they would be sent the programme for the Spring Term 1940. Memorandum No. 8 was 'Winter in the garden' (December 1939), containing practical tips for gardening; it suggests in the last paragraph that 'Where a wireless set is available, the pupils should listen to the very enlightening Science and Gardening broadcasts by Dr B.A. Keen and Mr C.F. Lawrence every Monday at 2 p.m.' A Board of Education memorandum (28 November 1939) notes that about two-thirds of schools said they were keen to listen in, but some (6 per cent) had difficulties (bad reception, school closures, time-tabling).[40]

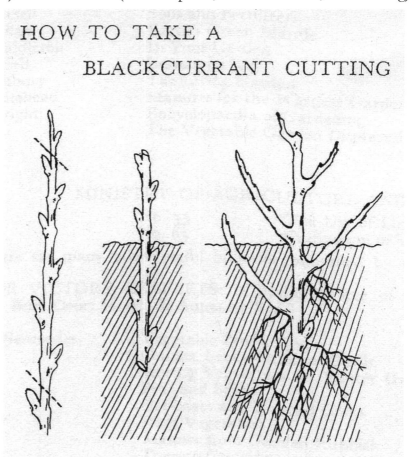

HOW TO TAKE A
BLACKCURRANT CUTTING

The usual method of taking a blackcurrant cutting. The top inch or so is cut off, leaving six or seven buds. About two-thirds of the shoot should be below ground. The part below the soil is not disbudded as in the case of red currants or gooseberries. New blackcurrant shoots appear both above and below the surface of the soil.

From the notes (25 September 1944) accompanying the BBC's *The Practice and Science of Gardening* weekly programmes for schools.

However, radio broadcasts quickly became popular with schools, partly to compensate for staffing difficulties, partly as a means of providing children with continuity, partly because children, especially those in country schools, could be encouraged to grow food and keep livestock. The number of schools listening in doubled by late 1941 to about 12,000 (out of perhaps 20,000 schools) (Gosden, 1976: 79). From 1940 and throughout the war, the BBC carried programmes titled *The Practice and Science of Gardening*, giving detailed advice on food production and (in the Spring Term 1942) on rearing livestock.[41]

Very revealing is a booklet issued by the Board of Education in 1941.[42] This consists of edited and numbered reports of the accounts sent in by teachers of their use of school broadcasts with children. For instance:

17. From a village school in the West Midlands. Seniors 11–15 listen to the News Commentary *and then use atlases to find points of interest. They also collect newspaper cuttings, which include maps. Each child makes a book of these cuttings with added notes. For instance a talk on 'The Raid on the Lofoten Islands' was a jumping-off ground for the geography of Norway. We revise the past history of the German occupation.*

20. From a modern school in the North West (13+). A talk which referred to Disraeli led to a lively discussion of the part played in history by the Jew. A little pedagogic manoeuvring and the presence of Lisel, our German Jewish refugee, transformed a faint incipient hostility with appreciation of the benefit to mankind wrought by the Jews.

28. [on The Practice and Science of Gardening *talks:] We are always on the alert to compare our practice with that suggested. Often the two coincide, e.g. our cropping plan closely follows that described by Mr Lawrence, except that we extend our rotation over four years, where he advocates a three-year course. On 17th Feb we got a good laugh when the sowing of onions was advocated while the ground outside was frost-bound and covered with snow and we had been unable even to start digging. The boys were delighted when in the intensive cultivation talk of 3rd March, the advantages of a hot bed were explained, as they had just made one.*

The BBC's broadcasts for schools included, from September 1941, a daily five-minute *News Commentary*, and this was continued during the holidays, and throughout the war. A series of programmes considered the histories, cultures and people of the allied countries – France, the USA and the USSR. Also developed were current affairs talks for sixth forms and later for fifth forms. Topics covered included consideration of values – 'the totalitarian answer' and 'the democratic way' and introductions to sociology and research methods. Throughout the war, the BBC encouraged schools to send in their views on the broadcasts; they also held meetings with groups of teachers, older schoolchildren, local education staff and regional education officers engaged in school work.[43]

As Jean Seaton notes (2006: 141), these BBC initiatives indicate that BBC staff were positive in their views of children, as people who could be asked to take part and as active, sensible, thoughtful people who could be engaged with directly, on equal terms. She quotes from a broadcast on *Children's Hour* (15 November 1940) by Stephen King-Hall, in which, discussing democracy and its implications for children, he addressed children, saying they must acquire the skills to engage with democracy by sensible activity. As a sensible child, you would 'take the trouble to find out the facts about problems yourself. . .train yourself to use your brains[,]... not believing everything you are told, or read or hear. Question everything but be sensible judges.' More generally, Seaton argues that, whereas in those years programmes for children included children and adults seriously talking with each other, nowadays no one makes programmes in which adults engage with children; programme makers have thus separated the worlds of children from those of adults (Seaton, 2006: 143). The view of children as sensible people who could do their bit comes through a 1945 retrospective description of *Children's Hour* during the war by Derek McCulloch ('Uncle Mac'). He says it aimed:

> *to give children stability and continuity in a world of chaos and change; to give children the best music, story, drama; to encourage their war effort in savings schemes, salvage, handicraft, harvesting and safety first; to avoid too much emphasis on direct war topics or*

hate of enemies but focusing on the part played by men and women in the Services; to avoid creating fear, to give direct and regular religious instruction.[44]

Films

'Going to the pictures' provided children with more messages encouraging them to participate in the war effort. Cinema-going was a well-established custom between the wars and even more so in wartime.[45] For instance, the Bolton Odeon, opened in 1937, could seat 2,354 people and had continuous programmes on weekdays and three on Saturdays (Gardiner, 2005: 148). In the 1930s, between 18 and 19 million tickets were sold weekly (the population was about 45 million according to the 1931 census).

A survey of children's leisure activities by Jenkinson, first published in 1940, showed that between 40 and 50 per cent of grammar school boys and girls went to the pictures once a week or more, and about 60 per cent of senior school boys and girls did so.[46] The Oxford study also showed that going to the pictures was part of many children's week.[47] A study in 1943 found that 32 per cent of adults went at least once a week and that this proportion was higher among young adults and children than among older people.[48] Most cinemas also had Saturday morning shows for children, and the history of Weston-super-Mare Grammar School (p. 63) records the jingle associated with these shows:

Every Saturday morning, where do we go?
Getting into mischief, oh dear no!
To the Mickey Mouse club, with our badges on,
Every Saturday morning at the O-de-on!

As well as American escapist films, popular films included British feature films about war, for instance *Convoy*, the most successful British film of 1940 and *Henry V* (1944), films that combined entertainment with propaganda (Chapman, 1999: 42). In those days, a cinema programme included a 'newsreel', perhaps a Ministry of Information documentary, a 'B' feature film and the main feature. Documentary films were five-minute (and later 15-minute) propaganda films, featuring, for instance, each of the armed services, or topical exhortations following crises – for instance following Dunkirk and the 1940–41 Blitz.[49] These films also praised the work of people on the home front, and the resilience of schoolchildren.[50] There were also 'story-documentaries' – fictionalised propaganda to promote the war effort.[51] This, then, was a setting in which children, like adults, enjoyed time out from day-to-day experience and hardships and (though they may have been sceptical faced with propaganda) might be cheered to see films about their own lives; children could also learn about how the war was progressing, and could link that knowledge with discussions and news bulletins at school. Documentary films were also shown in other settings, such as schools and village halls and via mobile vans touring villages (Swan, 1989: 155, 160, 169, 170).[52]

One of our interviewees, Teresa Letts, living in a small village in Kent, went by bus to the cinema once a week, and thus saw a wide variety of films – but always had to leave before the end of the film to catch the last bus back:

> INTERVIEWER: *Do you remember what you saw, what you liked?*
>
> *TL: Yes, I do actually. I wasn't allowed to see* The Wicked Lady *– so it was that era. I hated Will Hay, loved American features, Betty Grable and Carol Lombard.*

Another (Susan Sawtell) noted that at school, she learned about the progress of the war from her 'politically aware housemistress'. 'She put up maps and told us what was happening. And in the next-door house lived a refugee Jewish girl, who was, of course, deeply anxious about what was happening to her family. So that was a huge issue for me.' Her mother thought it important for her to know what was happening, so in 1945 'she insisted on taking me to a film about the relief of Dachau, because she said you need to know about it'.

Children's fiction

Children's literature was another arena in which children learned the value of their active engagement with the war effort. Children were explicitly exhorted – often entertainingly and amusingly

– to undertake all kinds of patriotic duties to support the war effort. Publishing for children was regarded as important at the time (while educational publishing collapsed) (Dudley Edwards, 2007: 650). If we take one classic series, Richmal Crompton's *Just William* stories are full of examples of William and his friends trying to offer their services. The wartime stories are pervaded with explicit stories of daily life during the war, and exhortations to help, and William tries hard to do so, often with very funny results. For instance:

> *William was finding the war a little dull. Such possibilities as the black-out and other war conditions afforded had been explored to the full and were beginning to pall. He had dug for victory with such mistaken zeal – pulling up as weeds whole rows of young lettuces and cabbages – that he had been forbidden to touch spade, fork or hoe again. He had offered himself at a recruitment office in Hadley, and, though the recruiting sergeant had been jovial and friendly and had even given him a genuine regimental button, he had refused to enrol him as a member of His Majesty's Forces.*[53]

Another series is by Virginia Pye, about the Price family and their friend Johanna. The stories show how children took on jobs in well-to-do homes as servants were called up; Dudley Edwards (2007: 639) notes that war led to people of every kind and age and upbringing being expected to do things they had never dreamed of. Thus, in the 1943 story *Half-term Holiday*, Pye writes about Priscilla, who was working on a farm:

> *She was glad too that because of her work on the farm, which she loved better than anything else, she could feel she had a job and that she was a necessary and useful cog in the war machine. She was no longer playing at farming, she was right deep in it.*
>
> (Pye, 1943: 20)

Children's comics, such as those published by D.C. Thomson, also played their part in enlisting children to participate in the war effort. *The Beano*, for example, was very explicit, containing blatant anti-German and anti-Italian propaganda, laden with images of war and fighting, that seems extraordinary, with hindsight. According to Heggie and Riches (2008: 79), '*The Beano* mobilised a battalion of heroes to inspire British children in their wartime endeavours'. The mantra was that every character should 'do their bit':

> *Whether by collecting old comics to recycle, supporting the Home Guard, bearing privation, or simply maintaining prudent war etiquette, everyone had to play their part. Primarily,* The Beano *concentrated on encouraging children. Every aspect of a war child's life, and indeed their potential contribution to the war effort, was covered.*
>
> (ibid.: 92)

If you keep waste paper saving going with a swing

maybe you'll soon see Hitler swing!

WASTE PAPER IS USEFUL!!

If you want to help your country
Here's how you can do your bit—
Gather every scrap of paper,
Don't destroy it—salvage it.
GIVE IT TO THE NEAREST SALVAGE MAN!

S. O. S.

Tramcar tickets, paper bags,
Old newspapers, label tags,
Magazines and old school jotters,
Cardboard packets, finished blotters—
Save all the paper waste you can
And give it to the salvage man.

The History of The Beano: *The story so far,* published by Waverley Books Ltd.
Images © D.C.Thomson & Co., Ltd.

The History of The Beano: *The story so far,* published by Waverley Books Ltd.
Images © D.C.Thomson & Co., Ltd.

Discussion: Concepts of childhood during the war years

As at any period, ideas about childhood and about children's relations to society and, at local levels, to parents and teachers, were mixed, inconsistent and shifting during the war years. But some ideas current at the time stand out.

Children as workers

There seems to have been no theoretical barrier during the war years to harnessing children's work towards the war effort. It was obvious that everyone should help by doing what they could. The fact that most children did work anyway in their households, and by 12 many were in paid work, meant it was no great step to enlist them as war workers. In practice, schools were good arenas in which to promote children's war-work – since children were captive and teachers could encourage and collaborate with the children. It was constantly emphasised in government pronouncements, however, that Britain – unlike Germany – was not going down the route of forcing young people to join organisations; since the country was fighting for democracy, democratic principles should be upheld.[54] However, these ideas were compatible with encouragement for children and young people to join groups, such as Scouts, and pre-military training groups, which also carried out war-work. We note too that one kind of incentive to get children involved may well have been to boost morale, on the grounds that people were happier if they felt they were contributing.

There is clear evidence, in the massive attempt to save the children through evacuation, that in wartime children were recognised as people valuable to the nation's survival. But protecting the children and providing for them through welfare measures was complemented by a focus on children's participation in the war effort. However, the future leaders of the country were entitled to more education than the 90 per cent, and the intelligence of the 90 per cent was hotly debated, as was their present and future status in life.

© Crown copyright.

An ambivalent view of children: A boy clearing up after an air raid is told that he should be evacuated.

Children as learners

It can be argued that during the war changes were in progress, building on earlier movements, towards conceptualising children as learners. There was increased emphasis on the idea that children were agents in their own education, as had been promoted in the 1930s by Susan Isaacs and other 'progressive' thinkers. Mary Somerville, head of BBC schools broadcasting during the war, surveyed the education field retrospectively and noted changes in educational theory and gradual changes in practice, from what children should learn, to what engaged children, with more emphasis on the arts, crafts, music and drama.[55] She noted that the BBC had responded to the changes with programmes on these topics; and certainly the schools programmes emphasised children as social actors in learning and doing. From his travels up and down the country (as editor of the *TES*), Harold Dent endorsed the view that children were increasingly engaged as participants in education.[56] And evidence from the Oxford study (see Appendix) provides convincing instances of changes to education practice during the war. Teachers had to use what was available – and rural studies, botany and local history could be experiential as much as book-bound. Apart from the effects of war, there may also have been a 'Hadow effect' – as curricula had to be developed for the 11–14s in the new secondary elementary schools and classes, so teachers and the Board of Education (1937) devised a widened curriculum with more emphasis on children's activity in practical subjects. Thus, it seems that the earlier model of teaching children a highly limited set of facts was giving way to a view of children as active agents in learning, and by extension to a view of schooling as a wider, deeper and more valuable enterprise for all children.

We note here, too, that as the war progressed and victory looked more certain, educationalists turned their attention to more basic consideration of the socio-political status of children across Europe and the perceived need for political and psychological re-education of children, in the context of international cooperation. A 1937 English documentary film, *Children at School,* had drawn attention not only to what schools could offer, but also to the 'multitude of old, decrepit, dark, under-funded and over-crowded English schools' attended by many; the film made the point that 'European fascists were getting ahead in their approach to education'.[57] So it is interesting that the New Education Fellowship, at its 1942 international conference, chaired by Butler, and attended by representatives of the allied nations, drafted a 'Children's Charter', which stressed children's rights to education. This, like Jebb's in 1929, was a statement of 'the basic and minimum rights of children to be secured and guarded, above and beyond all considerations of sex, race, nationality, creed or social position' (Boyd and Rawson, 1965: 122). The conference aimed to promote international cooperation to rebuild education services and to encourage teachers, children and young people in working together for better education across countries.[58]

Child–adult relations: Taking responsibility versus knowing their place

Some children found it necessary to take responsibility, whether willingly or not, for their own lives. And whether or not separated from parents, many had to participate in caring for others, such as younger siblings, and in the daily work of maintaining the household. Children had to be adaptable to the changing events of the war. Our interviews for this study indicate strongly that adults assumed that children would contribute; as we shall indicate in later chapters, this applied to all children, not just working-class children.

However, it is also clear that children's agency was limited by adult understandings of childhood. Many children were 'kept in their place', both at school and at home. Working-class children, and many girls in all classes, were allowed only low aspirations. Several interviewees told how they were diverted from university or college towards 'women's work', towards a future as wives and mothers, and towards contributing to family income. Children were taught the hierarchy of the education system – with private schools and direct grant grammar schools not for the likes of them (Hattersley, 1983: chs 12 and 13).

Central to understanding childhoods at the time is relations across the generations, between children and parents, and between children and teachers. The encouragement to participate in the war effort was framed by a set of social expectations that children should do what they were told, and that adults had the right to tell them – government spokesmen, BBC programmers, teachers and parents. The social status of children was as subordinates to adults, and the exhortations we refer to here are part of a structure of adult control over children's lives. The apparent willingness of children to 'do their bit' may in part have stemmed from their social positioning. Thus, for instance, our interviewees, commenting on child–adult relations in the past and in the present,[59] make it clear that parent–child relations were much more authoritarian then. They quote parents' standard commands: 'Do as I say. Don't argue. Don't interrupt us when we are talking. Get home on time or else!' Children returning as teenagers from abroad after the war found repressive parent–child relations as compared with, for instance, the USA, where they had experienced more respect and more freedom (Mann, 2005: ch. 28). Many interviewees noted that English children had little psychological freedom – that is they were prevented from knowing, especially about sex and family problems; on the other hand, children had more physical freedom during the war than now, as many people remember, looking back.

In spite of psychological distance between children and their parents, then, as now, family was important to children. This is made abundantly clear in the evacuation studies, where children missed parents and home more than any other aspect of their former lives.[60] Close child–adult bonds are indicated in mothers' unwillingness to let their children be evacuated. However, while there was a psychological view that child–mother relations mattered, social policies were content to separate children from parents – during evacuation, in hospitals, and in institutions for children whose parents could not afford to care for them.

There is some evidence that children and their teachers came closer together during the war years. Though some of our interviewees remembered school as authoritarian, some remembered teachers' kindness and care. Teachers had to take on many welfare roles, as we have noted, including comforting children and seeing to practical needs (Cunningham and Gardner, 1999); the Oxford study makes this clear (see Appendix). One teacher recorded in her diary her resentment about the extra tasks imposed on her – administering savings schemes, supervising dinners, sorting salvage (Lawn, 1987). As teachers' roles changed, so did those of children in relation to teachers: working alongside teachers in school gardens and allotments, working up money-raising shows and fire watching. Children reported a welcome change during the war years. One memory – from Barr's Hill House school – speaks for many:

> *Danger, privation and adversity had made a bond between my generation and the Staff which many of us believe never existed in quite the same way before or since. We felt a special generation and we had been together in a special place.*

(p. 49)

Notes

1 See 'Discussion' section of Chapter 7 and Dent, 1944a: 95–7.
2 Chapters 2–5 of Titmuss's 1950 book, written as part of the official history of the war, give a detailed account of the planning for the eventuality of war. The 1976 edition (which has some amendments to the original) is used here.
3 For instance, see for discussion of pacifism Simon, 1989.
4 Under the Children and Young Persons Act 1933.
5 Dent, 1942: 18. There were about 5,400,000 children aged 5–14 in England and Wales – 1938 figures.
6 Board of Education, 1943b: 6 (paras 17 and 19).
7 See also Barber, 1994: 1 and 62. We note that the percentages quoted vary somewhat according to source and to date.
8 Padley and Cole, 1940; Isaacs, 1941; Barnett House Study Group, 1947.
9 Johnson, 1968; Wicks, 1988; Holman, 1995; Parsons and Starns, 2000.
10 Padley, 1940: 41–4; Titmuss, 1976: 102–3.
11 For a full account of the evacuation of children from Britain, see Fethney, 1990 – who was himself a CORB evacuee; and Mann, 2005.
12 Titmuss,1976: chs VIII and XXV; also Titmuss, 1966.
13 See also Cunningham, 1991, 2006 and Hendrick, 2003 for later endorsement of this view. In a lecture given in the 1950s, 'War and social policy', Titmuss, 1966 refers to a leader in *The Times* (1 July 1940) calling for social justice, for the abolition of privilege, for a more equitable distribution of income and wealth, and for drastic changes in the economic and social life of the country.
14 Quoted in Williams *et al.*, 2001: 94.
15 See Mann, 2005: ch. 5 for many examples of antipathy to children leaving the country, including the three quoted here, and patriotic statements by several young people.
16 Opening paragraph of the Board of Education's 1943 White Paper: 'Educational Reconstruction'.

17 For good summaries of these welfare initiatives, see Titmuss, 1976: 509–14 and Hendrick, 2003: ch. 3.

18 Board of Education (1943b), 'Educational Reconstruction', para 94. Titmuss (1976: 510) saw these welfare initiatives as becoming established social services 'fused into school life'.

19 Williams *et al.*, 2001: 97; Williams, 2000: 158–79.

20 *The Cambridge Evacuation Survey*, 1941: Chapter X reports on a questionnaire to teachers about changes, difficulties and other views on the evacuation processes (see Appendix).

21 Children's views on their daily lives as evacuees were collected by the Barnett House Study Group, 1947: 56–61, and clearly children's views varied (as did the adults'), but it is interesting that both the Cambridge and the Oxford studies saw benefits to children.

22 Interview carried out by Susan Williams in 2001 – Williams *et al.*, 2001: 92.

23 For detail, see Appendix.

24 The government scheme is detailed by Macalister Brew, 1943: ch. 2, who also discusses, from long experience, how best to run youth clubs.

25 For instance, 200,000 boys enrolled in the Air Training Corps in the first six months, double what had been expected by officials (Dent, 1944a: 111). See Chapter 8 for discussion of pre-service training.

26 See Chapter 6 for children's agricultural work at harvest time and in other farm work.

27 Among the many histories of the passing of the 1944 Education Act, especially useful are Richmond, 1945: ch. 8; Barnard, 1968: ch. 32; Gosden, 1976: Part III; Barber, 1994. A useful commentary about relations between Butler and the *TES* editor, H.C. Dent, is given by Joan Simon (1989), who worked with him from 1940.

28 Board of Education, 1943b; and see discussion in Barber 1994: Chapter 4.

29 By 1934 there were at least 17 'progressive' schools, such as Beacon Hill, Dartington and Summerhill (Blewitt, 1934).

30 Gosden, 1976: 448–50 lists 53 publications (mostly books) urging reform, published in the war years up to the passing of the 1944 Education Act. See also for descriptions of many of these, Dent, 1944a: ch. IV.

31 Joan Simon (1989) gives details of these groups, which included, in a committee organised by R.A. Butler, T.S. Eliot, Karl Mannheim and Fred Clarke.

32 For good description and discussion, including reference to critics of Norwood, see Barnard, 1968: 263–6.

33 As had been proposed way back in the 1920s, and notably by Tawney (1924) in a paper for the Labour Party.

34 See Chapter 7 for discussion of technical education.

35 R.A. Butler, a Conservative, privately educated man, was moved from the Foreign Office to become President of the Board of Education, in July 1941. With colleagues, he steered through the Education Act 1944.

36 Conservatives wanted retention of social class distinctions in the education system; some left-wing spokesmen argued for multilateral schools ('comprehensives'), no fees, no selection by IQ test, and abolition of the public schools.

37 In their study of Sheena Simon (1883–1972), Martin and Goodman, 2004: ch. 6 detail how the 'public' schools were deliberately excluded from the

remits of the various committees. Butler himself was pleased about his achievement on this score (Barber, 1994: 53).

38   Making do and mending clothes was a necessary task for adults and children.

39   Some schools acquired the necessary equipment to show films.

40   The information in this paragraph is derived from the BBC Written Archives Centre (WAC), folder R16/12/4/2b.

41   Pamphlets produced to accompany schools radio broadcasts are held in the library of the IOE. For the war years they are volumes 37, 38 and 39. The full collection covers radio broadcasts from September 1926 until 1979. Television broadcasts are included from 1958 onwards.

42   *School Broadcasts and How We Use Them: By a number of teachers* (Board of Education, 1941). The schools were not named, but each account sent in was given a number.

43   The McNair Committee Report on Teacher Training 1943, for the first time put emphasis on the need for teachers to be trained in how to use school broadcasts (Cain and Wright, 1994: 31).

44   Quotation in the *BBC Handbook, 1945* (BBC, 1945).

45   See Graves and Hodge, 1985: ch. 9 on the inter-war years; Gardiner, 2005: 146–9 on the war years.

46   For description of the survey by Jenkinson (1946, first published 1940) see Appendix, pages 265–6.

47   See Appendix.

48   *Wartime Social Survey, 1943*, quoted in Chapman, 1999: 41. Another source says annual cinema admissions rose from 1,027 million in 1940 to 1,585 million in 1945 (Swan, 1989: 168).

49   See, for fuller accounts, Swan, 1989: 158–9; Chapman, 2007.

50   *They Also Serve* (1940) documented women's work at home, supporting the family. *Tomorrow is Theirs* (1940) describes how children were coping (and enjoying new experiences) in the emergency schools set up in cities and in rural schools to which they had been evacuated (British Film Institute, 2007).

51   Some of the most successful story-documentaries were *Target for Tonight* (1942), *Fires were Started* (1943) and *Western Approaches* (1944), and these were also shown in the USA to boost support for US involvement in the war (Swan, 1989: 159, 171).

52   The Ministry of Information organised a fleet of over 100 mobile projector vans which toured the country and showed films in schools, village halls, factories and churches (Chapman, 2007).

53   *William Does his Bit* by Richmal Crompton (1995 [1941]: 9).

54   For instance, among many anti-fascist statements, Macalister Brew (1943: 25, 263–9) is important in stressing that young people must not be conscripted into youth organisations, but must merely be encouraged to help in the war effort. For the compulsory membership of Nazi youth groups, see Stargardt, 2005: ch. 2.

55   Somerville, 1945: 64–6.

56   Dent, 1944a: 155–62; Richmond, 1945: 134. Dent had a series of meetings with Butler during the drafting of the 1944 Education Act (Simon, 1989); perhaps he had some influence on Butler's thinking.

57   Jon Hoare, 2007.

58   This initiative was part of moves to establish the United Nations Educational, Scientific and Cultural Organisation (UNESCO) after the war. It is notable that the Ministry of Education in collaboration with the Ministry of Information made a documentary about how the 1944 Education Act would change schooling. *The Children's Charter* film was made in 1945 by the Crown Film Unit (see the *Land of Promise* DVD issued by the British Film Institute, 2007).

59   Three studies of grandmothers' accounts of their childhood concur on many points: Brannen, 2004; Wade and Smart, 2005; Mayall, 2005.

60   Isaacs, 1941: 67; Barnett House Study Group, 1947: 30. In much more detail, Roy Hattersley (1983) gives an affectionate account of close relations in his working-class family.

Chapter 5

Younger children's work: Doing their bit

In this chapter we move on from our exploration in Chapter 4 of how children were encouraged to participate in the war effort, to considering how far they were aware of the war and what factors made them aware. Then we go on to consider children's activities towards the war effort. We draw mainly on school histories and on our interviews[1] in order to describe these activities, both at school and outside school. Of course, the histories and interviews record mixed experiences during the war, with some children (whether evacuated or not) unhappy and overworked; others enjoyed themselves and felt valued.[2] Perhaps we should repeat that our emphasis is on what they did, on how they evaluated their contributions and on adult expectations that they would contribute.

School histories of all types tell us about war-work carried out by children aged 5–18, both what children did towards the war effort at school and what teachers organised. Our interviewees also drew somewhat on school efforts, but mainly on the work they did in their own time, out of school hours. Some did not recall – or mention – any school-organised war efforts. In the section of this chapter detailing kinds of work children did, we draw mainly on elementary schools (5–14), as well as on interviews with people who were younger children during wartime. In Chapter 6 we deal with work in agriculture and other farm work, and in Chapter 7 we give separate attention to schools for older children, including boarding schools, because children there carried out work and had experiences that were specific to older children and to those attending private schools.

Reproduced by kind permission of St Mary and St Giles Church of England Middle School.
Woodcuts illustrating children's wartime experiences.

Children's awareness of the war

What did children know about the war and about their possible contributions to the war effort? Children had a number of sources of information and they varied in how far the war impinged on their consciousness and on their activities.

First, some children, both working class and middle class, had *direct contact* with the war, both in cities and in rural areas: they sheltered from bombing, they saw enemy action, dogfights, bomb sites, fires, troop movements in the area and armed forces' camps. Many children had relatives fighting in the war. Asked whether adults shielded her from knowledge of the war, Susan Sawtell (aged 7 in 1939) said:

> No way could we be shielded. It was terrifying – we were in the cold damp shelter. And the whole ground shook. It was frightening. . . And people's brothers were being killed. The headmistress would send for them and tell them. No, I was very conscious of it, no way was I being protected.

Others had little knowledge of the war, or were preoccupied with other things. Roy Hattersley (aged 6 in 1939), for instance, writes mainly about family, school, football, cricket and, later on, the Labour Party (Hattersley, 1983). Roger Sawtell (aged 12 in 1939) – who still has his wartime diaries – notes that, though he did fire watching at his boarding school and 'went to see a bomb crater':

> *I have to say, looking at this diary, the war was not an important part of school life at all. Games were far more important. And unlike Susan (his wife) I don't recall being aware of what was happening.*

Secondly, as we noted in Chapter 4 (page 98), there was considerable encouragement from *government departments*. Schools were inundated with leaflets urging teachers and children to get involved – in salvage, savings, gardening; many schools equipped themselves with radios, and some with a film projector and, for instance, showed a documentary or propaganda film each week. At Tedburn St Mary School (elementary) in Devon, the school history notes that anyone who was a child there during the war 'was almost made to feel that Tedburn School was the nerve-centre of Allied operations' because the headteacher involved everyone in implementing the urgent suggestions coming down from government (p. 9). Thus, among other national campaigns, four official 'weeks' were designated for specific fundraising drives: Wings for Victory Week, Salute the Soldier Week, War Weapons Week and Warship Week. In the 'Books for the Navy' scheme (organised by the Royal Naval War Libraries), people were urged to collect and donate unwanted books for distribution to the armed forces.

In May 1940, Lord Beaverbrook, the newspaper tycoon, was appointed by Churchill as Minister of Aircraft Production. As owner of the *Daily Express*, the *Sunday Express* and the London *Evening Standard* newspapers, he was able to campaign effectively for funds to build more planes, notably Spitfires and Hurricanes.[3] Towns and villages, including their schools, worked together for 'Spitfire Funds' (publicity suggested that a Spitfire cost £5,000, although actually it cost considerably more) (Gardiner, 2005: 308–11).

Reproduced by kind permission of the family and estate of C.K. Bird.

A Fougasse poster.

The Dig for Victory campaign was boosted by leaflets – at least 24 – issued by the Ministry of Agriculture, and these were listed in the BBC's schools broadcasting programme notes on gardening.[4] As we noted (page 102) the BBC schools broadcasting service also ran a five-minute news bulletin every morning from September 1941 – Monday to Friday, including during the school holidays.[5]

Thirdly, many *charities* asked for funds, including some charities linked to government efforts – for instance, the Women's Land Army Benevolent Fund, Mrs Churchill's Fund for Russia, the Red Cross, the Aid to China Fund, the Waifs and Strays Society, Earl Haig's Poppy Day.[6] Under the auspices of the British Ship Adoption Scheme, several schools 'adopted' a boat and sent goods (scarves, socks) to the men; in turn, men visited the schools and described their experiences. For example, at Barrow Grammar School, Lancashire:

> In 1943, Lower IVa adopted a motor launch and this example was taken by the whole school in 1944 when it adopted the submarine 'Upshot'. In July the crew and its commander, Lieutenant Wilkinson, an Old Boy, visited School to meet the boys in the classrooms and to present the White Ensign to the School. In return a Bible and School crest were presented to the captain on the School's behalf and a Jolly Roger by Unwin, the youngest pupil. . .A regular flow of comforts to the crew continued to link the boat to its adopted parents.
>
> (p. 114)[7]

Fourthly, some *schools* encouraged children's knowledge and enthusiasm, in a variety of ways. Schools, both state and private, fostered patriotism and awareness of world events through remembrances on Armistice Day, when children might process to the nearest war memorial with a wreath. The logbook of St Mary and St Giles Church of England Senior School at Stony Stratford, Buckinghamshire describes Empire Day in 1940:

> The Union Jack was flown and the first part of the Scripture period took the following form: Morning Prayers by Rev. E.A. Steer, singing of the Hymn 'O God our Help in Ages Past', reading of Viscount Bladuskie's message followed by a short address

by Headmaster on the difference between Empire Day this year compared with Empire Day in 1939 when the King and Queen were visiting Canada, special prayers for the forces and the people were then offered by the Rev. E.J. Payne and the short service ended with the singing of the National Anthem.

(p. 12)

As victory began to look probable, schools, especially those for older children, took a keen interest in the conduct of the war. Thus at Terra Nova School, a private boys' boarding school in Cheshire, an 'old boy' recalled that every day:

from D-Day in 1944, the school gathered at 1.00 p.m. in Room 1 to listen to the BBC wireless news and the progress of the Allies across Normandy: Arromanches, Caen, Argentan, Falaise and then on. He recalls the celebratory school bonfire on VE-Day in 1945 and again on the fifth of November that year.

(p. 98)

At Barrow Grammar School 'wall-magazines went up on the walls of some rooms with illustrations, articles and cuttings to keep the boys informed about the progress of the war' (p. 111). And at the School of St Clare, Penzance, in July 1943 'the noted authoress Phyllis Bottome spoke on the subject of persecution of minorities in Nazi-occupied countries' (p. 43).

Growing up in a Lancashire orphanage and attending Darwen Grammar School, Philip Oakes recounts the boys' reliance on an enthusiastic schoolteacher, Mr Buller, for news:

His bulletins on the progress of the war, who was fighting whom and where, the numbers of casualties and the tally of tanks and planes destroyed were like chapters in a novel which became more fantastic day by day. In a sense it was Mr Buller's war. We saw no newspapers and only rarely were we allowed to listen to the radio [i.e. at the orphanage]. Mr Buller told us what was happening; more than that, he interpreted events and described personalities so enthusiastically that they seemed to be his own creation.

(Oakes, 1983: 224)

Similarly, Susan Sawtell (aged 7 in 1939) describes her teacher's initiatives at a private boarding school, near Derby:

She put up maps and told us what was happening. . .She liked me because I was interested. She would talk to me about it. We would sit, we had meals at the table and we had to make proper conversation so we talked about it. And there were quite a lot of Jewish girls in the school and of course they were – and that was the other thing I was so aware of, you know – they had relatives and news was beginning to filter out [about the concentration camps].

Some parents encouraged children to follow the course of the war, using maps and conversation; other parents, according to our interviewees, didn't talk about the war, perhaps to protect their children from harsh news. However, messages were mixed, and some children had means of finding out, as Teresa Letts (aged 9 in 1939) explained. She had moved with her family from Bermondsey, London, to stay with relatives in Kent:

INTERVIEWER: Did you know anything about the war?

TL: Oh, I knew. I read the papers. Listened in. I had big ears. We listened to the radio and Lord Haw-Haw.

INTERVIEWER: Did they talk about what was happening?

TL: No, never. My father used to turn the radio off. But we expected to be invaded. There were the butterfly bombs that came and rested on all the trees. And the army was billeted just round the corner. . .and we used to have the tanks rolling by the door. Father would explain to me and bring out a map. And uncles sent letters from abroad, from Alamein. We had several relatives in the war.

Fifthly, as we note in Chapter 4 (page 103), newsreels and propaganda documentaries were part of *cinema* programmes. And documentary *films* were sent round to schools. For instance at Stoke Poges village school, near Slough:

A film projector was provided for the school and film shows regularly held, showing Ministry of Information documentaries, of which there were many during the war. These films were designed not only to give instruction to the populace but also to boost morale in the dark days of the War.

(pp. 23–4)

At Tedburn Elementary School, Devon, the history notes that the enterprising headteacher:

saw to it that Tedburn was in at the beginning with a school wireless fitted and operating on 21st October 1939, quickly followed by a film projector in January 1940. The weekly film became a fixed feature of the timetable. [And] the whole world came into the village school and the horizons of the children were lifted far beyond the hills of Dartmoor. Every detail of the progress of the war through Europe, North Africa and the Far East was followed.

(p. 10)

Finally we note that weekly *magazines* for children carried stories of patriotic daring, including the serialised stories of Biggles (air ace), and from 1940 his female counterpart, Worrals (an initiative suggested by the Air Ministry as part of the WAAF recruiting drive) (Cadogan and Craig, 1978: 230). These magazines also carried features urging children to do their bit, by, for instance, collecting salvage (ibid.: 230).[8] Many wartime *novels* for children focused on two topics: evacuation (both positive and negative accounts) and German spies, with children active in catching them (ibid.: 223).

We are not of course saying that awareness simply caused children to work for the common good. As already indicated, for some children the war was a sideshow to their more interesting pursuits. But some kinds of work were already in place before the war. Thus, as well as domestic work at home and locally, children in the 1930s were involved in savings schemes for charities, such as Barnardo's, Save the Children, Poppy Day and Waifs and Strays. The British Ship Adoption Scheme was established by 1935, when St Clement Dane's Grammar School, London, adopted a tramp steamer (p. 97). However, it does seem that encouragement – and in some cases pressure – came from many sides and perhaps built up a momentum that provided a social and moral context for increased contributions by children, alongside adults.

Further, children's awareness was influenced by where they lived and by their experiences. It was also mediated by parental and teacher views on how childhood should be lived, and what they should know. Perhaps most interesting is that government, through a range of measures, encouraged children's participation (see also Chapter 4, page 98). One justification for this could be that since many children knew there was a war on, it was better they should be encouraged to help rather than allowed simply to live in fear. Another reason must have been the potential of schools and of communities, including children, to contribute.

Children carried out varied work

In this section, we focus mainly on younger children, and especially on those who attended state elementary schools. This focus means that we are including working-class children, who in their daily lives would be accustomed to helping out at home and working out of school hours. A common theme in interviewees' accounts of the war years was that work by children was a typical component of childhood, and it provided an unquestioned basis for war-work. One interviewee, Audrey Balsdon, speaks for many: 'Work has always been part of childhood and anything we did in the War was just a continuation of what was expected of children.' Data from individual interviews, from written memories and from school histories, indicates that children's work typically included more than one type of work. However, it is important to note that children's contributions were (of course) slighter than those of adults. This point was made by several people who wrote in response to a radio programme on children's war-work presented by Richard Moore-Colyer in 2004.[9]

The history of Walkington Elementary School, Kent, shows that a wide range of activities took place:

> *As in the First World War, the school played a full part in the war effort. A jumble sale raised £40 to help pay for a Spitfire; a sale for Red Cross funds raised 50 guineas; a collection held on the last celebration of Empire Day (1940) raised £19.4s.5d for the Overseas League Tobacco Fund. Old books were collected for salvage, and nettles, horse chestnuts, and rose hips were gathered. A school garden – complete with bees and hives – was cultivated as part of the 'Dig for Victory' campaign, and showed a profit of five guineas on the first year's curriculum. Gardening was to become an important part of the wartime curriculum. A week's holiday was given in October to allow children to help the farmers to pick potatoes; this practice continued until 1954. The older boys were allowed to help on farms at other times during the year; in May 1942, for example, 'all the boys in the senior class are helping Mr Dove with potato planting'.*
>
> (p. 35)

Gillian (aged 5 in 1939) made a list of war-related activities in advance of our interview:

> *We picked rosehips and Mummy took them to the town hall for 1d a pint. My sister and I picked stones out of the vegetable garden and we got 1d a bucket for that. We collected silver paper – was it to build aeroplanes? – maybe not! We knitted squares to be sewn together to make blankets. . .Oh, yes and there was Dig for Victory – I remember the posters. We had parsnips, I connected parsnips with the Germans! Maybe someone took me into the garden and said this is one way to beat the Germans! And we grew broccoli, Brussels sprouts, kale – things that would stand through the winter.*

The logbook of Boughton Monchelsea School (elementary), Kent, demonstrates a range of activities over two years:

> *1939*
> *Dec. 23 During the week a carol party of native children and evacuated children collected £6.11.5d for a wool fund – girls to make knitted comforts for men serving in the forces.*

1940

*May 24 Empire Day celebrated in the morning by a short service.
35/- was collected for the Overseas League Tobacco Fund.*

1941

*Jan 15 From to-day the keeping of poultry will form part of
the practical training of the older children. Miss Joan Clark has
presented the school with six Light Sussex pullets. The house will
be bought from garden fund.*
Jan 30 Mr Voysey called to discuss pig keeping.
*May 19 Mr Gaynor (Plant Protection Co.) gave a demonstration
to the top class on the application of fertilizers and pest control.*
Nov 22 Two chickens stolen during Friday night.

1942

*Mar 20 Miss Smith, the vicar, Gen. R. Style and Capt.
Crombie R.N. visited to see School display of warships made by
the children.*
*Dec 23 at 11.45 a.m., the School assembled to present Mrs
B.B. Jolly (Red Cross) with the money received for the collection
of 14 cwt waste paper and 15/- from an afternoon concert.
The money she had received she was sending to the Prisoner of
War Fund.*

And so on, through the war years. The 'knitted comforts' referred
to above are helpfully described in the history of Stoke Poges village
school, which quotes from the *Slough Observer* (March 1940):

*The boys and girls of Stoke Poges are doing their bit, knitting for
the forces. They have completed three flying jerseys, two balaclava
helmets, one scarf (made by a boy), mittens and gloves, four pairs
of amulets, three pairs of sea stockings and socks. The whole school
helps in the work. To start with, wool and knitting needles were
bought out of school funds and every child contributes a half-penny
per week to keep supplies going.*

(p. 24)

© Crown copyright.

Cover of a book of knitting instructions, depicting people of all ages contributing.

Similarly, another logbook lists a range of activities at Amberley Parochial School, Minchinhampton:

> *Empire Day – collection from the children; children gave a concert to raise funds for local soldiers' comfort funds; children planted potatoes; War Weapons Week – children bought £82.10s savings certificates and stamps; blackberrying trips for the communal kitchen; Armistice Day – children to war memorial with wreath; hip picking – 5 stones of hips; 1 cwt of horse chestnuts collected and sent to Middlesex HQ; potato picking; children gave concert – £95.11.0 raised for Savings Campaign; collection of books for Salvage Books campaign.*
>
> (pp. 111–14)

Some elementary school histories note competition between war-work and school work, though this is a topic of particular concern among historians of schools for older children (see Chapter 7, page 194). But for any school, priorities could be sharpened, when disaster struck. The history of Wisborough Green School (elementary), Sussex, records the death by bombing of 29 boys and two teachers at a nearby school in 1942, and the next paragraph reads:

> *As the war progressed, practical activities became more important than lessons and children were sent out to gather wool from fences and hedges or pick blackberries or work in the school vegetable garden.*
>
> (p. 31)

The realities of the war affected schools' activities and children's consciousness. At Wittersham Church of England School (elementary), Kent, this point is graphically made:

> *As in 1914–18 the school carried on its daily work as best it could; the pupils raised money for wartime causes – for National Savings and for Wings for Victory – they heard lecturers on such topics as the navy's defence of wartime convoys, they suffered the daily discomforts of blackout of the village, of rationing and shortages of fuel and food, they listened to neighbours' news of prisoners of war and casualties, and they learned to share their lives to some extent with the city children who had come to stay in their homes and school.*
>
> (p. 18)

Kinds of work children carried out

In this section we focus on the five main topics described by our younger interviewees and in the elementary school histories. These are: (1) gardening and food production; (2) household and domestic work; (3) savings; (4) salvage; and (5) paid work. These are types of work that could be carried out by younger school-age children, as well as older ones.

A wartime advertisement encouraging children's involvement in the war effort.

Gardening and food production

As noted above (see also Chapter 4, page 98) government departments encouraged people, including children, to grow food. In September 1939 the first of the Board of Education's memoranda, titled 'The Schools in Wartime', urged teachers to 'look round for a suitable piece of land and open up informal consultations at once with the owner or occupier'. This might be a garden or allotment owned by people whose war-work hampered their ability to grow food. It also included school grounds. Recipes were published in newspapers and booklets issued by the government. Thus, *Food Facts for the Kitchen Front* (Ministry of Food, 1941) is notable for its emphasis on the many ways in which vegetables could be prepared, using methods which minimised loss of nutritional value and using a minimum of (rationed) fat. BBC schools broadcasts covered gardening from January 1940. Later in the war, a White Paper (1943–4) noted:

> *An intensive drive has also been made to encourage production in private gardens and allotments in the Dig for Victory campaign. The number of allotments has increased from about 800,000 before the war to about 1.5 million in 1943 and there has been a large increase in the garden area devoted to vegetable production, with the result that private gardeners have themselves produced a substantial proportion of the vegetables essential for the maintenance of health and working efficiency.*[10]

Work to increase food supply got underway quickly. For instance, at Tackley School, Oxfordshire, school records show:

> *In April 1940 six boys worked to prepare the new school garden and plant seeds. In May Mr Bevan, a horticultural instructor, called and gave advice on the new garden, brought some tools and promised cabbage plants.*
>
> (p. 59)

Some adults remember the satisfaction they felt at what they did:

> *Growing food was the one way they would let us help; they turned our school playing fields into allotments. Unfortunately, it had recently been laid down on a levelled corporation rubbish tip. Once the turf was lifted, we found ourselves trying to plant cabbages, carrots, and potatoes in soil composed of rusted tin cans, kipper bones and brown-edged copies of the* Daily Express. *I stole a lot of my dad's bone-meal – planted vegetables into solid pits of bone-meal. Everything grew amazingly well. . .the family enjoyed everything. Dad never found out where his bone-meal had gone.*[11]

At Beaudesert School (elementary), Leighton Buzzard:

In 1943 the needs of a country supplied with much of its food from abroad were placed before the normal timetable of the school and many boys spent much of their time working on local farms and in the school gardens. Vegetables were supplied to the School Dinner Centre and in September an entry in the Logbook declared that 'the gardens must be the chief concern for this week and the next'. Altogether there were a total of 420 absences recorded in the first two months of the Autumn term as a result of agricultural employment.

(p. 76)

Gardening at home featured in many interviewees' accounts, as we have noted. Some families had allotments in the cities. Frank Chappell (aged 4 in 1939) notes:

We had an allotment in London (Peckham). My father was a great gardener, he kept chickens too. And I had a patch on the allotment to garden. And we did a bit of gardening at school.

And others, notably in the countryside, intensified the cultivation of the land. Joan Barraclough (aged 6 in 1939) remembers that her family moved to a house with an acre of land in a Berkshire village:

My mother's aim was to make us as self-sufficient as possible. We were too small to be of much use in all this but we knew we had to help: planting vegetable seeds, weeding, picking fruit, feeding hens, coating the eggs with waterglass to preserve them and collecting sack-loads of dandelions, cow parsley and other tasty morsels from the hedgerows for the rabbits housed in hutches in the barn.

And evacuees, billeted on farms, took part in farm work. This work has led to comments that children were exploited by farmers and such exploitation has indeed been documented (e.g. Starns and Parsons, 2002). However, some memories are of positive experiences, such as this one from a boy billeted on farms and writing his memories in the Leedstown School, Cornwall (elementary) history:

Again, I was well looked after and learned to help with the milking and ploughing, and various farm activities. . .I often travelled with

Mr P on his horse and wagon to deliver his farm produce. The horses were named Bob and Girlie.

(p. 62)

Household/domestic work

Helping at home was an established custom for the majority of children; and during the war years, as mothers and fathers were called up to war-related duties, children took on more of the tasks of running the home. This substitution work could be especially important where working-class families were running a business at home. One interviewee, Joyce Bateman, found herself, aged 10, in charge of the family smallholding in County Durham, because both parents were called up to full-time work, her mother on shift-work at an ordnance factory and her father in farm work. Her elder sister also had to work at a factory and her elder brother was in the RAF. At home, they had no electricity, no gas and no running water. So she had to collect water from a pump:

> *I had to feed the hens and pigs and see to the greenhouse, dig up potatoes for dinner and then peel or scrape them, set the table and then rush off to school, often racing back at lunchtime to finish the chores I might have forgotten in the morning. Depending on what time Mam was working, the chores varied from week to week. From peeling pickling onions to shredding red cabbage or vegs for piccalilli. . .Saturday morning was black-lead the fire-range and clean the brass fender and all the other brass things from the hearth. Then there were 26 steps to swill down, scrub the big bench in the back yard – it had to be kept spotless as this was where we chopped up pork, skinned rabbits and hares and plucked pheasants etc.*

This is only part of her account of jobs, and she goes on to say that she was both lonely and frightened:

> *The worst part was night. . .Having to light the lamps after pushing the board up to stop light escaping – then I would sit in a corner on the settee and listen for someone to come. I hated it. No-one seemed to have time to spend with me but hey! Everyone was worried and busy and I didn't expect a fuss. Mind you I never got one.*

An important task for girls at home was caring for younger siblings. However, many interviewees experienced this as an unquestioned task in families, so they often did not mention it unless we asked whether they did childcare. During the war years, girls were increasingly kept at home to care for children, as well as to do household work, as is shown by records of school attendance.[12] Where mothers as well as fathers were working out of the home, someone had to care for babies and for ill children, run errands, deal with the rent collector or insurance man, queue at the shops for food, do the cooking, washing and cleaning.

Joy Ewer was aged 9 in 1939. The family moved around in accordance with her father's peripatetic work, building air raid shelters. Her mother was often depressed:

> On and off during the war I looked after my brother, because she was depressed. And my father would pick up children from where we [had] lived, cousins, relatives and bring them to wherever we were living. So there would be several children. And we older cousins would look after the baby cousins and I remember on one occasion we had twin boys, my brother and another boy of similar age and we used to push them around in a double pram, full of pee. . .It was the norm, I think and my mother would have expected it. . .Absolutely normal. You had no choice. Sometimes I'd get out on my own. Which I did as often as I could and I'd hide in a corner of a field and read.

Another interviewee, Elizabeth, was the eldest of nine children, living on a farm and aged 11 in 1939. She did domestic work, farm work and childcare. She said, of her young brother:

> He wouldn't go to school unless I took him. We were very close. He was just like one of your own. [And before school, on the farm where she lived] very often I would clean the grates for lighting fires, clearing the ashes, and then tidying up before going. And if there was time I might have to milk a few cows before going.

An important kind of childcare was helping evacuees settle in and make the best of local life. For instance, John (aged 8 in 1939) told of a succession of evacuees coming to live with the family in Cambridge:

We got them into the Scouts as well. They joined the Scouts and joined in where they could. So we did help out there. We made them welcome. They went to school as well, got integrated into school.

At their elementary schools, too, children engaged in domestic work. The rapid expansion of the school meals service during the war was built up with the minimum of staff. So children helped with the preparation, serving and clearing of meals (Dent, 1944a: 160).

Savings

Schools worked at many ways of making money – putting on shows, making things to sell at fetes. Over 90 per cent of schools had savings schemes and it was reported that by March 1942, schools had contributed £23,500,000 in savings (Gosden, 1976: 85). During the 1943 Wings for Victory campaign, schools had been set a target of £3 million, but actually raised over £10 million (Dent, 1944a: 160). Children's creativity was encouraged too during these campaigns: for instance, to design posters for their schools. An exhibition of these was held at the Royal Academy in London in 1942, the first time children's art had ever been exhibited (Dent, 1944a: 160).[13]

Along with gardening, savings schemes are the commonest types of war effort mentioned in the elementary school histories. The headteacher of Trewirgie Infants School, Cornwall (pp. 55–7) describes the efforts made during the four big savings weeks. During each week 'a giant-size indicator' was erected outside a shop in each village, 'to catch the eye of young and old as they wended their way home from business, workshop, school'. She reports that the amounts collected doubled during the war years. Each village and each school organised its own events, so this was a community enterprise, involving children and adults. Weston-super-Mare Grammar School history records that 'most town halls in the land sported some sort of huge barometer reflecting the town's progress towards reaching their savings target' (p. 31).

The history of Nash Mills School (elementary), Watford, records that these efforts were appreciated:

Although routine matters like crowning the May Queen took place, the war dominated activities. The National Savings Group target

for 'Salute the Soldier' was £50 and the school raised £301.
Postcards arrived from soldiers thanking them for books collected
by the children and for tobacco bought by the children's contributions
to the Overseas League Tobacco Club.

(p. 35)

And our interviewees filled in detail of savings schemes, and the pressure on everyone to contribute. Audrey Balsdon (aged 13 in 1939) recalls:

I also was the Savings Monitor at school and every Monday had
to go round the classroom asking for National Savings. Everybody
saved 'for victory'. . .I am sure more children of whatever age were
aware of the need to save not only money, but paper, elastic bands
and all manner of everyday items. We weren't allowed to waste
anything and I am sure that is still true of my generation, as we see
the way food and other things are wasted now. In those days, nothing
got thrown away.

And Tony Rees (aged 7 in 1939) explained in his written account:

On a given day each week in my infant school, children were
told to bring in what they could save to be exchanged for savings
stamps that were stuck in a book. When you had fifteen shillings'
worth you sent them off to be exchanged for a savings certificate
which was guaranteed to be worth £1.0s.6d in ten years' time.
My mother's two sisters each gave me a shilling each week to save
and by the time we went to live in the country in October 1940 I
had four certificates worth £3, which means that the scheme must
have got going just about immediately when schools re-opened in
October 1939 after the outbreak of war. The pressure to save
was pretty strong. One incentive was to set targets. £5,000, we
were told, would buy a Spitfire plane, £10 million would buy a
large warship. The former was a feasible target for a school over a
year or two, the latter for a city the size of Birmingham during its
annual savings week.

While, we gather, most charities seemed to people to be deserving causes, Rose (aged 6 in 1939), brought up in a Communist family, remembered standing on the street in London, towards the end of the war, with a collecting box for Mrs Churchill's Fund for Russia, and she said she was shocked at the number of people who refused to give. She had been brought up to believe Russia was a great society.

Financing the war also included making things to sell, as Teresa Letts (aged 9 in 1939) told us:

> And then you had fairs in the summer, a village fete on the village green. We would have to raise money. 'Say Thanks with Tanks!' And we used to make things to sell, or raffle them – pipe-cleaner dolls, rag dolls; my father made a doll's house and we made curtains and knockers and furniture out of balsa sticks. And bigger dolls' toys – we made cots from shoe boxes and dolls to go in them. And fairy dolls, we used to make for the Christmas tree. . .We made rag rugs on hessian, scarecrows for the gardens, we soaked beech leaves in glycerine for the winter; made brooches out of beech husks. I learned crocheting and made crocheted collars. Paper doilies we made out of paper, folded and cut. We grew lavender and in the drawers you had wallpaper with lavender stuck down, with a piece of muslin over it.

Salvage

Of the many schemes to get children involved in the war effort, one remembered by many was organised by the WVS: the 'Cogs' scheme (that is, children were encouraged to regard themselves as cogs in the war-work machine). Hundreds of thousands of children joined Cogs corps, as part of the salvage-collecting enterprise. *The Times* noted in 1941 that the scheme was based on 'the knowledge that all children like responsible worthwhile work to do. Schools were asked to co-operate and most did.' A Cog song started: 'There'll always be a dustbin'.[14] The Gamston Elementary School (Nottinghamshire) history recorded a Cogs scheme:

> Nottinghamshire introduced a scheme to encourage children to collect paper. If you collected 25 books you became a Lance Corporal, 50 books a Corporal, etc. A boy who had collected 250 Punch magazines all at once, was made a Field Marshall – the first in Nottinghamshire.

(p. 142)

Tony Rees recounts how he enthusiastically collected waste paper and filled the garage with it, until his mother, in desperation, urged him to write asking the council to collect it:

> *A few days later I had my answer. . .appointing me to be a Senior Salvage Steward, and enclosing a yellow lapel badge of office. The letter explained that there would soon be a delivery of three bins, one for paper, one for metal and one for bones. . .Apart from the yellow badge and consequent envy of the other children, the only perquisite of my appointment was that I, in turn, could choose Junior Salvage Stewards, who would be sent their badge on my nomination.*

Many people recall the pig bin stationed at the end of the street, so that people could put their waste food there, to be used by those keeping pigs. And one of the jobs done by children was to take vegetable waste to the bin each day. Powell Corderoy School (elementary), Dorking records:

> *The younger children formed a branch of the Children's Feather Brigade, which collected feathers to make into pillows for the hospitals, and children of all ages joined in picking blackberries, which were then delivered to the local Fruit Preservation Centre to be made into jam. . .During the annual Egg Week, one year, to collect eggs for the Dorking Hospital. . .the school contributed a record number of 540 eggs, and when a nationwide Book Salvage Fortnight was organised the school contributed over 10,000 books and magazines.*
>
> (p. 66)

Foraging or 'scrounging' for blackberries, mushrooms, acorns (for pigs), rose hips and nettles was a topic in many memories. This kind of work, necessary in poorer families (Humphries, 1981: ch. 6), was more widely useful in wartime, to supplement rations. Frank Chappell (aged 4 in 1939) and his siblings would be sent out 'scrumping' in London:

> *Our mother used to give us a shopping basket to fill – apples, plums, nuts – we climbed into the garden of a big house. It had been locked up for the war and the owners gone away. But we*

saw the back of the house had been blown out, so we climbed in: there were elephants' feet waste bins, chandeliers, lots of books, Victorian children's books – I took a few!

And Teresa Letts described herself as 'a scrounger':

The war was lovely, it was freedom, I lived where I wanted, how I wanted. My mother used to call me a gipsy because I was never in. I used to bring home all sorts of things. Mushrooms, fruit, wild berries, flowers.

Paid work

Some children did paid work, and there is some evidence that rates of work varied, with more evacuated children doing paid work than those who stayed put. As the Appendix shows, of the sample children evacuated from London to Oxford, 30 per cent were earning money whereas fewer of the local children (14 per cent) and of children living in London (8 per cent) did so. One reason may be that pocket money, even if normal in pre-war households, might not be readily available to many children living away from their parents. Some of the money earned could also have been given to the foster parents, to eke out the government subsidy for evacuated children. Paid work may not have been a direct contribution to the war effort (though some was), but it did perhaps mean that children were able to feel useful and to keep themselves cheerful, using the money for sweets (rationed) and for trips to the cinema. Frank Chappell, evacuated to Wales, did a paper round. Another of our interviewees, June McMahon, evacuated to a rural area, aged 9, told us:

JM: We got this little job at the manor house – we got paid 6d a week (each) and we used to wash up every night. [Then she was sacked, because she stole a peach.] So then we got another job with Mr and Mrs N and that was on a farm. We used to chop firewood, and collect the eggs, we used to feed the chickens and we used to do all sorts of things.

INTERVIEWER: Did you like that?

JM: Well, it wasn't a problem. It didn't seem like a chore. . .And we were paid about the same, for a lot more work. He had a lot of apple trees and he didn't mind if we – Help yourself! And of course we used to go, I think they call it 'gleaning'. Because Mrs F [foster mother] had chickens too and at one stage a pig. So we did the gleaning for them. There was a pigsty in her garden.

As we describe in the next chapter, children's agricultural work was paid, during the Second (but not the First) World War. Of course, most of the children who feature in this chapter left school at 14 and worked in factories, offices or on the land, or for household enterprises. The 1930s youth unemployment problem was alleviated by the war because of manpower shortages, so young people could find work that was directly useful (unlike many peacetime pre-war jobs), or they were directly recruited into war-related work. For instance, Eddie's career is followed in the history of Piggott School, in Berkshire; at 14, he 'went straight to a course at Woodley Aerodrome, and by the age of 17 had qualified as a skilled fitter' (p. 10). As we shall describe in Chapter 7, training in technical work for the war effort was also an important development during the war.

Discussion

It is clear that government ministries and charities were keen to enlist children in the war effort. Firstly, war conditions reduced the availability of imported food, and the Dig for Victory campaign was almost certainly recognised by everyone as a contribution to the nation's larder. Secondly, waging war most certainly did require huge funds and any means of encouraging the population to contribute, including children's efforts, had to be worthwhile. A third important problem was the shortage of manpower; so children's contributions were substituting for the work of adults. This aspect is not very well documented, except in the examples our interviewees gave us, and in the discussion by Titmuss of what the school attendance records show (see note 12), but children, especially girls, were a reserve force who kept the home fires burning; in doing so, most of them were continuing with the kinds of domestic work they had done before the war, though now some had more to do.

So the second point we reiterate here is that it was expected for the vast majority of children to help out – as our interviewees told us. Children were not at this time conceptualised as scholars, solely or at all; childhood could, and in practice did, include work. Thus, while some interviewees thought they were helping the war effort – others did not conceptualise their work in these terms. It was just what you did. Childhood included contributing to the division of labour, in households and in society more generally.

Perhaps schools were an obvious target for ministries and charities, since children and teachers together could devote some of their school hours – and out-of-hours time – to war-work. While morale-boosting may have been one motive for encouraging young children to do their bit, it does seem from our evidence that children and their teachers did make contributions to the war effort. However, it is interesting in another respect that government departments targeted schools. Schools, it seems, were not conceptualised solely as places of learning and preparation, set apart from social and political enterprises; schools were constituent agencies in the national enterprise and the children who attended them could be asked to drop their school work in favour of collaborating with their teachers for the good of the nation. This call to help had occurred in the First World War too.[15] In this sense, children as learners were second in priority to children as workers. We have here indications not only that war made for unusual demands on the people, but that schoolchildren could readily be classified as part of the people.

Explicit rhetoric about service as a concept underpinning the school ethos does not feature much in these elementary school histories, as it does in histories of grammar and private schools, but duty to respond to government requests does. Loyalty to God, King and Country was embedded in elementary school events. Since about half the elementary schools were church schools (mainly Church of England and Roman Catholic),[16] this ensured that those children were taught to revere both God and Country. In non-church schools, too, a daily assembly with hymns and prayers, celebrations of Armistice Day, visits to the church for harvest festivals and visits by local clergymen would site Christianity and patriotism firmly in school life. Furthermore, many of the elementary school histories are of village schools, and their war-work was often part of a village enterprise, as we have exemplified. It is also tempting to suggest that the war offered opportunities welcomed by some teachers to widen the children's experiences. Keeping chickens and growing vegetables provided an active form of education, as well as release from school desks. Though the downward pressure of the 'scholarship exam' may have worried some teachers and some children, it might be taken seriously for only a minority of the most promising children (since the chances of success were slight, and costs daunting), so it may be that, compared to grammar and private schools, academic success was less of a preoccupation at many of these schools.

We also note that many children probably experienced childhoods, in some of the conventional meanings people ascribe to childhood nowadays: that is that children should have freedom to explore, to play, to be independent. Many of those who recalled their childhood chose to mention that they found enjoyment where they could – some of those evacuated enjoyed country life and some of the country children enjoyed roaming around the countryside with them. Some noted that children benefited from freedom – parents not having the time to control them: Benny Green (1994) recounts teenage exploits out and about in London. Some children enjoyed seeing the aerial dogfights, playing war games, collecting shrapnel and becoming experts in aeroplane recognition.[17] Other children, we hear, were purposely protected by their parents, again in the name of one component in ideas about childhood: that it should be carefree. Thus Teresa Letts's father, who, we noted earlier, had ambivalent views on whether she should be allowed to know about the war, also insisted that she should have an enjoyable childhood, free from household chores, even though her mother was heavily overworked:

No, my father said, leave her alone. She's got enough to put up with. Enjoy things while you can. He didn't want me helping with the washing up. She [mother] would say, but she won't know how to wash up and he would say, she'll have plenty of washing up later on. Let her enjoy this world as much as she can.

But he also insisted on absolute obedience to parental diktat:

Oh, yes, I had to do what they said. There was no argument about that. If they said be in by eight, you had to be.

For some children, undoubtedly, the war years were very hard (Joyce Bateman, in charge of the family's smallholding, is a prime example). But here we are up against the assumption that in childhood life should not be hard; this may well be a more modern assumption, and it would therefore be with hindsight that we would view the hard work of some children as not natural to childhood. It is also difficult, looking back, to know how important, in shaping people's ideas, were the tough choices and difficult lives of adults at the time; how far parents and others responsible for children thought it justifiable, especially because of the war conditions, to ask of children that they work even harder than they did in pre-war times.

The notion of childhood as a time of protected innocence – especially about adult problems (marital tensions, sex, poverty) is evident in some of the accounts; it persists alongside the view of some (but not all) parents and other adults that children should know about the war (through maps, radio, cinema, relatives' activities in the armed forces). So some children were kept informed about the war, others were not. However, schoolteachers seemed to have assumed that children should be taught patriotism and this provided one basis for harnessing children's work in the service of their country.

Notes

1 See Chapter 1, pages 16–21 for a description of our data sources.

2 For instance, the history of Trinity Grammar School, evacuated to the countryside, gives detailed memories, good and bad, of children's wartime experiences.

3 Gardiner, 2005: 304–12; Anderson, 2008: 80.

4 Topics covered in the 'Dig for Victory' leaflets included: onions, leeks, shallots, garlic (Leaflet No. 2); manure from garden rubbish (No. 7); jam and jelly making (No. 10); storing potatoes for food and seed (No. 13); garden pests and how to deal with them (No. 16); making the most of a small plot (No. 23).

5 See Chapter 4, Note 41, for information on the BBC schools broadcasts archive.

6 History of Badsey Schools, Evesham – a state elementary school.

7 As we explained in Chapter 1, we refer in the text to page numbers of the school history. The 'Schools histories' section lists all the schools to which we refer, along with the author, title and publisher of the history.

8 See also Chapter 4: pages 105–7 for comments on *The Beano*.

9 This material is held at the Museum of English Rural Life (Reading) in a folder relating to Moore-Colyer's work.

10 *Statistics related to the War Effort of the UK, 1943–44,* Cmd 6564, viii, 597, p. 17.

11 Anon, quoted in Westall, 1985: 151.

12 Titmuss, 1976: 415–18; also Gosden, 1976: 68.

13 The development of 'progressive' interest in children as artists during the twentieth century is told by R.R. Tomlinson, whose 1947 book includes paintings by children during the Second World War.

14 This information is quoted from Anderson, 2008: 79.

15 Many school histories devote chapters to the war effort in both world wars.

16 See, for discussion of church schools, Barber, 1994: 24.

17 Tony Giles (2002) became so expert that he was awarded an Efficiency Certificate by the RAF in recognition of his 94 per cent accuracy in recognising aircraft (the certificate is reproduced as the frontispiece to his memoirs).

Chapter 6

Bringing in the harvest

In this chapter, we describe the extent of children's involvement in agricultural production, drawing on school histories and our interview data, as well as propaganda and other documents from the time. We describe how children's contributions were evaluated. Finally, we suggest that children could effectively be seen – in theory – as a kind of reserve army of labour; that from the children's points of view, the work was very physically demanding, occasionally appalling, but that they felt they 'did their bit', however small, to help in national food production at a time of crisis.

Background

As in the First World War, schoolchildren were an important source of labour in agriculture. Though concerns about the ill effects of 'heavy continuous muscular work' on children were voiced in the run-up to the war (see Chapter 4: page 92), it became clear that children of school age would have to be employed in agricultural work if Britain was to be able to feed its population. Several million acres of meadowland were ploughed up each year in the struggle to increase food production. According to the Ministry of Information, between 1939 and 1943, 6.5 million extra acres of grassland were ploughed up, and 98,000 skilled men had been lost from the land. By 1943, the estimated net output of the soil of the UK was up 70% on pre-war output.[1] Wheat production increased by 109%, barley by 115%, oats 58%, potatoes 102%, sugar beet 37%, vegetables 34% and fruit 55% (Ministry of Information, 1945).

Faced with a growing shortage of adult male labour, the government had to look to other sources of labour, particularly that of women and children, to work the increased acreage. One of the first measures of the war, in early October 1939, was to pass a Bill to postpone raising the school-leaving age to 15.[2] A subsequent series of government measures relaxed child employment legislation to allow schoolchildren to work on the land. The Board of Education issued the first of its annual 'potato' circulars in 1941, asking local authorities to arrange for school holidays to be fixed, if necessary at short notice, in those periods when the needs for seasonal agricultural labour was greatest, so that children over 12 years of age could be employed in agricultural operations during the holidays, and also that schools should organise parties to visit local farms on certain days in term time in order to help with the work of planting and lifting potatoes.[3] In May 1942 new regulations freed more children to work the land during term time, where local education authorities were satisfied that 'by reason of a shortage of labour any agricultural work of a seasonal nature will be seriously delayed unless school children in the area of the authority are employed in that work'.[4]

Children over 12 could work, with parental consent, for not more than 36 hours a week, or seven hours a day. It was also suggested that, wherever possible, children under 14 should be employed only for half-days so that they could attend school in the morning and work in the fields in the afternoon, or vice versa. This was more or less identical to the half-time system, described in Chapters 1 and 2. War Agricultural Executive Committees were also asked to discourage the employment of children under 14, so long as any other source of labour was available.[5] However, we know from our interviewees and from school histories that younger children took part too. It is impossible to assess the extent of children's contributions in terms of hours spent working on the land, or the amount of produce planted, sown or harvested, or the acreage of land they cleared. Official statistics were not kept (in contrast to the First World War, described in Chapter 3, page 63). The important point is that, according to the official view, children's work was voluntary – this is emphasised over and over again in contemporary reports – and it was paid.

The most thoroughly researched aspect of children's involvement in agricultural production is the case of 'school harvest camps', that is, camps for schoolchildren, accompanied by their teachers, run in the summer school holidays. These were organised by state and private schools, urban and rural, and were attended by boys and girls, in increasing numbers throughout the war years. Rural schoolchildren also helped out on local farms, in the holidays and while at school, in much less formal arrangements, and these are the experiences of agricultural work remembered by most of our interviewees.

Museum of English Rural Life, University of Reading.

Schoolgirls, Girl Guides and members of the Girls' Training Corps (GTC) gleaning beans for cattle fodder in Essex.

School harvest camps

The school harvest camps, or 'school agricultural camps', have been well researched by the agricultural historian R.J. Moore-Colyer (2004). In 1940, there were 249 camps for 8,000 boys organised by both private and state schools. However, the arrangements had been *ad hoc*, and after an accident, a more formal system was introduced by the Ministry of Agriculture:

Much concern is felt by secondary teachers at the development of the case recently heard at Birmingham Assizes when heavy damages were awarded against a headmaster for alleged negligence in allowing a party of 20 boys to work on a farm without supervision (a boy lost an eye when hit by a clod of earth intended for another boy in a fight).[6]

This case led to teachers being 'unwilling to organise camps unless a formal structure embodying indemnification against legal action could be elaborated'[7] and it was agreed that camps should be better organised. The Ministry of Agriculture set up the Schoolboy Harvest Camps Advisory Committee (SHCAC) under the chairmanship of Robert Hyde, Director of the Industrial Welfare Society. This was 'a small body of experienced people to guide and advise schools on a number of matters that were likely to arise if the movement grew' (Hyde, 1952: 469). The Board of Education issued guidance as to how camps were to be financed and organised, down to detailed instructions about diet, pay and insurance. Table 6.1 shows the numbers of children involved in the scheme, which lasted until 1950.

Table 6.1: The School Harvest Camps Scheme, 1941–45[8]

	1941	1942	1943	1944	1945
Camps	335	654	1,068	997	774
Boys in single-sex camps	12,000	26,425	41,372	45,968	28,130
Girls in single-sex camps	–	3,869	20,424	15,593	12,130
Children in mixed camps	–	848	6,892	5,679	4,320
Total	12,000	31,142	68,688	67,240	44,580
Total boy/girl weeks of work		124,568	274,752	268,860	178,320

Museum of English Rural Life, University of Reading.

Propaganda photograph of Mr L. Hugh Newman, a lepidopterist, organising bands of children to catch butterflies in cabbage fields.

According to Harold Dent, boys under 16 were paid a minimum of 6d an hour, and those over 16 were paid 8d an hour (Dent, 1944a: 119). The fact that children were paid wages was explicitly contrasted to the situation in Germany, where the government had introduced a similar system with the instruction which stated: 'The children will regard their auxiliary work in agriculture as honorary service but to encourage joyful alacrity in their work, the farmer must give them pocket money.'[9] The British Ministry of Agriculture insisted:

> *There was no question of 'conscripting' youths on Nazi lines, nor will the plan involve any regimentation of youth labour. The idea is to invite these young men to offer themselves for farm work at their local Employment Exchange where they will be placed with farmers who are willing to accept their services.*[10]

Moore-Colyer describes the considerable organisation required to establish the camps, and farmers' appreciation of children's work, for example:

> *So delighted were growers in the Fylde district of Lancashire (where children from twenty schools picked 2000 tons of potatoes in 1943) that they provided camp participants with illuminated scrolls as expressions of gratitude.*
>
> (Moore-Colyer, 2004: 202)

Reproduced by kind permission of Lord Wandsworth College.
Lord Wandsworth College boys pulling a haywagon.

While there were official statistics of the numbers of children involved in school harvest camps, there were no statistics kept of how many children were employed in agriculture outside the camps. Dent suggests that thousands of others helped from their homes:

> *During term time elementary and secondary school pupils by the thousand engaged in part-time agricultural work. Altogether, it is estimated that during the year schoolchildren did about 3,000,000 hours of work on the land.*
>
> (Dent, 1944a: 117)

Many school histories draw on school magazines of the time to record children's activities in these organised camps. Several include children's poems and drawings, and teachers' descriptions of the camps. Some give detailed accounts, logging the amount of time spent in work, the amount of produce, and the numbers of children involved. Nearly all of them record the hard work involved. For example, the school history for Barrow Grammar School called it 'a hard but profitable holiday' (p. 110).

Agricultural camps were run by both urban and rural schools. For example, George Dixon School, Edgbaston, Birmingham, set up camps in Warwickshire. According to the school history, 'the boys travelled to the location either by train or on their bicycles. There they found a quasi-military regime, led by Mr Walker. Days were organised as follows':

7.30 a.m.	*Reveille and prayers*
8.00 a.m.	*Breakfast, followed by briefing and identification of daily tasks*
Midday	*Cold sandwich lunch*
5.00 p.m.	*End of working day*
Evening	*Supper, games and baths*
9.00 p.m.	*Parade and evening prayers*

Mr Walker remembered that 'the famers and the Warwickshire Agricultural Committee gave unstinted praise to the boys and their efforts. They were magnificent' (p. 41).

The history of Stationers' Company School, Hornsey, details some of the practicalities. In the summer of 1942:

Photo courtesy of Cheltenham College Archives.

Boys harvesting carrots at Cheltenham College, Gloucestershire

Mr Davis organised the Harvest Camp for three weeks at Stockcross near Newbury. The boys cycled from London to Stockcross, and then used their cycles to travel from the camp to the farm each day. After an early breakfast the boys would arrive at the farm by 8 a.m. The first job was 'shocking' [i.e. stooking]. . .When the harvest was in on the first farm, the gang was at work by 8 a.m. on the next farm, more mechanised than the first, to clear out the tractor shed and pitch up sheaves to the cockpit of the threshing machine. The day ended at 8 p.m.: time sheets were completed and the boys cycled back to camp, where the staff, headed by Mr Davis, doctored their wounds, and Mrs Davis patched their torn garments. The boys who took part were clearly very appreciative of the support given them by the staff – and produced an additional verse of the School song, 'respectfully dedicated to BD'. This begins:

'We are the campers who gather the harvest in,
Stooking and sweating at five bob a day,

Living on sandwiches packed into ma's best tin,
Moaning and groaning and earning war pay.'

The history adds, 'This account of the Harvest Camp drawn from the jaunty report at the time by P.H. Carter in the School Magazine, reflects something of how cheerfulness and willingness to contribute to what was called "the war effort" expressed itself in a group of Sixth Form pupils at the turning point of the war' (p. 73).

The history of Trinity, a London grammar school, describes children's involvement in harvest camps in Hertfordshire, and includes accounts of their memories. Jenny (Lunnon/Suckling) recalls:

And finally pea-picking camps at Terling in '42 and '43. When at Hatfield Peverel the boys had done some pea picking, but not many girls were involved until those wonderful camps where we slept in the village hall and the boys in the upper area of the apple packing shed. The lower part was our dining room and communal area. We returned home looking like gypsies after several weeks out of doors. We were often transported by lorry to distant farms singing popular songs of the day – Run Rabbit Run, Down Mexico Way, and Deep in the Heart of Texas.

(p. 75)

Reproduced by kind permission of Don Grammer and the Trinity Old Scholars Association.
Students from Trinity Grammar School pea-picking at a harvest camp in Hertfordshire.

Bedford Girls Modern School describes how girls were involved in agricultural camps from 1942 onwards:

In 1942 four weeks were spent at Bourne, Kesteven, by two sets of 22 girls and 3 mistresses who each worked for a fortnight. The following year from 40–45 girls at a time took part in lifting potatoes, while in 1944 the quarters were in the Carre's Grammar School, Sleaford, and the work flax pulling for three weeks, and potato lifting for the last. The fourth and last camp was at Hacconby near Bourne, Lincolnshire where potato lifting and thistle spudding[11] were the chief jobs. Miss Pugh, as a Guider with some experience of camping, was a regular staff member and gives a vivid picture: 'Viewed in retrospect the conditions were appalling but we were prepared to put up with anything to be able to help our country'. . .'The work was mostly potato picking, though we did do a bit of fruit picking and weeding sugar beet. The potato lifting was back-aching work. A machine called a "spinner" turned up rows of potatoes and they had to be picked up by hand and put into baskets…A basic wage was paid but bonuses were added at so much per hundredweight over a minimum and some girls earned what were quite princely sums in those days'.

(pp. 86–7)

The history of Kingston High School, Hull, records evacuees' reminiscences. Barbara Dawson, for example, recalls:

A great adventure was participation by some of us in a journey to Bourne, in Lincolnshire, to help with the harvest. We were the youngest pupils able to take part in 1944 and we were each allocated to a particular farmer. . .Most of our time was spent weeding carrots and sugar beet. . .although I believe we did stook barley. It was a back-breaking job and. . .the reward was 28 shillings a week. [The farmer] also gave a bonus – he booked seats at the local cinema in Bourne for the two Saturdays we were able to go. . .When we first arrived at the house we were each given a palliasse cover and told to fill it with straw from the barn. Thus, we were provided with our beds for the two-week stay, and our 'beds' went on wooden floors in the attic. . .Hot water was very scarce and at times non-existent. It was very difficult removing soil, sweat and general grubbiness with cold water at the end of a day working in the fields. However there were many good memories. We had great fun there.

(p. 40)

The school log for St Edmund's College, Liverpool, records the following:

July 18th: Miss Wilson will take girls from LVI and VI to Stonehouse near Worcester for fruit picking.

1942: Girls will begin pea picking at Wheathill Farm July 23rd to 27th.

1942: October 26th–30th: School closed for girls to help in potato picking (at Ranford and Altcar).

1943: Sept 27th: Party of girls began potato picking at Formby. Other parties to Formby and Melling. No girl to miss more than 20 sessions.

1944: October: Lots of potato picking – Formby and Melling.

(p. 90)

And the school history also contains reminiscences from former pupils:

I remember volunteers were needed for two weeks potato picking at Formby. Trying to pretend that we were helping with the war effort, my friends and I volunteered our services; had we been more honest, perhaps the thought of two weeks holiday was more compelling – but we would live to regret the rash decision! It turned out to be two weeks of sheer misery – up and out at 7a.m. – icy cold hands trying to pick potatoes – gloves became soggy and heavy as the day drew on. However, it was an experience to remember. How could I ever forget aching joints, back pain, frozen red hands!

(M. Phillips, pp. 97–8)

M.J. Moody, a member of the party which went fruit picking in the summer of 1941, recalled:

I loved the peace and quiet of the countryside after the nerve-racking nights we had been through. We picked blackcurrants, loganberries and the raspberries which were the last to ripen. At the end of the day our crop was weighed individually and we were paid so much per pound. I earned enough for my keep for the month, to pay back my train fare to my mum and to buy myself a second-hand bicycle which was my pride and joy.

(p. 98)

One of our interviewees, Roger Sawtell, born in 1927, recalls a harvest camp:

We lived in tents – it was lovely, I'd never been camping before. At nine o'clock lorries used to arrive to take us round to the local farms. We did the stooking. . .we did that day after day. And sometimes we went to the canning factory – I remember they were canning soft fruit. I think we were on a sort of conveyor belt, sorting out plums, throwing out the bad ones.

The overall impression from the school histories is that agricultural work was very hard physical work, but fun, and that children enjoyed being out of school.[12] However, there are some negative accounts. For example, Bolton School, in 1941, ran a harvest camp for pea picking:

The Parbold camp was. . .limited to 25 senior boys who were not then involved in public examinations. This was perhaps the first of all War Agricultural camps for schools. It was used for propaganda purposes, and boys found their photos appearing in the most unlikely pages of society magazines.

(pp. 214–15)

The same school recorded illness during the camp, and three boys contracted polio. 'Most tragically, J.C. Davies died. He was one of the most promising of his generation' (p. 215).

The school history for Shrewsbury, a private boys' school, regretted that the national mood was turning away from honoured and honourable traditions:

In comparing the number of boys who volunteered for farming in term and holidays with those of the previous war, it is only fair to the latter to remember that their service had been purely altruistic, and the boys received nothing for it, while in the Second War the principle was accepted that the labourer was worthy of his hire, and the boys combined the virtue of doing useful work with the advantage of a pleasant addition to their incomes. No doubt it was necessary as part of a nationwide movement away from the principle of unpaid service that had long been the pride of ex-public school men in public life.

(p. 214)

However, published in the Bishop's Stortford College magazine in 1942, is a boy's poem (pp. 127–8) that provides a critique of such rhetoric by encapsulating the exhilarating, exhausting experience of potato picking:

All the morning, gasping, bending
In the furrows all are seeking,
From the earth the taters grasping:
By midday their backs are breaking.
For an hour midst hay reclining,
Eating, they forget their troubles;
But when they have finished chewing
They must pick up more – Potatoes.
Still the pains of toil enduring
Worked the aching band of heroes:
Where they turned their wide eyes, straining,
All they saw were more – Potatoes.
Now the day of toil is ended:
Wearily to bikes they stagger,
Shoulders o'er their cycles bended,
Plod towards the School back yonder.
Joyful, seated on the saddle,
They forget the dread Potato
Strength returning, pedal faster,
(One bright lad crashed by the wayside).
Finally beneath the showers
Scraping mud from dirty elbows,
They forget the bending hours
During which they picked – Potatoes.

And the author's verdict: it was 'a holiday with pay, in which there was never a dull moment' (p. 128).

All this evidence suggests that children from all kinds of schools were involved in a range of agricultural tasks in organised camps, but the task that seems to have absorbed copious hours of effort and was understood by commentators as an important contribution to the war effort was potato harvesting. The accounts reflect a range of experiences – children appear to have felt that they were making a contribution, but the work could be physically very demanding, and living conditions were basic and uncomfortable. In some cases the experience was positive when contrasted to living in urban areas that were the target of bombing raids.

Helping on local farms during school terms and holidays

Less systematically documented, because it was more informal, was schoolchildren's help on local farms. While the school harvest camps were well organised and would not have drawn on the labour of under-age children, it is likely that on local farms the under-12s (12 was the minimum age for work) were involved. Murray acknowledges that 'there were countless children who helped, particularly with potato lifting, from their own homes'.[13]

Several of our interviewees, including some under-12s, describe working on local farms. Rose Pockney recounted a week's work in 1942, when she was 10. The village school was closed for a week so that the children could do 'tattie picking'. They were told to report to the farm in boots and gabardine. She recalls: 'The tractor went round and round the field and turned over the plants and we had to pick up as many potatoes as we could before the tractor came past again.' She got 19 shillings for five or six days work, and felt hard done by – 'I was a mercenary little girl and I wanted the money.'

One of our interviewees, aged 11 in 1939, growing up on a farm, noted that much work had to be done by hand:

I helped with the harvesting. There was no machinery then. You had to go and help, and you'd do most of it by hand. And rake, there was a special rake for turning hay, and gathering it up into one heap. It was really hard work. . .That was our life and that was it. I did the hoeing of swedes and things like that. Everything was done with hoes. It was in 1947 when we had our first tractor. There were no tractors anywhere. It was very rare that you would see a tractor.

John Balsdon, born in 1928, grew up near Sidcup, in Kent, about a mile from the local farm where he worked during the summer holidays of 1941 and 1942 when he was 13 and 14 years old. He provides a description of stooking:

I would start when the cereal crop harvesting began. A tractor towing a cutter left the crop on the ground. Several workers (usually farm-workers' wives) would gather armfuls and bind them into sheaves with a stalk twist. My first job was to gather up sheaves and form them into cone-shaped stooks. This allowed any moisture to dry out. Those sheaves were then pitch-forked on to either a horse-drawn cart or a small open lorry. I did this work and then graduated on to being a stacker on the cart or lorry. The loads were taken off to a temporary store until the harvest was complete and then a steam engine towing a mobile threshing machine would arrive. . .The thresher was belt-driven from the steam engine's flywheel. . .Feeding sheaves into the thresher was hard work. All the work was hot and quite tiring, but not exhausting.

John describes how he stayed on after the harvest:

[I was] in the charge of an old wizened Romany farm-worker who lived in one of the farm cottages. He taught me how to harness up a farm horse for towing a brake (rather like a small plough) which I would then guide down between endless rows of various brassicas. This was easier work than harvesting but rather lonely after the companionship in the harvest field. I remember leaving at the end of one week. . .for I had put in some extra time, and was gleefully clutching 8 shillings.

Peter Rivière, born in 1934, recalls agricultural activities while at prep school 'pulling up ragwort. . .I remember the whole school used to have afternoons in the summer, when we all turned out, to the local farm and pulled ragwort – out of grazing fields.'

Some of the school histories provide evidence of rural children helping local farmers during the war, but this had been a widespread practice anyway, as noted in Chapter 3. For example, the history of Great Rissington School (elementary), Gloucestershire, describes how:

> *The pattern of school holidays was changed in 1942 to allow older children to help out on local farms. The school was closed for a special period of two weeks at the beginning of August, and again for three weeks at the beginning of October for potato picking. This pattern continued for the rest of the war and is reminiscent of the 19th century when harvest time determined the start and finish of the school holidays.*

(p. 89)

At the same school, Rupert Duester recalls potato picking at Barrington Park:

> *The children had to pick up the potatoes and put them in sacks or buckets which were then loaded on to a horse-drawn cart. It was hard work and 'certainly no picnic', though they enjoyed being out of school. They had to work quickly, filling the buckets and getting out of the way before a machine came round to dig up the next row. Italian prisoners of war from the prison camp at Northleach also assisted with potato picking in this area.*

(ibid.)

Charlie Pratley, who left Great Rissington Elementary School at the age of 14 in 1944, remembers being allowed out of school when he was 13 to help in the fields with various tasks including stone picking prior to haymaking, dock pulling in the wheat fields and mangel pulling (for cattle food in winter).

At Merton Court School, a private preparatory school, some boys were evacuated to the village of Butleigh, near Glastonbury, in Somerset. John Waters recalled how he and his fellow evacuee were:

very happy at the farm and lived with the farmer and his wife as if we were their children. We had our meals with them, and helped with the bread, butter and cider making. Our great friend on the farm was Jack, the farm labourer who, at that time was 19 years old. We helped Jack with rounding up the cows and hand milking them, hay making and riding the cart horses to and from the farm to the fields.

(p. 103)

John's map of the farm indicates his close knowledge of the farm and its work (see below).

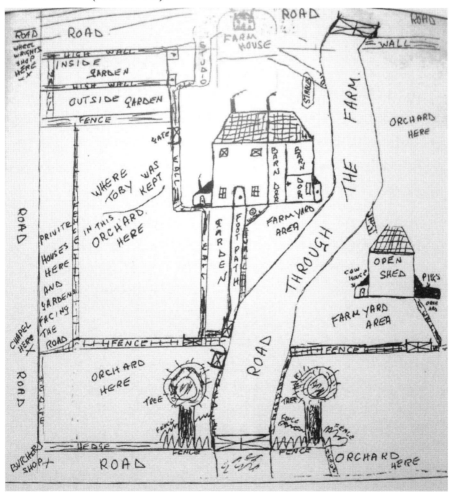

Reproduced by kind permission of Merton Court School.

Sketch of Holman's Farm by 11-year-old John Waters.

It is difficult to estimate how many children were involved in agricultural work, but some school histories do give an idea of extent. For example, at the Royal Grammar School, Worcester, it was noted that:

> *Another service actively undertaken by boys was the driving of tractors on farms. 28 boys were trained for this. Three-quarters of the School helped on farms during the summer holidays, and boys were also given leave of absence for the purpose, during term-time, 'when vitally necessary'.*
>
> (p. 245)

Another kind of work was collecting herbs. According to the *Scouter* magazine (May 1942: 73) the Ministry of Supply asked people to collect medicinal plants, and in 1941 about ten tons were collected, mostly by Scouts, Guides, Women's Institutes and schools. The school history of St Clare, Penzance describes a more unusual crop:

> *25th July 1944: seniors picked seaweed for the Ministry of Supply – For what purpose? There was a second expedition moreover, this time to Marazion, on 10th–11th July 1945. It has now been discovered that the girls were probably picking a type of red seaweed called Gigartine Stellata from which was obtained a gel-like substance, agar (extract from Rhodophycean Algae), that was used as a medium in the culture of bacteria. The normal supply from Japan would not have been possible in 1944–45, and it is probable that the gel was required by the Government for use in the early days of penicillin production.*
>
> (p. 44)

Sadie Ward, social historian of war in the countryside, notes the usefulness of children because they were a flexible, readily available source of labour: she claims that 'The young excelled at the really back-breaking jobs, such as potato-picking and pea-pulling, at which they were invaluable during "catchy" weather when speed was of the essence'.[14]

Colin Dibb (aged nearly 11 in September 1939) sent us a written account of his memories. He grew up on a 50-acre farm in Lancashire. Milk production was the main enterprise, until the War

Agricultural Executive Committee instructed his father to plough up ten acres and plant cereals. They also grew some vegetables to sell. One of Colin's main jobs was the milk round (from the age of 6, with his father, and later on his own):

> *In the summer of 1943, when I was fourteen, father was seriously ill for about one month with septicaemia. Fortunately I was on summer holiday and was the only one who knew the milk round (except for the horse!) So, I set off at 9 a.m. every morning with the horse and milk float and delivered the milk, returning about 1 p.m. I had no mishaps of any sort and, on Saturdays, collected the weekly money. Looking back, it was a big responsibility, but I do not remember my parents worrying about me – this was what sons were raised for.*

He also had to collect the ration coupons for the milk. He was not paid for this work, but got some 'tips' from customers. His second main job was milking the cows, by hand, twice every day of the year. 'I started pre-war when I was seven and continued through the war and after until I left in October 1946 for university.' Thirdly, he took part in haymaking – this involved cutting the hay, turning it the next day and spreading it out till it dried. Then it was gathered in rows across the field, and if rain threatened it was made into 'little foot cocks, which was a very skilled process at which I was very good, using a hand fork with two tines to create a cock which would shed the rain'. Then he would lead the horse and wagon, loaded with hay, to the barn to be stacked. 'When father was ill, the farm man and I, with some casual help, successfully completed the hay harvest.' Fourthly, Colin worked on the oat harvest, stooking the oat sheaves, which then had to stand in the field for at least two weeks – 'to hear the church bells twice' – while the sheaves 'fed out' and matured, before being stacked. These are only brief excerpts from a detailed account, which shows how farming families expected sons to work for the family business, and in wartime, there was extra work in cereal production and vegetable cultivation to be done. Colin combined all this with academic school work – having passed the scholarship to grammar school in 1939.

How was the work evaluated?

This section examines how children's contributions were evaluated, by commentators at the time, farmers, trades unionists and children themselves.

The government/official view

In the official history of agriculture in the Second World War, the agricultural economist Keith Murray discussed manpower during each year of the war and recognised children's contribution, particularly to potato picking. Since 1939, 'the potato crop had increased by almost 1,500,000 tons, or 31%: such a crop could not have been harvested successfully without the very special efforts and the use of schoolchildren and volunteers' (Murray, 1955: 102). Murray suggests that 'Schoolboy [*sic*] camps had been phenomenally successful...rates of payment were raised and the Ministry of Agriculture undertook to help with rents, railway fares, and the salaries of camp organisers' (ibid.: 159).

Contributors to *Agriculture*, the official journal of the Ministry of Agriculture, certainly acknowledged schoolchildren's contributions. In a piece entitled 'Leicestershire schoolchildren help the farmers', it was claimed that:

> *So great was the help given to Leicestershire farmers during 1941 by school teachers and schoolchildren in both city and county, that it was freely admitted by the War Agricultural Executive Committee and the National Farmers' Union that without it the potato crop of the country would never have been gathered.*
>
> (Measures, 1943: 84)

Boys and girls harvested potatoes, though girls were paid slightly less per hour than boys. The opinion was 'they were not so mischievous as boys and were more conscientious. In most instances, however, farmers did actually pay the girls at the same rate as the boys; some even went so far as to make bonus payments' (ibid.). The author comments:

> *The city children apparently enjoyed the work. Viewed against the background of the U-boat menace and the need to release every available ton of shipping to carry [sic] the war against the enemy,*

the harvest this year will be even more crucial than it was in 1942. Every man, woman and child that can be spared will be required to cooperate with our farmers to ensure that there is no disparity between the yield and the harvest.

(ibid.)

Children's agricultural work also featured in propaganda material, such as a Ministry of Information booklet (1945) about agriculture published 'to inform people about the progress of the war and the home-defence operations', and as a 'tribute to those who had contributed to the war effort at home':

Schoolchildren gave great help everywhere. Those from the country were used to seasonal work on the land. But great numbers came from the town and city too, from public and council schools alike – boys and girls to whom the produce of the farm had never been much more than items on a shopping list. It was a great adventure for them; they came in loud, excited groups, bursting with curiosity for the new world. . .They helped with every kind of job: the boys potato planting and lifting, tractor-driving, harvesting, flax pulling, root-hoeing and singling; the girls potato-planting and lifting too, weeding, pea-picking, fruit picking, flax pulling – their neat swift fingers unrivalled at such labour.

Surrounded by the clamour of war, they appreciated very well the reality of what they were doing; they knew their work was important and, of course, they were being paid for it.

There was never enough labour. . .Harvesting, suddenly, became everybody's business.

(ibid.: 91–3)

In official statistics, there is brief acknowledgement of children's 'assistance'. As noted, statistics do not include children, but the text does recognise their contribution, alongside that of the Women's Land Army:

An extremely important part in the food production programme has been played by the Women's Land Army. . .In addition, farmers have been assisted by schoolchildren and adult volunteers who have spent their holidays on the land.[15]

The role of evacuees was also recognised. A Ministry of Information pamphlet described the situation of evacuees, and the 'benefits' of evacuation to the children concerned. The pamphlet contains photographs of children 'helping on the land':

> *It is true to say that practically all the children have improved in physique, general health, poise and bearing during their stay in the country. . .[There] children can get fun from very different things – fishing, rambling, cross-country running – but especially from helping in the many and varied jobs on the farm or in the garden. In their spare time children have learned to feed the poultry, to keep the runs and houses clean. . .They seem particularly to have taken to looking after animals – calves and pigs – and many have become expert milkers. Boys have often developed into experienced helpers on the land, learning how to use their tools and to guide simple machinery with practised skill; while some of the girls have become quite proficient milkmaids and dairy maids.*
>
> (Ministry of Information, 1941: 10)

Documents such as this refer to children 'learning' and 'helping'; but the evidence suggests they were doing valuable productive work. As Murray notes, 'It is unfortunate that complete statistics are not available to show the immense contribution made by volunteer workers to the successful collection of the great crops in 1942 and 1943' (Murray, 1955: 209). He adds: 'it would have been impossible to plant and lift over 1 million acres of potatoes if children had not been permitted and willing to assist in the busy period before 1944 when prisoner of war labour became relatively plentiful' (ibid.: 58).

Thus in 1943, when it was clear that many children would be needed to help with the harvest, again the Board of Education issued a circular appealing for the cooperation of the local authorities. 'This appeal is made on behalf of the government as a whole, and the purpose is not to help farmers to make profits but to safeguard the country's food supply' (*TES*, 27 February 1943). The Minister of Agriculture and Fisheries appealed directly to schoolchildren, asking them to see it as their duty to take part in agricultural work:

> *This may mean surrendering some of your leisure and recreation time, and engaging in what in many instances will prove to be long,*

*hard and wearisome tasks, but the service you will give will be a
direct contribution to the winning of the war.*

(*TES*, 10 April 1943)

And a 1944 Board of Education memo asking for help with the
harvest included an appeal from the Minister of Agriculture:

*This year the military situation will demand a supreme effort. The
cultivation and harvesting of crops will be carried out in even more
difficult conditions than last year. . .There will again be a heavy
demand for potato planting and lifting, and in certain districts for
root hoeing and other important work in term-time.*[16]

A further circular modified the conditions under which children
are employed in agricultural work: 'a child shall not be employed
in any agricultural work involving heavy strain, and in particular
shall not be employed in extracting sugar beet crops from the
ground' and 'no child shall be employed in any agricultural work
under the control of a gangmaster as defined by the Agricultural
Gangs Act 1867'.[17] In 1944 a Home Office circular called for
the ending, as soon as possible, of the Defence Regulation
which allowed exemption from school attendance – subject to
conditions – for employment in seasonal agricultural work. 'The
circular asks for observations and comments regarding the effect
of employment on health, education, character, and aptitude, as
well as suggestions concerning further prohibitions or restrictions
which seem desirable' (*TES*, 1 July 1944). This circular reflects an
attempt to balance exhortation to children to continue to do farm
work, while also wishing to protect children from exploitation
and injury.

Educationists' views – the *TES*

At the start of the war, the *TES* was wary about the engagement
of children in agricultural work. An early leader article, entitled
'Lessons of 1916', complained that:

*Children are again allowed to take employment at 14, and in East
Anglia a local education authority has found it inevitable that
children of 12 should be allowed to help in agriculture, in spite*

of the offer of troops, the training of the Women's Land Army, and the existence of several hundreds of thousands of able-bodied unemployed. Within a month of the outbreak of war the symptoms which caused such alarm in 1916 have shown themselves.

(*TES*, 7 October 1939)

However, by 1942 a *TES* article by 'a correspondent' examined children's agricultural work in some detail, and expressed some of the dilemmas of the time:

The Defence Regulations 29 and 30 have reversed the educational policy of a century. Children may become half-timers once again, even if only for limited periods, with all the educational disadvantages that this entails. Yet the employment of children, apart from its economic value, has at least one good thing to be said for it. The nation is in danger. The call goes forth to the entire population. Even children are not omitted. They are part of society. If they are not asked and encouraged to contribute their mite to the total effort, they feel useless and unwanted in the middle of a battle they see going on all around them, and out of such impotence social neuroses are born. It is better, surely, that children should be worked a little too hard in war than they should feel socially neglected. A child brought into the war effort is better than a child brought into the juvenile court. There is not much doubt that children like farm work, it gives them status and feeds their pride. They are glad to join the wage earners and happy to feel the bonds of school loosened.

(*TES*, 15 August 1942)

The author then suggests that the law should be better enforced and that notices could be posted ('in non-legal language') in villages about the regulations surrounding the conditions of employment of children. He asks, 'Notices are exhibited where the protection of wild birds is necessary – why not therefore for the protection of children?'

Farmers' views

There is evidence that farmers were initially sceptical about employing schoolchildren, as they had been about taking on women. According to Ward (1988: 19):

While many farmers were pleased by the willingness of their young helpers, there were inevitably complaints. One farmer telephoned the Labour Committee to protest that a master in charge of a camp had refused to allow his boys to spread sludge, while another grumbled that the four lads who had been working on his farm had been 'larking about'. Even so, the experiment worked well enough to be repeated in later years.

Ward notes that farmers had been sceptical of schoolgirls' labour (their scepticism of the Women's Land Army is well-known), but again their views shifted. According to a Lancashire farmer, Mr Heyes of Bickerstaffe, 'we farmers have said all sorts of things about unskilled labour, but the way some of these dainty High School girls have tackled the job out in the fields, seven and eight hours a day, has fair capped me' (ibid.: 49–50).

A.G. Street, a Wiltshire farmer, wrote a regular column in the *Farmers Weekly*.[18] His views on casual labour also shifted over the course of the war. On 7 August 1940, he noted a good supply of teenage casual unskilled labour for harvesting: 'Too many boys are more hindrance than help, and six boys are as many as we can handle efficiently on this farm' (Street, 1943: 87). A year later, he noted that:

All last week my harvest field was inhabited by soldiers, nurses, schoolgirls and schoolboys, most of whom had never before stooked one sheaf. In spite of the fact that a large proportion of the wheat sheaves were awkward and bowzy, after a little practice these new hands did far better than I expected.

(ibid.: 187)

By 1942, Street was describing 'rural camps for schoolboys' as 'admirable' (p. 283). Dent (1944a: 120) also noted that despite initial suspicions, many farmers:

are loud in their praise for the boys and girls who have worked for them, and it is not unusual for a farmer to 'book' a party from the same school for the following year. Some schools have indeed returned each year since 1940 to the same site.

The trades unions' view

Throughout the war, the TUC frequently raised concerns about the use of child labour in agriculture, though it was generally acquiescent (Griggs, 2002: 185). For example, the General Council of the TUC was critical of the Board of Education's proposal that children should visit farms during term time to help with planting and lifting potatoes, and suggested that children should be engaged only in 'light work' with a maximum of four hours work a day for 12–14 year olds, thus accepting that the work was inevitable, and needed to be regulated (TUC, 1941). On the other hand, in 1942, E.G. Gooch,[19] President of the National Union of Agricultural Workers, responded to new Board of Education regulations freeing more older children to work the land during term time, by arguing that:

> *the place of children under 14 was at school or play. Farming had not yet reached the stage when its salvation depended upon the labours of the workers' young children.*[20]

Thus, there were wide-ranging views, and some changed over time, as it was pragmatically accepted that children could, should and would contribute their labour in agricultural production. While it is unlikely that, during the war, the *TES* or anyone else would publish tales of appalling hardship and exploitation of child workers in agricultural labour, children did give negative, as well as positive, accounts. But many people (recorded in school histories and reminiscences) claimed that children 'loved farm work'. Whenever the subject of children's agricultural employment came up in the House of Commons, someone eagerly pointed out that 'children regard it as a pleasure',[21] that it was a 'very healthy education'[22] or that 'children love working on farms'.[23] Kenneth Lindsay, Secretary of the Board of Education, argued in the House that 'the Board are strongly in favour of giving every opportunity to schoolchildren over the age of 14 in evacuation areas to enter rural life'.[24] Mr Butler, President of the Board of Education, gave a revealing reply to a question about 'the acceptability of child labour':

The Right Hon. Baronet gives a rather sinister implication to what is a perfectly normal war-time occupation for children. I think when he reflects upon the trouble taken by the Government to ensure that conditions are satisfactory, he will not feel so disturbed about it.[25]

Health and harm in agricultural work

In June 1943, the Board of Education set up a compensation scheme for injuries sustained by children aged 12–14 employed in agriculture. Dent (1944a: 118–19) notes that during their hours of employment in agriculture campers would in the ordinary course be protected by statute and common law in the event of accidents. But it was felt to be essential that children should be insured against all kinds of accidents at all times. Later commentators, looking back, were more likely than contemporary commentators to note the damaging effects of children's involvement in agricultural work. Gosden (1976: 81), discussing children's contributions to the war effort, suggests that:

> *there were circumstances in which they could retard children's education. . .the employment of schoolchildren by farmers in some of the eastern counties certainly damaged the elementary school system in those areas and set back the education of many of the older children – even though it may have helped the agricultural war effort.*

Gosden suggests that there was 'plenty of evidence that children below the minimum age of 12 were being employed' (ibid.: 84). However, he argues that on balance the employment of children was justified:

> *If children had not been allowed to help with potato lifting and if a food shortage had developed, the effects on the whole community, including the child population, could have been very damaging.*
>
> (ibid.)

Children's evaluations of agricultural work

One kind of comment by children was that they learned from their agricultural work. According to the history of Westminster City School, evacuated to Kent:

Over the years the boys picked plums, apples, loganberries and damsons, kept rooks away from crops, helped with the harvest, pulled up and cut down weeds, gathered vegetables, and in a few cases helped with hop picking. . . at the end of the day, and certainly at the end of the week, many boys had cultivated a healthy respect for those who worked on farms in all weathers.

(p. 73)

Evacuees to rural areas also recorded life there as learning; one woman recalls her billet in Sussex: 'I learned how to pluck geese and to live like a farm child. . .I really got my education there. I learned about flowers and wildlife generally' (Wicks, 1988: 89). Howkins, in his social history of rural England, draws on Mass Observation archive material and relates the observations of Emily Baker, a Sussex schoolteacher, who suggested that 'many [evacuees] clearly enjoyed the change, like the 10-year-old girl from Greenwich who a week after evacuation was helping to drive cattle, turning out cows to the manner born'.[26]

In an article in the *TES* about children's involvement in harvesting, 'a correspondent' gives examples of 'what children think' – they liked earning money:

Many boys in the village brought home £2 in the first week. The second week of the holiday earnings dropped off because the temperature suddenly soared and the children felt the heat badly in the shadeless fields. . .All this work is piece work, and the amount a boy earned depended on his strength and patience. . .No farmer or boy who had heard of the limit of 36 hours, or even on any one day, imagined it applied to the holidays. Often schoolboys were bringing home larger wage packets than boys over 14 who were permanently employed. More than one small boy boasted to me that he was earning more than a soldier.

(*TES*, 15 August 1942)

There is also evidence that close working relationships developed between children and adults – not only with the teachers who organised the camps and accompanied the children and worked alongside them, but also with other agricultural workers and the farmers themselves. For example, the history of Repton, a private boys' school, reports:

The series of Harvest Camps began with the camp at Brockhampton, Hereford, on a truly magnificent site, in an area where the farmers were for the most part very pleasant to work with – in fact, friendships formed have lasted long after the camps were over – and where really useful work could be done. The cooperation between Staff and boys reached its height in these enterprises.

(p. 129)

Dent (1944a: 119) also emphasised benefits for children's relationships with other workers:

Of the pleasure and satisfaction felt by the campers, and the benefits they have derived from the vigorous work in the open air, there can be no doubt; and among the happiest camps in 1942 were those in which school boys and girls worked alongside young people released from shops and factories by their employers.

Discussion

As many of the above quotations indicate, it seems that adult views about children as agricultural workers changed during the war. Initial fears and scepticism were modified through the impacts of children's agency, their demonstrated willingness, competence and usefulness. We argue that children changed adult understandings of children. Moore-Colyer concludes, 'in a very British sort of fashion, common sense prevailed in the pursuit of the common good. One way or another the wartime cereal and potato harvests were gathered in, much of the effort being contributed by people with little previous contact with the land' (Moore-Colyer, 2004: 206). This 'British' behaviour is presumably thought to build on a flexible approach to what is proper and on appropriate responses to the immediate crisis, while eschewing the system under fascism of forcing young people to take part. The crisis could, in effect, set aside pre-war recommendations on protecting children from hard physical work (e.g. the Spens Report, see Chapter 4, page 92). At the same time, it is important not to present an overly urban bias to this story. Children who grew up on farms were very likely to have done agricultural work as a matter of course, especially given the low level of mechanisation and high levels of labour needed at peak times of the year.

Museum of English Rural Life, University of Reading.
Tommy Bridger, 8 years old, from Knebworth, Hertfordshire, driving a tractor to pull out roots on the family farm (1943).

During the war years and beyond, children's contributions were clearly necessary for agricultural production. One can speculate, drawing on people's reminiscences, about the effect this had on their experiences. Did they feel they belonged to a greater mass, and moreover were a vital part of that greater mass? Perhaps by participating in wartime food production, not just for their families, but (as propaganda frequently proposed) for the sake of the whole country, they felt a sense of belonging and satisfaction from their work. Our interviewees suggest that what they did was largely typical – part of the life of children at the time. What was new in wartime was the scale of children's involvement, the involvement of privately educated children, and the highly organised participation of children from urban areas, in hard physical labour in school harvest camps, and in a collective effort. The work they undertook was clearly important to the survival of the nation but this vision of children as workers clearly conflicted with the nascent ideas that their proper place was in school, as learners. In structural terms, one could argue that they constituted a reserve army of labour, in the classic Marxist sense, for the purposes of gathering in wartime harvests.

Notes

1   *Agriculture,* 1943: 217.
2   Bills Public 1938–39 (274) ii 655. See also Barber 1994: 2.
3   Board of Education, Circular 1541, 20 February 1941, cited in Gosden, 1976: 462.
4   Defence (Agricultural and Fisheries) Regulations 1942, No. 802: 105.
5   Reported in the *TES*, 9 May 1942, and in Gosden, 1976: 462.
6   Cited in the *TES*, 26 April 1941.
7   Public Record Office (PRO), Ministry of Agriculture and Fisheries (MAF) 47/7(34) cited in Moore-Colyer, 2004: 193.
8   PRO, MAF 105/45(214) cited in Moore-Colyer, 2004: 202.
9   Cited in Hyde, 1952: 468–70.
10 Cited in Ward, 1988: 18.
11 Thistle-spudding involves pulling out thistles, and excavating the root with a 'spudder'.
12 While school histories might be thought likely to be overly positive about schools' and children's achievements, there is plenty of evidence to suggest that schools, or the authors of the school histories, were realistic in their assessments.
13 Murray, 1955: 209. Murray wrote the Agriculture report for the official history of the Second World War.
14 Ward, 1988: 49. Drawn mostly from the farming press, especially the *Farmers Weekly* and the *Farmer & Stock Breeder.*
15 *Statistics Related to the War Effort of the UK, 1943–44.* Cmd.6564 viii 597: 17.
16 Cited in the *TES*, 25 March 1944.
17 Cited in the *TES*, 8 April 1944.
18 Street's articles are collected in his 1943 book, *Hitler's Whistle.*
19 E.G. Gooch was the Chair of the Norfolk WAEC and continuously and vociferously opposed the involvement of children in agricultural work. Thanks to Professor Brian Short (University of Sussex: pers. comm.) for pointing this out to us.
20 Reported in the *TES*, 16 May 1942. See also Moore-Colyer, 2004: 191.
21 Major General Sir Alfred Knox, *Hansard* HC Vol. 351, 19 October 1939.
22 Vice-Admiral Taylor, ibid.
23 Sir L. Lyle, *Hansard* HC Vol. 379, 7 May 1942.
24 *Hansard* HC Vol. 351, 19 October 1939.
25 *Hansard* HC Vol. 379, 7 May 1942.
26 MO Archive Diaries No. M5376m, schoolteacher, Burwash, Sussex, 8.9.1939, cited in Howkins, 2003: 126.

Chapter 7

Older children's work: Serving their country

This chapter is about older children's work. We are considering here: (1) those who left elementary school and embarked on paid work; (2) those who while still on the rolls of elementary school also did some part-time paid work; (3) those who worked unpaid at home, doing domestic tasks and working in family businesses; and (4) those who continued in grammar schools and private schools up to the age of 16 or 18 – and engaged with the war effort during and outside school hours. In very many settings and in many differing ways, children helped to keep the home fires burning and turned their hands to specific tasks urged on them by government.

Working-class lives and work

We start by noting, again, the huge class differences in how children spent their time during the war years, a tiny minority in grammar and private schools, and most out at work. At the start of the war, about two million young people aged 14–18 were in paid work.[1] In 1941, The Board of Education estimated that about 75 per cent of boys and about 67 per cent of girls over 14 were in full-time employment.[2] By July 1941, average weekly earnings for young men under 21 had increased by 60 per cent compared with those in October 1938, probably because of the very long hours being worked.[3]

During the war there was also a large increase in the numbers of schoolchildren who were in paid work during term time: for instance, from 68,000 boys in 1937 to 81,000 in 1943, and from 3,700 girls to 12,000 (Cunningham, 1999: 161). A Home Office enquiry in 1944 showed that some 15 per cent of schoolboys aged 12–14 were regularly employed on some paid work during the day. These figures were nearly 20 per cent higher than before the war, and the figures exclude seasonal agricultural work during term-time (Titmuss, 1976: 417–19). As Titmuss notes (ibid.: 418), numbers of girls in paid employment did not rise in the same way, but school attendance reports indicate that girls were increasingly kept at home to do shopping, childcare and housework, as substitutes for their mothers who were out at work. One reason for these increased rates of child work was Home Office concern to maintain food production (Cunningham, 1999: 157); another must have been families' increased need for children's wages during the varying crises of the war years. As Titmuss notes, schooling may have seemed less important to parents than family survival (ibid.: 417–19).

In 1939, much of the work available to school leavers was routine, repetitive and dull, offering little in the way of mental stimulation. For girls, the main types of work were in shops, offices, and factories and as domestic workers (Jephcott, 1942: ch. 2). Boys worked as messengers and errand boys, in factories and shops. Most embarked on a working week of up to 44 hours, and some, responding to wartime pressures, worked even longer hours.[4] The compulsory registration of young people aged 16 and up, in 1942, revealed such long working hours among at least a quarter of young workers that they could not be asked to do voluntary work as well.[5]

During the war years, concern for the healthy development of these young workers continued,[6] and so did proposals for post-war reactivation of day continuation schools, as a bridge between education and industry, where the young worker could 'recover and refresh himself' and acquire a better understanding of the inter-relations of society, work and education.[7] Notably, Jephcott (1942: 96–7) argued that war conditions provided 'an eye-opener' to boys and girls: that their work was valuable for the community. She proposed they be taught, through a range of means (radio, magazines, cinema, youth clubs) that their work did indeed contribute to the war effort. Increasingly as the war continued, the rapid expansion of factories turning out essential goods provided better employment opportunities, and more work in engineering, mining, building and textiles, and these, though poorly paid, trained young people for better future work. As we describe in Chapter 8, young people flocked to join pre-military organisations, such as army cadets, which could suggest they wanted to do their bit, and/or that the life offered was more interesting than that offered in most of the available jobs. An indication of how girls' work changed between 1939 and 1943 is given in official statistics.[8] For girls aged 14–17, increased numbers worked in auxiliary services, civil defence and munitions, and in agriculture, mining, national and local government, transport, shipping, public utilities and food manufacturing; there was a complementary fall in numbers working in textiles and clothing distribution, and a huge drop in numbers of girls working as domestic servants or unemployed.[9]

In the next section we give some detail on an important type of training and work, undertaken by boys (and some girls), and offering expanded war-related opportunities to working-class children.

Technical education and munitions work

The inadequacy and the expansion of technical education

The war years saw expansion of technical education, which enabled children, especially boys, across the social classes, opportunities to participate. Technical, academic and practical streams of secondary education had long been advocated, to suit the assumed 'needs' and interests of varying children, and the Hadow Report of 1926 had endorsed these proposals.[10] For very many reasons, progress in the inter-war years was slow on these proposals. Apart from the economic downturn and the low status of education for the masses, 'academic' education had the highest status, bolstered by its prevalence in the 'public' schools (Chapter 3, page 75). On technical education, opposition during the 1930s came from socialists and from psychologists. Socialists wanted broad-based secondary education for all, with some emphasis on widening children's chances of an 'academic' education at grammar schools; they (for instance, many in the TUC and WEA) resisted the idea of vocational education, which they saw as training for specific kinds of work, and therefore perpetuating existing social class differences. Psychologists – importantly Burt and Valentine – thought it was not possible to determine a child's bent towards academia or practical work at 11. However, they did think that the curriculum at secondary level should include more practical subjects (Sanderson, 1994: 90–4).

By the late 1930s when war was looming, proposals to develop useful skills were again made. Thus the Spens Report (1938)[11] recommended the expansion of technical education – offering a five-year course for children selected by exam at age 11 – and this proposal was supported in the Norwood Report (Board of Education, 1943a).[12] The White Paper of 1943 spoke in favour of technical education, but prejudice in favour of 'public' and grammar school 'academic' traditions, and the costs of providing more technical schools after the war, led to a 1944 Education Act framed in very general terms. In practice, establishing technical schools had low priority after the war (Sanderson, 1994: ch. 6; McCulloch, 1989: 41–6).

Reflecting on the waste of human skills and resources in the 1930s, in the context of an education system which offered only basic instruction to the many, the Bolton School historian recalls a powerful speech by Ernest Bevin (Minister of Labour in the Churchill government from 1940) at the school in 1943:

> *[Bevin's] telling with deep emotion of what he found in 1940 – on the one hand, the imperative necessity for massive expansion of the war industries, and, on the other, a mere handful of skilled men for the benches of the factories, which in many cases had yet to be built.*
> (p. 225)

During the late 1930s and 1940s there was an expansion of junior technical schools (JTSs) for young people aged 13–16 and of technical colleges for people aged 16 and over. Numbers of JTSs rose between 1938 and 1946 from 243 to 324, and numbers of young people attending them doubled from 29,000 to 60,000 (Bristow, 1999: 121). These schools offered two-year or three-year courses for young people, providing training for engineering, instrument factories and textile work. During the war this technical bias was useful training for future work in the armed forces, for instance, as engineers and radar staff in the Royal Navy and as maintenance staff in the RAF (Bristow, 1999: 120). Numbers of technical colleges also expanded so that by 1939 there were over 200 (Richmond, 1945: 121).

The Board of Education asked technical schools and colleges to increase the training of recruits for war industries. The government also initiated various schemes to promote scientific and technical education. One was a State Bursary to any boy passing Higher Certificate in certain combinations of physics, mathematics and chemistry, if he was over 17. This defrayed all expenses to a university for one or two years and would permit some boys to take a degree. At Luton Modern School, 'training for the radio industry was offered to any who had reached School Certificate standard physics and mathematics' (p. 188). From November 1942, the government established engineering cadetships for boys aged 16–18 (Dent, 1944a: 135).

The technical schools and colleges turned out two sorts of products: trained skilled workers and manufactured goods (Dent, 1944a: 132). Men and boys from the forces came to train, using the equipment in technical colleges. The JTSs: (1) trained boys in tool-making for the aircraft industry; (2) provided pre-nursing courses for girls; (3) provided textile training, especially in Lancashire; (4) offered courses of training for work in agriculture (plant growth, stock-keeping, farm machinery), metalwork and woodwork; and (5) gave training for the building trades (Sanderson, 1994: ch. 5). Work carried out in the four technical colleges in Essex was show-cased in an exhibition in 1941, including demonstrations of fitting, turning, welding, instrument mechanics, radio mechanics, electrical installations, camouflage, war-time applications of science, testing of material, foremanship, civil service courses, dressmaking and cookery, nursing and ambulance training, and posters for the national food and war savings campaigns (Dent, 1944a: 135).

An interesting commentary on the possible weaknesses of selection by exam (the 11+) for secondary schooling is given in the history of Loughborough College School, which, alongside its academic grammar school, established a 'building school', in response to a 1942 request from the Board of Education to expand training for boys in the building trades. Boys who had 'failed' the 11+ entered the building school at 13, and some did so well there that they joined the grammar school, and took the School Certificate; some went on to study architecture or obtained posts in the drawing offices of local engineering firms. The headmaster observed that 'for many boys the building school has represented a second chance at the age of 13' (p. 153).

Some examples of munitions work in and out of schools

Training young people and providing manufactured goods for the war effort was not confined to the technical schools and colleges. Some secondary schools were also able to make a contribution since they were equipped with machine-tool rooms, where boys worked on making parts for machines.

At Coatham Road School, Redcar, teaching staff extended their work to include instruction in:

> *Maths, the Morse Code, Navigation, Electricity and Internal Combustion Engines. The aim was to help provide air crews, mechanics, riggers and fitters to pass on from Squadron 300 [in the Air Training Corps] to training Wings to become NCOs and useful personnel.*
>
> (p. 121)

Three senior schools in Cambridge worked in collaboration with Pye Radio Ltd, making components for radios during school hours and after school. In Slough, over 4,000 junior and senior children were making earplugs for Veedip Ltd, after school. This work in both cases was on a voluntary basis (Gosden, 1976: 86).

Another kind of opportunity was taken up at Twickenham County Grammar School for Girls:

> *During the Easter holidays 1944, the local ordnance factories took over the school hall and turned it into a factory. About 160 staff and senior girls came each day to pack small metal objects into cardboard boxes. . .The work was voluntary but they were paid the rate for an eight-hour day. . .The commanding officer came on the last day to tell them they had been packing spare parts for lorries for the Normandy landings. They went home feeling six feet tall after that, and were also proud of the Merchant Navy ship which had*

been adopted by the school and which had been sunk to form part of the Mulberry Harbour on the Normandy beach.

(pp. 26–8)

Among private schools, Oundle in Northamptonshire was unusual in its tradition of education in engineering and technology. The school possessed a foundry, a machine shop and a woodworking shop. These facilities were pressed into service for the war effort, with boys volunteering to work through the holidays. The machine shop produced shell casings and firing pins for rifles and guns, while the woodworkers made thousands of boxes for hand grenades (Stranack, 2005: 51). Similarly at Brighton College, Sussex, a machine shop was established, and after initial problems with the accuracy of the work, the production line became more efficient and was able to supply a factory with steel bomb rings. Boys and teachers worked together in two-hour shifts at least three times a week (Stranack, 2005: 6–7).

© Wolf Suschitzky and courtesy of Oundle School Archive.

Students at Oundle School carrying out Government-commissioned work by using an oxy-acetylene torch to cut holes in an artesian well shaft.

The history of Wrekin College (a private boys' boarding school) notes that boys worked as packers in a nearby ordnance depot:

> *Boys went on half-holidays and even on Sundays to Donnington, to assist as packers in the Ordnance Depot there, which someone happily described as 'the army's Woolworths', for it issued everything from stopwatches to mechanical diggers.*
>
> (p. 92)

Enlisting people to help was not confined to targeting the schools. To increase aircraft production in 1940, the manufacture of components was distributed to over 15,000 subcontractors, including small garages and engineering works across the country and even to homes, where women held filing parties to smooth down the rough edges of mysteriously shaped pieces of metal 'for an hour or two after tea'. School workshops were filled with small boys 'diligently lipping the sharp edges of stamped-out aircraft seats with fibre-headed hammers that seemed too big for some of them. It was everyone's war and this work gave a sense of participation' (Wood and Dempster, 1961: 97).

Another enterprise was organised by Morris Motors to salvage aircraft parts and rebuild aircraft. In 1940, they ran the Civilian Repair Organisation (CRO) which created a chain of repair depots, including training schools. From February 1940 to July 1940, numbers of repaired aircraft rose from 20 to 160 per week (Wood and Dempster, 1961: 199).

Children who stayed at school beyond 14

This section is about work by children who stayed at school to 16 or 18.[13] Most of these older children were relatively privileged in terms of affluence and social class. Many of the private schools and the grammar schools that emulated their traditions emphasised the children's duty to train for leadership and for service to society.[14] While they may have traditionally conceptualised 'service' in terms of professional and military work serving the nation and the Empire, the war years provided new opportunities for putting this tradition of service into practice on the home front, including working for 'the community'. Some had long traditions of training boys for later military service. School histories tell of assemblies recording the exploits of 'old boys' now serving in the armed forces; sometimes one of these young men would come and talk to the school. Deaths of former students were mourned in assemblies and recorded on war memorials in the school. In some histories, such as that of Woodroffe School, we learn that the school magazine published accounts of war exploits, sent in by former students (pp. 213–21).

Older children attending boarding schools are a distinctive subgroup. Because they were there night and day, they and their teachers could organise activities out of lesson times; gardening and animal husbandry could take place in evenings and weekends; and girls could form knitting groups in the evenings to provide goods for the armed forces.

Awareness of the war took specific forms in schools for older children. Children and their teachers organised varying means of studying the war. Debating societies considered topical issues, such as democracy, fascism, pacifism, the purposes of the war and retribution as a war aim. Bolton School had a Reconstruction Club, planning for the future after the war (p. 220). Many schools, such as Barrow Grammar School, had visiting speakers, some from the armed forces, to talk with the students:

> *Sid Solomon, that 'cultured communist' criticised the muddle in Britain, gave talks on 'Russia Today' and later looked forward to 'Post-War Reconstruction'. In 1941, Flitton's talk on 'Modern America' was interrupted by an air raid warning and continued in number eight shelter. Mr Schloss, that improbable German, spoke of his experiences in escaping from France which were almost as hair-raising as his subsequent adventures in this country.*
>
> (p. 112)

At Steyning Grammar School in Sussex, the Free French headquarters, based in London, arranged a series of lectures and discussions (no date given) for the boys, to help mutual understanding and pave the way for post-war exchanges between French and English boys (p. 99). In September 1941, Luton School Literary and Scientific Society had a lecture from a refugee teacher,

Dr F.W. Pick, on 'Goebbels at Work' (p. 190). And in March 1944, girls at the Hollies (a grammar school) in Manchester, 'were given a lecture by a Belgian who had lately escaped his country'. He gave the students 'surprising details of his life under the invader' (p. 82).

Types of work

As well as carrying out the tasks described in Chapter 5 (salvage and savings schemes), these older children were encouraged to work in ways that younger children were not – for instance, serving in canteens, visiting wounded soldiers in hospital and preparing school premises to receive schools evacuated from the cities. Some older children substituted for adults called up for war work by teaching in elementary schools and working in war nurseries. Schools for older children were expected (by local authorities) to carry out fire watching and both staff and students formed rotas to do this. Furthermore, secondary schools (whether state or private) were generally better resourced than elementary schools, for instance in having woodwork and metalwork rooms which could be used for war-work. They were also more likely to have grounds which could be ploughed up for substantial food production work. And, judging by the school histories, they were more likely to have equipment for showing films to the students and could thereby promote children's active participation.

As we noted in Chapter 5, most school histories that record war-work refer to several types of work. Thus, the history of Rendcomb College, Cirencester, helpfully lists the range of war-work being carried out just after Dunkirk (May–June 1940): (1) the school made collections for the Red Cross; (2) senior boys trained as runners in air raids; (3) boys attended first aid lectures; (4) they collected waste paper and ran savings groups; (5) they worked with the Home Guard to block roads; (6) they did all the mowing at school; (7) they lifted a local farmer's potato crop, did a farmer's haymaking and cabbage planting and provided tractor drivers; (8) they sowed a crop of barley for poultry; and (9) they sawed logs for fuel and excavated and timber-lined forty yards of ARP trenches (p. 90).

One of our interviewees, Patrick Morrow (aged 16 in 1939), provided a list of remembered activities, outside school. He had left school and was studying with a private tutor. But he combined this with war-work: he joined the Local Defence Volunteers (which became the Home Guard), dug trenches, did fire watching, unloaded timber in a local sawmill, did harvesting work, worked in a brewery, sold savings stamps, cooked potato peelings for chickens and helped his mother with beekeeping.

We deal here with the main types of work carried out: food production, other war-work at school and community work, including helping the armed forces.

Food production

Just as younger children dug for victory, so did older ones. Some school histories report that the school became almost self-sufficient in vegetables, and many report extensive work on local farms, as well as on 'farmping' holidays.[15] At Earl Colne's Grammar School in Essex, there was massive attention to food production:

> In April 1940 a miniature four-field farm was laid out, to be cropped on the old Norfolk rotation, and two new twenty-rod allotments were prepared for Forms III and IV. By the end of that year the school had turned out three gross of canned fruit and vegetables and had produced another 1,000 cans for the Women's Institute.

Later additions were of 150 fruit bushes, 1,000 tomato plants and bees; and vegetables were being sold in commercial quantities (pp. 134–5).

However, the poor conditions of some school grounds made for difficulties. The history of Barrow Grammar School notes that heaps of mud and builders' rubble hampered vegetable growing:

> But until these problems revealed themselves, the boys set to with a will. Here was applied education in the style of Squeers at Dotheboys Hall and, in any case, it was a novelty, for only a minority of boys came from homes with gardens. 1941 saw a good crop. . .By 1942, 160 boys and about half-a-dozen staff were looking after some 90 gardens. . .but it proved to be a losing battle with the weeds and the rubble. By 1943 the obituary notice appeared in the school magazine: 'The hay crop in the school garden will soon be ready for gathering'.
>
> (p. 110)

Older children, like younger ones, went foraging in groups organised by their school. For instance, at Whitehills Boys' Grammar School in Buckinghamshire:

> *Blackberry picking was reintroduced and each class went for one half-day a week, for three weeks. 120 pounds were picked and taken to the Germain Street School canteen to be made into jam, together with at least 200 jam jars. There was a collection in April 1945 for sick returned prisoners of war in Amersham Hospital. Mr Cox [the headteacher] took 300 eggs, a crate of apples, some oranges, Horlicks and milk chocolate contributed by the boys.*
>
> (p. 16)

Some private schools with large grounds gave high priority to food production; indeed, at some points gardening took priority over more conventional kinds of school work. At Cheltenham College, 'The production of vegetables became a major aspect of physical exercise, which for some boys took the place of games.' And the history quotes a table giving the harvest from 1941 to 1944 (p. 198).

A visitor to Wellington School found that boys did extensive 'land work' during term time, as well as seasonal harvesting:

> *Every square inch of the land that could be turned to useful purpose was put under cultivation. They [the boys] have acres of vegetables under cultivation, which the boys work under the supervision of [a teacher] who is a great agriculturalist. I gather from [the headteacher] that they practically have to buy no vegetables outside.*
>
> (p. 374)

The history of Rendcomb College explains how high productivity was achieved:

> *On planting day, academic work went on until 11 o'clock, then followed four shifts ending at 9 o'clock. From this field seven to ten tons of potatoes a year were raised. Parties of boys worked all over the district from Syde, Miserden and Beechpike to Chedworth and Withington. The production of food came to have a quasi-religious quality. The College Magazine records: 'Sept. 19th Blackberry Sunday was followed by Potato Monday, the festival lasting till Tuesday'.*
>
> (p. 93)

Livestock were kept at all types of school, but boarding schools were well placed for this work, since the animals could also be cared for outside the formal curricular hours. At Beaumont, a Roman Catholic boys' boarding school:

> *There were geese in the playground, pigs in the orchard, cows everywhere, hens in the cow field and turkeys on the lawn. They used to roost in trees near the ambulacrum [sic] path, and a boy was nearly expelled for shooting one.*

(p. 63)

Reproduced by kind permission of the Old Rendcombian Society.
Students feeding hens, 1941.

Other war-work on school premises

Preparing and repairing work

Many schools in reception areas had whole schools billeted with them, often at short notice, and this involved reorganising space for the incomers – a job carried out by both staff and children. For instance at Bolton School, the imminent arrival of evacuees from the Channel Islands prompted:

obvious scope for action and a joint committee of staff and pupils of both Divisions [i.e. girls and boys] set to work. The Scouts, together with a group of girls under Miss Elliott, had, within two days, repaired, furnished and made ready for immediate occupation two large houses which had been empty for some time. This was a clear indication of immediate response by pupils to calls for help and their capacity to cope with such crises; but no less of their readiness to cooperate on the basis of the whole foundation; something we had been slow to grasp. We also realized that we had been no less blind to the needs of the many in our own town in recent years who had been over-run by economic defeat. . .Most relevant was the immense benefit to the general development of the boys and girls which could arise from such experiences as this 'Operation Guernsey'.

(p. 214)

In some cases evacuated schools moved into premises which required adaptation. For instance, after many moves around the Kent countryside, Westminster City School (from London) found itself in possession of a 'fine mansion', just evacuated by American troops:

A working party of senior boys cleaned up to make the premises ready, and desks and apparatus were sent from Palace Street [the London premises] to enable a start to be made in the Autumn term.

(p. 70)

Many schools sustained damage during the Blitz. Twickenham County Grammar School for Girls, London was declared to be in a neutral zone (not an evacuation area or reception area) but, in November 1940, 50 incendiary bombs fell on the school buildings and grounds. No one was hurt, but a large water tank burst and flooded the floor below:

Much hard work with spades was needed to clear the staffroom floor of the black charred debris, and the stench was appalling. The school had been collecting toys for an East End School and a large Noah's ark was floating gaily on the flood water. A chain gang of staff and girls passed the remaining contents of the rooms (public and private) down to the library for drying.

(p. 26)

Maintenance – civil defence

At the start of the war, regulations were established by Air Raid Precautions (ARP) which prohibited any assembly of people in locations that lacked adequate air raid shelters. Outside contractors came to schools to build defences such as extra walls and air raid shelters – although this took time and hindered schools, which could not continue with their normal timetables and classes.[16] But schools were required to establish more minor defences themselves, in the form of sandbags, trenches and blackout precautions. At Barrow Grammar School, for instance, following air raid instructions, boys spent a week in September 1939 filling sandbags 'and placed them so that the School looked like a fortress' (p. 109).

Reproduced by kind permission of Pam Weatherley and St George's VA School.

Young people in a fire-fighting squad.

Throughout the war, an important feature of secondary school life was civil defence. Schools were asked to patrol their premises night and day. In many school histories we read of combined forces of staff and older students (including some girls); in others, either staff alone or senior students alone took on these duties. From the many examples, we give some to indicate the range of this major kind of activity:

Members of [Reading] School also took on Civil Defence duties. . .They had attended lectures by the School ARP officer and lectures and demonstrations by outside experts. Sixty-eight senior boys took part and all had practised with the twenty stirrup-pumps distributed in various places around the school buildings. There were regular drills and inspections of fire-fighting implements which comprised not only pumps, but Redhill outfits, picks, axes, ropes, ladders and tins containing reserve supplies of water. Every Wednesday one of the Day Houses took over the duty of inspection for the following week and each party had particular fire-fighting apparatus assigned to it. The boarders were excused these weekly duties, as they were on duty at certain hours in the morning, noon and evening. It was noted that eventually the duties became a matter of routine and as nothing had happened in terms of actual 'action' some of the initial enthusiasm was slightly dissipated.

(p. 72)

In other cases, the patrols did see 'action'; for instance, the history of Malvern College (a private school) records that:

In August [1940] two Malvern boys on holiday on the outskirts of South London were on duty with the local Home Guard platoon and helped to bring down a German raider with concentrated rifle fire.

(p. 130)

A grammar school, Hackney Downs, in London, experienced a direct hit in June 1942:

Swift action by the Fire Service, Wardens and volunteers (including the boys) confined the flames to the roof and top floor. The attack took place during the period of the Certificate examinations, but fortunately the stationery and question papers were stored downstairs. Temporary accommodation was found in Gawood and the examinations proceeded with a minimum of fuss, though many of the candidates had been up half the night.

(p. 48)

Senior girls too took part in fire watching, for instance at Friary School, a private secondary girls' school:

Fire watching, of course, had to go on, and for years a rota of staff, teaching and domestic, helped out by a few elder girls, old girls and parents, slept in the building. No one enjoyed it, but everyone made the best of it, and sometimes found it rather fun to make cocoa over the remnants of the fire in Miss Hodge's office [headteacher], after having been called up to patrol the outside of the building in a tin hat.

(p. 91)

Home Guard duties were not confined to school premises – in some cases, groups of boys and staff also patrolled in the local area. For instance, a company of 17 year olds and staff of Shrewsbury School, together with 'a platoon of local residents', was responsible for 'the sector of the defence perimeter of Shrewsbury from the Longden Road to Port Hill':

As in all other Home Guard companies there was a cheerful and unconventional camaraderie about the parades and, as in all these too, there was a glorious lack of military punctilio, and an officer would address a man on parade with equal naturalness by his surname, his Christian name, his nickname or 'Mr'.

(p. 215)

According to Hurstpierpoint College's magazine, the Home Guard platoon had the tasks of manning road blocks, organising wireless communications and 'learning how to deal with an enemy tank using Molotov cocktails' in 1940 and 1941. One of their last tasks was to 'patrol the Downs the day after D-Day in case of German retaliatory measures' (p. 202).

Other children joined ARP local groups. For instance, Derek Fairbairn's father organised the local air raid watch committee in 1939 and Derek and his brother (aged 11 and 14) had the job of checking 'that all the people who were on the rota, knew they were on the rota and knew they were supposed to go out'. He also served as an ARP messenger:

but there weren't any messages that I can remember I ever took. I wandered around with my helmet on, I don't think I did anything useful but it was very exciting being out when the raid was on – it was quite dangerous, but I didn't realise it at the time.

Domestic work at school

At some schools, the training of children for their future working lives included domestic work. For instance, at the Royal Hospital School near Ipswich, which trained boys for entry to the navy, boys made their beds, swept and cleaned the house each morning before breakfast, and a rota of boys served meals. But at other – private – schools, boys had been waited on by servants before the war. When schools' domestic staff were called up for war service, notably at boarding schools, children took over their duties. Thus, at Rendcomb College during the war:

> *A group of twelve–fifteen senior boys would stay behind for the first three days of the holiday and work on a carefully planned scheme, washing, scrubbing and generally cleaning the building. The pay was generally agreed to be poor but the food above average and the sense of freedom from school rules and regulations rather pleasant.*
>
> (p. 93)

School historians commented on the social change implied in these new tasks. At St Lawrence College, Kent a 1942 note in the logbook records:

> *Perhaps the most drastic change is the number of tasks we now do which once we took for granted. We no longer have anyone to roll the pitches, to make our beds, to clean our shoes. Our latest innovation is sweeping our Common Rooms, while volunteers have been helping with the washing up. It is not pleasant pushing a heavy roller through the damp cold mist, or carrying a pile of porridge plates, but no one has questioned the necessity of it.*
>
> (p. 20)

At Cheltenham College, too, the boys took their turn as orderlies, laying tables, serving meals and clearing up afterwards. In the wake of clothes rationing in 1941, the boys also abandoned their expensive and elaborate uniforms for austere Churchillian boiler suits, and the school history notes the social importance of these changes:

> *College before the war still lived in the world of 'upstairs–downstairs': there must have been many social preconceptions swept away at this time, which the young could adjust to as if they had never been.*
>
> (pp. 194–5)

Similarly at Rendcomb College, blue boiler suits were introduced to save clothes 'points' and in an attempt to protect the grey flannel uniform suits from wear and tear. Suddenly the boys looked like 'an assembly of motor mechanics' (p. 93).

However, some histories, especially of private schools, note concerns that academic achievements might suffer through the diversifying of children's activities. These schools depended on academic results to attract parents and fees, and at some schools numbers on the school roll had been falling in the 1930s. In 1943, the headteacher at a private girls' school said in her speech at prize-giving that many girls were lacking the essential qualities of industry and application and had little or no ambition to master difficulties:

> *The distractions of everyday life which tend to dissipate energy and attention are having a serious effect on the mind and body and I would remind both parents and pupils that it is in the Junior and Middle School that good foundations are laid, and it will save fret and anxiety in the fifth and sixth years if girls learn to think and work in the lower forms.*[17]

The archives of the Royal Latin School in Buckinghamshire record that some people disapproved of children's domestic work at school. In 1943, a survey of parents' views was carried out there and 50 parents replied, ten of whom 'objected to their children peeling potatoes, and six objected to the chore of washing the dishes' (p. 113). Indeed, the question of whether academic standards fell during the war years is discussed in many of the histories of schools for older children – with varying views and varying recorded impacts on students' achievements. Some histories welcomed the widening of children's activities, especially those directed at food production; others deplored the disruption to time-honoured traditions. Drawing on records made at the time, the history of the Royal Grammar School, Worcester, notes that in addition to farm work each summer and during term time:

> *The gymnasium was fitted out as a Decontamination Centre, in case of gas attack. Some senior boys were trained by the Medical Officer to staff the Centre. Other duties undertaken by boys included fire watching. Four fire-watching teams, each of three boys, were on duty*

during school hours, and boarders took over at night. 'At all times', says the Headmaster's Report, 'when boys are about in the grounds in any numbers, "spotters" from boys who have volunteered have been chosen to give notice of the approach of enemy aircraft'. . .On the domestic front, it is recorded that 'Boarders now do most of the work in the house except for scrubbing and cooking'. One wonders when School work was done.

(p. 245)

And what the disruptions of war could mean for individual children is vividly evoked in the history of Sandown Grammar School, Isle of Wight:

It was no unusual thing for the staff as well as the senior boys and girls to be on duty all night and at school next day. One girl was dug out from her Morrison shelter in the early hours of the morning after her house had been hit by a 'V1'. She then reported for duty at her first aid post and at 9.30 that morning she was at school taking a School Certificate English paper. She took the second English paper in the afternoon and got a credit. There was the boy who went out before breakfast to shoot rabbits and used his gun instead to persuade two German airmen to accompany him to the police station. They were rather troublesome, but did not make him late for school.

(p. 75)

Community work

In pre-war years, schools had varied in their interconnections with the local community. Many village schools, for instance, were often closely integrated into village life, with people such as vicars and policemen and local experts (e.g. gardeners) visiting the school, and the school taking part in local festivities and other events, including fundraising. But some schools (perhaps especially private and boarding schools) had been relatively isolated or insulated from such interactive contributions. As we noted above (pages 188–9), the historians of Bolton School thought the demands of war had enlightened staff about possibilities for both students and staff to work in and for the community. One task was helping people who were bombed out of their houses. The history of Barrow Grammar School records that, after bombing raids at Easter 1941, when many local people became homeless and were housed in a reception centre, 'Staff and senior boys and girls spent many hours there', helping to entertain the children and serve food (pp. 109–10).

Bruton School for Girls, Somerset, mounted an ambitious project when the school:

> *was converted into a holiday resort for women and children from bombed areas of Bristol. Two parties of about 90 people, ages ranging from 11 weeks to 80 years were hosted for a fortnight. Sunny Hill old girls who helped out at this event chiefly remember total chaos, enormous gratitude from the guests and a great sense of a worthwhile contribution being made.*
>
> (Stranack, 2005: 8)

Many of the children from Trinity Grammar School, evacuated from London to a small village, were billeted in small cottages with cramped spaces for the evacuees, and no electric light. So outside school hours the children began to roam the streets and paths. Older children at the school decided to help to organise the younger ones, so that they were not a nuisance to local people. This work included:

> *The setting up of village patrols to ensure none of the evacuees were getting into mischief. . .Some of the children caused concern by wandering the streets after dark. The excuse for this was the need to see friends and the difficulties of doing this in the homes of their hosts.*

Since it was also difficult for these grammar school children to do their homework in the cottages, the school captain and vice-captain arranged to keep the school open in the evenings under their supervision, to provide quiet study places (pp. 56–7). Sixth formers at Leighton Park School, Reading:

> *took on themselves to help out at local primary and nursery schools whose young male teachers had already been drafted into the armed services. Regular visits were made to coach soccer, cricket and gymnastics.*
>
> (Stranack, 2005: 41)

More direct war-work for the community included a range of tasks, unpaid and paid. One boy records life in the village to which his grammar school had been evacuated: cycling a 10-mile paper round, delivering telegrams, manning the telephone exchange in his dinner hour and working as part-time volunteer for the ARP. He noted:

And my first regular task was to hurtle round the village on my bicycle and blow a whistle to denote that an air raid warning had been received – and when the 'All clear' message was received I was to hurtle round again, but this time ringing a very loud bell.

Later a siren was installed for these tasks, but:

I still went on regular duty at the ARP post to carry urgent messages to places not equipped with telephones. A lifetime friendship developed with a Warden with whom I went on duty at the ARP post, where we always played chess to pass the time…After the war my wife and I stayed with them at the farm on many occasions.

(p. 32)

Helping the armed forces

Some work in the community involved direct contact with the armed forces. Again, private schools played an important part in this work. For instance, in the summer of 1940, men rescued from Dunkirk were housed in the village of West Malvern, Worcestershire, near St James's School:

The troops were in a dreadful state, many traumatised, and the staff and senior girls of the school joined the rest of the community in helping them to find accommodation, food and clothing.

(Stranack, 2005: 61)

The historian at St Mary's in Wantage, Oxfordshire, thought the war had little impact on the girls, but the arrival of an army contingent altered perceptions – and practices:

The staff realised, however, that the presence of the Cheshire Regiment, stationed in the town, was unlikely to be completely ignored by the senior girls, and eventually the School's gym became converted into a canteen for the soldiers. Dances were organised on

Wednesday evenings and there were entertainments organised in the School hall on Saturdays.

(Stranack, 2005: 63)

Fraternising with the armed forces could be advantageous in other ways. At Barnard Castle School:

The school was surrounded by military activity with a number of army and air force bases close by. Good relations were built up with these local units, particularly the South Wales Borderers who took the school under their wing. Sporting fixtures – particularly rugby and cricket – were arranged and every opportunity was taken to play these matches 'away' as the post-match meals at the military camps were vastly better than the school could provide.

(Stranack, 2005: 3)

At the Hollies School, the girls assembled in the hall to hear an officer from their adopted ship talk:

He told them that he had been torpedoed and shipwrecked three times and spent days each time in an open boat. His fears at the time were as nothing compared to how nervous he felt facing the sea of faces before him. However, he showed little signs of fear as he spoke about the Zealous's *battles at sea and unfurled a German flag captured from a German battleship during a battle with the Narvik flotilla. At the request of the* Zealous's *crew, the flag was presented to the girls 'whose Masses and prayers had, without doubt, brought the gallant crew through many and terrible dangers'.*

(p. 79)

The girls were themselves zealous in sending parcels and magazines to the ship's crew, as well as in praying for their welfare. At this school, too, fundraising efforts included, as well as the usual charities, special efforts to help fund a home for merchant seamen made homeless during the war.

St Clement Dane's Grammar School, London, 'adopted' a ship, and experienced 'several grim reminders of the tragedies of war':

During the early Spring [1941] the school ship, The Chinese Prince, *which had been adopted in 1937, was torpedoed in the Mediterranean. The vessel sank in four minutes and the lifeboats, though launched, were all overturned, only eighteen members of her crew of sixty-five being saved. Her master, Captain W. Finch, who had regularly corresponded with the school, was rescued but died of exposure after fourteen hours in the sea.*

(p. 97)

More indirectly many children attempted to contribute to the well-being of men in the armed forces. An 'old girl' recalls life at Barr's Hill House, a private girls' boarding school; she argued that the war made these privileged girls 'more socially conscious':

We knitted for the Merchant Navy, we made fingerless gloves for the Russian Army in response to an appeal by Mrs Churchill, we made soft toys and dolls as well as clothes for the children of the USSR and we also contributed 1000 tablets of soap to the same cause. We knitted vests for babies in the occupied countries (these were known as occupied vests). We collected money for various causes, including Lady Cripps' Aid for China, and we collected mountains of books for repulping. . .We had a school allotment, too, where the most energetic amongst us (and that did not include me!) 'dug for victory', and provided the dining room with enough cabbage to see us through the winter. . .Several girls were doing voluntary work at the Coventry and Warwickshire Hospital, and others helped at nursery schools.

(pp. 43–4)

And at Bruton School for Girls, Somerset:

A frenzy of knitting consumed remarkable amounts of wool, about a hundredweight a year. Each of the four houses adopted one of the services – army, navy, air force and merchant navy – to benefit from their labours, and large quantities of blankets, mittens and other garments were despatched with increasing frequency.

(Stranack, 2005: 8)

The history of Bedford Girls Modern School indicates a strong tradition of dramatic productions and many wartime shows were put on, both in continuation of that tradition and to raise money for charities. Thus girls put on *A Midsummer Night's Dream,* raising money for Save the Children, and *Twelfth Night,* which raised £90 for the Partisans of Yugoslavia. The author adds that:

To these major activities must be added the continuous round of semi-routine fundraising efforts. Flag days, parties, entertainments, fetes, fairs, all were patronised. Funds were raised for Lord Robert Workshops, the District Nursing Association, Youth Club Equipment, Welfare of the Blind, Earl Haig's Poppy fund, Red Cross, Relief of Larissa, the Lord Mayor of London's National Air Raid Distress Fund, Russian Relief, the Ex-Servicemen's Welfare Association, Merchant Navy Comforts Fund, Warships Week, YWCA Fund for Women in HM Forces, Parcels for Russian Soldiers, a named bed in Stalingrad Hospital and the contributions of cash and clothing to Dr Barnardo's homes, the evacuees next door and other needy groups in Bedford.

(pp. 84–5)

Queen Mary's, Clitheroe (grammar school), made a point of keeping contact with former students (700) who were now serving in the forces:

The proceeds of each School play during the war were distributed amongst the old boys serving in the Forces. Each of them received a postal order for 2/6 and a letter from Mr Hardy [headteacher]. After the production of Mr Chips *in 1944, Mr Hardy sent postal orders to over 500 old boys. They were surprised and delighted to be remembered in this way, and Mr Hardy received hundreds of letters saying what a pleasure it was to know that they were not forgotten by their old school. Extracts from these letters were regularly printed in the magazine.*

(p. 82)

This school also forged links with the Royal Engineers, who were stationed nearby, and school teams played them at football and cricket. The Engineers presented a cup to a winning team at a sports day and their band played to 'enliven' the occasion (p. 82).

Individual memories include individual initiatives. Roy Hattersley (1983: 88) volunteered to work on a ward for shell-shocked soldiers from the Normandy landings: sitting with them, listening to their stories and writing letters for them, until the head of the ward said he was too young (at 11) for such work. Patrick Morrow helped to look after a group of soldiers who had just arrived back from Dunkirk. Later, during the Battle of Britain, he was encouraged by his father, who was chaplain at the local hospital, to:

go and have chat with a pilot who had just been shot down. He had not been severely wounded, but he was laid up in bed. A sergeant, I can almost remember his name. They were heroes, these people, a young chap in his early 20s.

Joy Ewer worked in a canteen for soldiers. She had little schooling during the war (because the family moved house frequently), and when she was about 13:

After a while some women noticed that I wasn't at school, and someone from the WI [Women's Institute] came and encouraged me to come and work in a canteen, a long low building along the lane. And it served tea and, I don't remember, coffee and baked beans and cheese on toast. To British soldiers. The Americans weren't invited. . .And I used to serve the tea and cooked the baked beans. We had these huge urns for the tea. And it was a very peaceful place. Because most of the soldiers who used it, used it to write letters. . .And they were very sweet and kind to me.

Audrey Balsdon (aged 13 in 1939) also worked in a canteen:

Every Sunday afternoon for a while we went to the YMCA in Woolwich and served tea to servicemen. This was our voluntary work, I suppose. We were two shy young girls and hated doing it because we often couldn't understand what the men wanted, as there were all sorts of accents we had never heard before. We used to hide under the counter, but we don't know if the poor guys ever did get served.

Discussion

This chapter has pointed to huge differences in young people's daily lives, between the majority and the minority, and the varied contributions each group made to the war effort. The expansion of war-related jobs enabled some young workers better opportunities, both to help the war effort and to better themselves. A frequent comment in the histories of the schools for the minority is that their sense of being privileged urged them to war service. A rationale commonly advanced for schools for the privileged was service: such schools train young people for service to society. While before the war this idea was linked into ideas about Empire and leadership at home and abroad, during the war schoolteachers and students learned about a broader, more democratic, or perhaps more practical kind of community work: participation, cooperation, mutual help on the home front.

© Royal Mail Group Ltd 2010, courtesy of The British Postal Museum & Archive.
Young people sorting the mail, 1942.

This chapter has shown that school students took part in a range of war-related activities, and teachers, whether willingly or not, released students' time for this work; many worked alongside students. The demands of the war provided incentives to rebalance time spent in 'school' work and time spent in war-work. Some of the tasks brought these older children close to the front line, but it seems that if adults were worried about exposing children to the realities of war, to contact with wounded soldiers or indeed with soldiers at all, they did not prevent it. Hattersley's comment that he was excluded from helping in the local hospital ward on grounds of age is an exception. As our examples show, some of the older children came directly into contact with the war and its armed forces.

War conditions encouraged many to reflect on what education is for; the accounts suggest that the situation provided opportunities for young and old to participate in and reflect on the educational value of a wide range of activities. New directions for the curriculum were an important theme for the editor of the *TES*, Harold Dent (1944a: 155–60). Based on his visits to schools across the country, he argued that changes were taking place, for the old narrow 'academic' curriculum was giving way to broader approaches to learning, with new emphasis on opportunities for creative cross-curricular learning and on the educational value of practical activities, such as gardening and understanding the natural world. He thought that school activities in the future would be more relevant to the life and work of society.[18] The 'progressive' movement in education, mainly led by psychologists, may have been influential.[19] The expansion of technical work in schools and colleges during the war also led commentators to identify the value of practical and immediately useful work. As Richmond puts it, the 'reality principle' was being applied, for instead of being engaged in 'formal exercises', young people were now making '*real* shell-cases, *real* spare parts, *real* machine tools'; the reality principle was also being applied in education more generally for, under war conditions, 'The school's four walls were breaking down: outside activities were coming to be an integral part of its daily life' (Richmond, 1945: 134–8).

The exigencies of war perhaps served to show that a common perception among educated, privileged commentators – that most young people presented undesirable deviations from the norm of the privileged few – was due for rethinking. This topic we take up in the next chapter. If young people at private and grammar schools rose to the challenge of contributing to the war effort, it was in the context of the fact that most young people were putting in long hours of work on the home front, for instance in factories and workshops. The war years provided opportunities to think about the value to the country of the majority of young people.

Notes

1 Jephcott, 1942: 96. See also, for children's working lives, Chapter 3.
2 Cited in Bathurst, 1944: 294.
3 Ministry of Labour *Gazette*, December 1942.
4 According to Jephcott (1942: 91), writing in March 1942, 14–15 year olds could be asked to work for 48 hours a week, 16 year olds for 60 hours a week.
5 See, for fuller treatment of this topic, Chapter 4.
6 See for instance the *TES*, 27 July 1940.
7 Ministry of Labour and National Service Memorandum on planning for the post-war entry of young people into employment, 1942: 8.
8 *Statistics Related to the War Effort of the UK, 1934–44*, Cmd 6564, viii, p. 603.
9 We have not found similar data for boys.
10 Board of Education, 1926: ch. XL.
11 The remit of the Spens Committee was to consider 'secondary education with special reference to Grammar and Technical High Schools'. See Richmond, 1945: 120.
12 The remit of the Norwood Committee was to consider 'suggested changes in the secondary school curriculum and the question of school examinations in relation thereto'. See Barnard, 1968 [1947]: 263.
13 We note that in most cases it is not possible to specify the ages, or in some cases the sex of the children undertaking the activities illustrated in this chapter. Such information is lacking in our sources.
14 See for instance McCulloch, 1991, especially chs 2 and 3.
15 'Farmping' referred to camping holidays to help on farms.
16 For instance, at Bolton School, delays in providing shelters meant that only small groups of boys could enter the school and boys had to be taught in a 'work-at-home' scheme (p. 209).
17 This report of the headteacher's speech is given in the history of the Friary School, p. 98.
18 In 1945 the Crown Film Unit, sponsored by the Ministries of Education and Information, produced a documentary film, *The Children's Charter*, which portrayed the new world of schooling being developed after the 1944 Education Act (Russell, 2007).
19 The work of the New Education Fellowship may also have been influential in changing practices. See, for discussion, Jenkins, 2000.

Chapter 8

Children in organisations: Working for freedom

This chapter will focus on organisations through which children and young people could contribute to the war effort, enjoy the social life offered, work as a group to improve the quality of their own lives and foster social solidarity through community work. Belonging to one of the many organisations with roots stretching back to early in the twentieth century or before meant that children, by long-standing tradition, were encouraged to improve their health through physical exercise, and to endorse the values of the organisation – many of which promoted Christian belief and practices. From the point of view of the war effort, one advantage of belonging to a large organisation was that small contributions from a group or individual could be put together to form a substantial contribution by the organisation as a whole. Children could feel that, though their own contribution might be small, it was part of a larger and well-organised enterprise. The major organisations all stressed loyalty, steadfastness and helpfulness, as is indicated in their mottos: Serve One Another (Red Cross); Sure and Steadfast (Boys' Brigade); Be Prepared (Scouts and Guides).[1] This chapter continues with the theme of service to the community which, as we saw in previous chapters, was a guiding light for many schools.

In Chapter 4 (page 93) we noted government efforts from 1939 to engage young people with organised groups and, as the war went on, to encourage them to undertake pre-service training. Youth Committees (under the local education authority) were to work with and provide funding for voluntary organisations to promote their work. From 1942, all 16–18 year olds were to be compulsorily registered and invited to come for an interview to discuss what they could do. Some of these efforts were overtly aimed at dealing with the perennial moral problem which some adults perceive young people represent or embody.[2] Thus, according to some commentators during the war years, young people who left school at 14 and went into dead-end jobs were at risk of moral and physical deterioration (see Chapter 3, page 60).[3] Rates of 'juvenile delinquency' increased during the war.[4] The moral problem presented by youth, as perceived by the Youth Advisory Council (1945), resulted from three key characteristics of an unstable, social, economic and moral background which underlay young people's growing up during the war years:

> To thousands of young people their father is a stranger, their mother is somebody whom war work has taken away from home for the whole of a long working day, and their school is a weakened influence only.[5]

The compulsory registration of young people led to (or was followed by) an increase in take-up of membership of youth organisations, especially of the pre-military organisations, of 15–20 per cent.[6] While government attempted to organise young people, some of them organised themselves. According to Dent (1944a: 110), a poster was sent out in July 1940 to the 250 villages in East Suffolk, urging young people 'to form squads to do work of local and national importance'. In three months young people had formed 142 squads and in six months nearly 200. About 70 per cent of the young people had never belonged to any youth organisation. They directed the groups themselves, with self-chosen young leaders, and they carried out a range of work: (1) salvage; (2) farm and garden work; (3) civil defence duties; and (4) they organised concerts and ran small clubs. Other similar groups sprang up around the country.

Young people in schools also formed their own youth service squads. Thus at Marling School (grammar), Stroud, boys formed three squads:

> They took over the cultivation of the school vegetable plots of which there were three. They volunteered to work the gardens of those who were on military service; they worked on farms and gathered scrap

metal and waste paper; they collected woollen articles for the Red Cross and wrote letters and sent gifts to prisoners of war.

(p. 81)

And the history adds that this initiative was then copied at other local schools.

As the historian of the George Dixon School, Birmingham, explains, a corps was established at the school in March 1942 and for girls this entailed:

work both in and out of school. Tasks included collection of salvage, adopting a war nursery, extending cultivation of the school field and helping at Queen Elizabeth hospital. The following month [April 1942], Miss Ritchie noted that 42 girls had assisted in the hospital and 30 had attended the City Road War Nursery.

(p. 41)

Youth organisations

The Board of Education's 1939 Circular 1486 lists the following voluntary organisations: Boys' Brigade, Boy Scouts, Church Lads' Brigade, Girl Guides, Girls' Friendly Society, Girls' Guildry, National Association of Boys' Clubs (including the Association of Jewish Youth), Girls' Life Brigade, National Council of Girls' Clubs, Welsh League of Youth, YMCA, YWCA and National Federation of Young Farmers' Clubs.[7] However, the circular noted that 'considerably less than half of boys and girls (aged 14–20) belong to any organisation' (para. 1), and the circular aimed to tackle this perceived problem. Another set of figures is given by Gosden (1976: 219): in 1940 there were about three million boys and girls aged 14–18. Of these, 15 per cent were in full-time schooling; 15 per cent had some part-time schooling; 20 per cent were in youth organisations, and some of these were also getting some schooling; and 50 per cent were not taking part in any educational activity or youth organisation. Both sets of figures appear to reflect a view that young people should be subject to adult control.

In this chapter we give examples from the wide range of organisations, and of what children in these organisations did.

We draw on a range of types of information. We have consulted internet sites, records and histories of these organisations, and archived journals and other papers, including people's memories.

Boys' Brigade

The information given here comes from the Boys' Brigade website and from the book on which it draws.[8] This was reputedly the first uniformed organisation for young people in the UK. It was a Christian movement, using military methods, founded in 1883 in Glasgow. Its founder, William Smith, stated its aims: 'The advancement of Christ's Kingdom among boys and the promotion of habits of Reverence, Discipline, Self-Respect, and all that tends towards true Christian Manliness'. Boys were organised in squads, companies and battalions, and paraded with bands and colours. Camping was an important activity. From the start, interestingly, some commentators opposed the military aspect of the organisation (McFarlan, 1982: 21), but it proved popular with boys, and by 1933 when Jubilee celebrations were held nearly 112,000 boys had been members of the Boys' Brigade over its first 50 years. Membership in England and Wales in 1940 was 44,530.[9] During the Second World War, many boys moved over to the wartime organisations and served at first aid posts, in the auxiliary fire service and in air raid precautions and rescue work. This movement meant a dramatic fall in Boys' Brigade membership (but it recovered after the war and embarked on new activities, for instance raising money through sponsored walks for Oxfam).

A parallel organisation for girls – the Girls' Guildry – was established in 1900 and was 'a unique combination of a senior Sunday School class, friendly club and a female equivalent of the Boys' Brigade'.[10] It aimed to develop in girls 'capacities of womanly helpfulness' (Springhall, 1977: 130). It too was uniformed, and activities included military drill. As with the Boys' Brigade, the movement was more popular in Scotland (where it originated) than in England, but figures suggest that by 1939 there were over 6,000 members in England (ibid.: 130–1). (Later, in the mid-1960s, several of the girls' organisations amalgamated to form the Girls' Brigade, with a membership of about 100,000 girls under the age of 21.)

Junior Red Cross

The Junior Red Cross was started officially in 1924 with the aim of promoting good health, service to the sick and suffering, and the development of international friendship and understanding. Clubs – or 'links' – were mostly based in schools, but could be sited elsewhere; and children could join links from age 5, with youth detachments for 16–20 year olds, who, by 1944, numbered 18,000 boys and girls.[11] One source of information (Brown, 2009: 43) gives age-divisions as follows: Red Cross cadets were aged 12–15, and the Youth Detachment members of the Red Cross were aged 15–20, or they could become full members of the Red Cross at 16 if they passed an exam in first aid and, for girls, home nursing. Similar was the Cadet Nursing Division of the St John Ambulance Brigade and the two organisations collected jointly during the war years.

The *Junior Red Cross Journal* is a useful source of information for messages beamed to children during the war years, and also about children's war-work.[12] Each edition of this quarterly journal included an editorial on some aspect of national and international news, often with exhortation to young members to engage with the war effort. It also included: (1) stories and poems; (2) texts of plays and pageants which children might use in fundraising efforts; (3) information about what groups and individuals were doing for the war effort across the country; (4) suggestions for helpful activities; (5) accounts of the exploits of men in the armed forces, and (in later years) of life in prisoner of war camps; (6) articles of general interest (for instance, on the history of the penny post, life in Finland, country life in England); and (7) information about Red Cross activities in other countries.

For instance, the December 1939 issue (No. 63) refers to the evacuation of children from the cities and notes that 'You country juniors have a great chance of helping the town boys and girls who are living with you to enjoy the beauty and pleasure of country life'; it adds that helping others will also enhance their own enjoyment of country life (p. 615). An article called 'War Work for Juniors' includes instructions for knitting gloves, scarves and socks for soldiers; boys are told they should collect waste paper. And 'for the relief of suffering among children', especially those in Poland, juniors can knit for them too (p. 618). This issue (like all the others) also lists very many Junior Red Cross activities taking place around England: sewing parties, entertainments to raise funds, collections of sacks of books for hospitals, making toffee, iron-holders and 'lavender ladies'[13] to raise funds, collecting silver paper, running jumble sales, knitting blankets and carol singing at hospitals.

The *Junior Red Cross Journal* is explicit in emphasising children's duty to contribute, and it often bases its encouragement on the battle for freedom. This suggests that the organisation did not want to shield children from this war; we read especially of the sufferings of children brought about by the conflicts raging in mainland European countries and about the consequent duty more fortunate children have to help in whatever ways they could. A striking editorial on the opening page of the September 1940 issue (No. 66) is titled 'The Fortress'. It quotes from John of Gaunt's speech in *Richard II* extolling the sea defences of England: 'This fortress built by nature for herself, Against infection and the hand of war' and agrees that the sea defends the country against 'the invader' – 'but it has to be defended within and without and that means discipline and loyal obedience from all within it to the orders given by people in authority'. Then the editorial goes on to list some of the duties of Junior Red Cross members:

> *You should know the position of Air Raid shelters, the address of the ARP Warden, how to get in touch with the Fire Station and the Police, how to use the telephone. . .If you are old enough and strong enough, join a pump party and in any case join a savings group or put something, if it is only a penny, aside each week to buy savings stamps.*

Another example comes later in the war, when a new Director of the Junior Red Cross (Audrey Eckersley) was appointed; the *Journal* carried a letter from her to the links:

> *Most of you have Fathers, Brothers and Sisters serving in the War, many of them leaving behind their loved families and homes. Let us, too, join with them in their fight for Freedom by each one making his or her own personal contribution.*[14]

From the thousands of activities described in the *Journal*, we give just one example of children's efforts. In April 1941, two girls, aged 10 and 12, organised a sale for Red Cross funds, which raised £12.9s.9d. 'These little girls have been working for the sale since January and all the articles sold were either made or collected by them, bunches of lovely spring flowers proved very popular with their customers.'[15] Many of the school histories describe fundraising for the 'Red Cross and St John Fund'. For instance, at Weston-super-Mare Grammar School:

> *Money collected for this fund was allocated to buy parcels containing food and other necessities for British prisoners-of-war...By the time the school fund was wound up in June 1945 the boys had collected £455 – a goodly sum for those days.*
>
> (p. 31)

And the logbook of Boughton Monchelsea Elementary School in Kent records, for 23 December 1942, a ceremony to present funds collected:

> *At 11.45 a.m., the School assembled to present Mrs B.B. Jolly [Red Cross] with the money received for the collection of 14 cwt waste paper and 15/- from an afternoon concert. The money she had received she was sending to the Prisoner of War Fund.*[16]

Within the overall aim of serving their country, the main kinds of work the Red Cross links did were fundraising for the Red Cross in its national and international work, contributing goods and helping people directly. Fundraising was through, for instance, running entertainments and jumble sales. As well as knitted goods and parcels of food, books and useful items (such as razors) were assembled and sent to prisoners of war. Direct work included helping old people at home, changing library books for housebound people and taking round tea in hospitals.[17]

Scouts and Guides – common ground

The Scouting and Guiding movements had always emphasised service as a central tenet. According to the social historian Janice Anderson (2008: 103),[18] Scouting and Guiding took on new characteristics during the war. The founder of the Women's Voluntary Service (WVS), Lady Reading, worked with the Scouting and Guiding movements at national level in order to encourage their collaboration with the WVS when war broke out. This work included welcoming newly arrived evacuees with food and drink and leading them to billets, running groups to entertain evacuees and looking after the youngest. Thus, while Scouts and Guides had always worked for badges, there were now new awards: the National Service badge for the boys and the War Service badge for girls. Also, the work might include: (1) distributing gas masks; (2) directing traffic; (3) helping in first aid posts; and (4) for some of the older ones, acting as telephone operators or as messengers, delivering telegrams (often with bad news).

Boy Scouts National Service and War Service badges (images are not to scale).

But international membership (among both Guides and Scouts) had begun to decline from 1938, as these movements were prohibited abroad, for instance in Germany and Italy, in favour of national youth movements (such as the Hitler Youth).[19] There was also a drop in numbers in the UK, explained as the result of falling birth rates, shifts of population from cities to unorganised suburbs during the evacuation process and schools taking on some of the elements of the Guide programmes (for instance fundraising, community work, fire watching). And many older Scouts and Guides moved on to the pre-military training groups or worked for the Red Cross.[20] However, some joined groups in schools and in the community where they were living, and some new groups were formed, especially in rural areas. Our interviewee, John Chambers, explained that he encouraged evacuees to join his Scout group in Cambridge (Chapter 5, page 135).

Since Guides and Scouts were international movements, this gave the UK branches great strength when efforts were made to raise money for specific projects, especially in wartime when groups in other allied countries were eager to help the UK and the defeated countries. Thus, in 1940, when the Girl Guides Association advertised for money for ambulances, Guides responded from all over the Empire, and from the USA. In England, Guides earned money to contribute by doing odd jobs – painting gates, babysitting, weeding. Altogether £46,000 was raised and this paid for 20 ambulances which were handed over to the navy.[21] The Scouts International Relief Service was started in 1942, and this worked with other relief organisations, raising money and sending goods to the occupied countries. In May 1944, for instance, all UK Cubs, Scouts and Rovers were asked to donate by raising money during a bob-a-job week, and raised £32,000 (Saunders, 1949: ch. 7).

Scouts

Judging by the histories of the Scout movement[22] and by its weekly journal the *Scouter* (price 2d), Scouts – including Cubs (8–11), Scouts (11–18) and Rovers (17–25) – carried out many tasks during the war. This was a large movement, with, in 1941, about 279,000 members.[23] The *Scouter* adopted a cheery, optimistic tone, offering adventure stories, practical tips, cartoons and nature notes; it stressed Scouting as fun, adventure, togetherness and, increasingly, bravery. Editorials, like those in the *Junior Red Cross Journal,* emphasised service:[24]

> *You can help –*
>
> *Keep calm in all emergencies*
>
> *Be chivalrous to women, children and old people*
>
> *Obey orders promptly*
>
> *Get on with your training*
>
> *Get your Pathfinder and Ambulance Man Badges*
>
> *Wear your uniform and a smile*
>
> *Remember the Scout Law.*

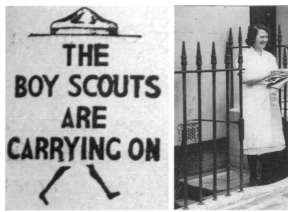

A Scout's logo during wartime (left) and Scouts collecting waste paper (right).

Increasingly as the war went on, and stories flowed in, the magazine recounted examples of selfless service, for instance in its report on the bombing of Coventry in 1941, when Scouts and Rovers helped put out fires and looked after people injured and bombed out of their houses.[25] These examples sat alongside the contributions to be made in, for instance, agriculture and gardening. Thus, in June 1940 an article titled 'Are you "Farmping" this year?' explained that traditional camping could be combined with farm work, and articles on digging for victory gave practical tips on what to grow, how and when.[26]

Some Scout groups were disbanded in the wake of evacuation, others were established in both cities and rural areas, and in some cases schools organised a Scout group. Scouts traditionally worked for badges (in recognition of their skills in, for instance, pathfinding, camping, knots or cooking), and during the war years 60,000 Scouts earned the National Service badge. The war-work included: (1) helping to welcome and place evacuees; (2) message-taking (when phone lines were down); (3) salvage collection; (4) fire watching, fire-fighting and rescue work (especially in London, Coventry, Liverpool and Glasgow); (5) erecting shelters, manning listening posts; (6) cultivating the land, harvesting, hop picking and wood chopping; (7) helping with postal deliveries; (8) running parties for children; (9) collecting and distributing food for the poor; (10) fundraising to help the armed forces; and (11) working in hospitals and in air raid shelters. And Sea Scouts comprised part of the force manning the Thames River Emergency Service.[27]

One dramatic example will have to serve for many. Scouts aged under 16 formed 'after-the-raid squads' to rescue people after air raids. On one occasion they had worked for hours, 'they had dug and scratched among the torn and splintered woodwork and plaster and rubble and had brought out shell-shocked and blood-covered victims'. Just as they thought they had finished, they heard a moaning cry:

> [The Patrol Leader] turned quickly aside and climbing over a tangle of debris, got into the house. A minute or so later he came out carrying the naked body of a young girl. Blood dripped from a terrible gash in her neck which was stained crimson. Staggering over the debris, the Patrol Leader thrust his burden into arms of his Scoutmaster, who had just arrived on the scene, gasping out: 'Take her, Skipper. I'm going to be sick.'[28]

Reproduced by kind permission of the Bedfordshire County Scout Executive Committee.
Illustrations of Scouts working as fire-fighters, messengers and rescue workers.

More mundanely, as the history of William Ellis Grammar School, evacuated from London to the country, records:

> *There were of course always the farmers to help, especially during the summer holidays and the school had its own allotments which kept the boys busy. One particularly close tie was formed with Mr C.F. Brotherton, the local Scout leader, who aroused an enthusiasm which led to the whole of the Third Form and many of the Lower IV joining the Leighton Buzzard Scouts and forming the Raven patrol as a William Ellis patrol.*
>
> (p. 168)

A detailed account of one kind of Scout work refers to building Morrison shelters. Peter Smith says:

> *These were the indoor shelters, steel frame with a steel top and mesh sides, the idea being that people slept in them or got into them in an air raid; the shelters would be strong enough to withstand a ceiling or roof collapsing on to them. They arrived in kit form and were quite heavy, and we were asked to assist householders erecting these. In many families there were no menfolk available. Usually two or three of us worked together because they took some manhandling. I know our troop put up just over a hundred altogether.*[29]

The international Scouting movement facilitated money-raising for people in distress both in the UK and in other countries.[30] There were, for instance, over one million Scouts in the USA and they were keen to help (Saunders, 1949: 191, 246). In 1942 the Scouts International Relief Service was initiated and along with other relief organisations raised money for the work; for instance in May 1944, all UK Cubs, Scouts and Rovers were asked to donate, and through a bob-a-job week £32,000 was raised (ibid.: ch. 7).

John Chambers, a Scout living in Cambridge, gives a vivid account of his contributions:

> *JC: We used to go to a farm just outside of Cambridge. . .especially during the summer time. We would walk behind the binder, because they used to just cut it and bind it into sheaves and used to throw it out the back, then we used to have to go walk round, keep walking round the field continually, picking two up, four of us would walk together and make stooks all the way round the field, and that was one of the jobs we used to have to do, and we done a lot of that.*
>
> INTERVIEWER: *Did you get paid for it?*
>
> *JC: No (chuckle), the farm would supply us with milk…we used to work on that, we did a lot of work there, about 11 onwards. Yes, it was hard work, but yes we did enjoy it, with all the lads together, that did make a lot of difference, and we did enjoy ourselves.*
>
> INTERVIEWER: *Any other things?*
>
> *JC: Some of us done fruit picking, the older ones. Some older ones also went up into Leicestershire for potato picking, but they were allowed time off school, to go do that, because school started again then, and that's when they harvest the potatoes. I wasn't old enough to do that. But back on the farm we…helped single out sugar beet, and one of the hardest jobs was stone picking. We would walk the fields picking up stones by the bucket load. It was quite heavy work, and it was quite hard on your hands because there's a lot of chalky soil that way, and a lot of it was flint, so you quite often cut yourself. I think they used them for hardcore.*

Guides

Like other youth organisations, the Guides organisation promoted the concept of service, suggested useful activities and engaged in training work. Though evacuation disrupted some groups in cities (and some cities lost their groups), some evacuated Guides joined packs in their new locations. Guides helped to welcome and billet evacuees, and ran centres to keep young children happy and occupied. In the years ahead they collected and sorted salvage, ran messenger services for the ARP and Home Guard, cultivated allotments and helped in hospitals and canteens (Liddell, 1976: 12–13).[31]

Courtesy of Girlguiding UK.
The Guides logo, 1922–1966, and a Guide packing Red Cross parcels.

The *Guider* journal, published weekly during the war years, includes, like the *Scouter* and the *Junior Red Cross Journal*, a wide range of articles and gives a useful flavour of the ethos of the times. The editorials included reflection on the hard times of the war years and the duties of Brownies (6–10), Guides (10–14/16) and Rangers (16–21). The journal carried articles on nature study, camping, suggestions for useful activities, competitions, general knowledge quizzes, letters, book reviews, serial stories, information about national policy events (for instance, progress towards the 1944 Education Act is discussed in January 1944), and how to make, for instance, 'camp gadgets' and handcraft items, including toys. There is detail about funds raised and by whom, awards for good work and activities in other countries.[32]

Just one example, from the history of Merchant Taylors' School, Liverpool, gives a further list of the range of activities undertaken:

> The Guide Company had been doing sterling work since the outbreak of war. One local effort they assisted in was the scrubbing of all the floors in Little Crosby Hall, which had been lent to the army as a hospital. The learning of first aid took on a new importance and urgency, and in 1941 the Company responded to an appeal from the WVS for girls to work at camouflage netting.
>
> (p. 116)

A Brownie (born around 1930) remembers the day in September 1939 when:

> war was declared and on the day after my mother received a telephone call for me to collect my Six and report to the school opposite my father's shop, called Garden Fields. We were among many others there, WVS, Scouts, police, Mothers' Union and teachers. We were told that lots of children were coming on trains from London and our job would be to take groups round the local area and ask householders if they would take one or two in. This was very exciting for us as the children were all about our own age and we soon got talking with them. As far as I remember we took several groups and all were taken in.

Other activities she remembered were running errands and helping on the wards in the local hospital, collecting salvage, pitching camp and cooking. Another memory was of being allowed to stay up on VJ Day to listen to the news – 'this was very moving'. And finally, when she was 14:

> As my mother had died in 1944, I had to leave school and run the shop, so my childhood was finished, but what a lovely war we had.[33]

As the *Guider* shows, Guides were frequently exhorted to keep fit, to eat sensibly, to benefit from fresh air. And again, the government took a hand, initiating in 1940 the Home Emergency Scheme, a forerunner of the pre-services training groups for girls, to train girls (aged 14–18) in discipline, physical fitness and all-round usefulness (Liddell, 1976: 19–22). The Guiding movement always linked together physical fitness, practical skills and competences and an ethos of helpfulness. Given these emphases, the girls were well suited to help during the war for they comprised groups much better trained and educated than the general run of girls in England.

Illustration in an article by Seaman, J. (1941) 'The Importance of Being Healthy: Exercise'. *The Guider* (Vol. xxviii).

Illustration of a healthy, active Guide.

Looking abroad and to the future, the Girl Guides Association (GGA) set up schemes to raise money and train girls to help with reconstruction in the UK and in other countries after the war. This effort was part of an international movement – the Guides International Service (GIS) and it drew on support from the World Association of Guides. The GGA became a member of the Council of British Societies for Relief Abroad (COBSRA). Older girls were trained to be fit and competent, to be able to drive. In 1944 a group went to Greece to help in reconstruction. After Holland was freed in February 1945, groups of Guides and Scouts worked there and, later, after VE Day, they worked in Germany; the work there went on until December 1952 (Liddell, 1976: ch. 3).[34]

Woodcraft Folk

As we have suggested, the main youth organisations – those enrolling large numbers of young people – emphasised character-formation and service, and some promoted quasi-military work, in the context of a Christian ethical framework. An organisation which attracted much smaller numbers is interesting because it was based on an alternative *raison d'être*. The Woodcraft Folk was founded in 1925 as a non-militarist, pro-socialist alternative to the Scouting movement (Davis, 2000: 8).[35] It aimed to be a democratic and egalitarian organisation; it was co-educational and motivated by a socialist vision of the future (ibid.: 34). It was rooted within 'a synthesis of "recapitulation" theory, pacifism, internationalism, socialism and the eugenic ideal' (Springhall, 1977: 116). An offshoot of its work was the Forest School which ran in the 1930s and drew its philosophy from the Woodcraft Folk movement, from Native American traditions, from the Quakers and others; it promoted the importance of boys and girls, children and adults learning to live and work together, close to nature. Forest School Camps began in 1948 and have continued with this work, providing holidays for children.[36]

From the start, the Woodcraft Folk movement had links with the co-operative movement and in 1927 it received a small grant from the Central Education Committee of the Co-operative Union (ibid.: 41). However, the relationship between the Union and the

Woodcraft Folk movement was stormy during the 1930s and 1940s, apparently because the Union tried to take control (Davis, 2000: 41). According to Springhall (1977: ch. 7) the Labour Party and trades unions failed to support the movement. During the Second World War some Woodcraft Folk members took a pacifist stance, while others decided to support the war effort because of its anti-fascist aims (Davis, 2000: ch. 6).

It was much less popular than the Brigade and the Scouting movement, perhaps because it was too 'progressive' for many parents to contemplate (Springhall, 1977: 117). Its membership was drawn mainly from left-wing middle-class families. Notably, too, the movement (unlike Scouts and Guides) did not attract the patronage of the royal family. Its membership was 4,521 in 1938; this halved in 1940, though it rose again by about 300 by 1946 (Davis, 2000: 103). It seems that Woodcraft children were encouraged to promote peaceable ways of working together for a better world, in contrast to the more conventional contributions encouraged by a government fighting a war. The children's activities included discussions about ways forward towards cooperation between societies, in the context of camping and learning to live in the countryside (Tizard, 2010: 93–6).

At a rough count, based on the available information, there were during the early war years about three-quarters of a million young people enrolled in the Boys' Brigade, the Girls' Guildry, the Scouts, the Guides and the Woodcraft Folk (no information is available on the Junior Red Cross members).[37]

Pre-military training

Boys

As some examples showed in Chapter 7, schools for older children were asked to engage directly with war-work (in the Home Guard, for instance), and the armed services mounted initiatives to recruit boys into pre-military training units. Thus, the history of Woodroffe (grammar) School, Lyme Regis, records:

There was great excitement during those early war years as there were large demonstrations laid on, in the main by the army, to attract volunteers from the Sixth Form. Many bangs, and tanks everywhere – 'Top Fields' provided the venue.

(p. 30)

Many boys were keen to join the pre-military training groups, some based in schools, others at military training bases (Chapter 4, page 93). The general lower age limit for boys was 16, but the Army Cadet Force (ACF) had an entry age of 14; by December 1942 it had enrolled 170,000 boys. The Air Training Corps (ATC) was established in January 1941 for boys aged 15.5 and up, and officials thought that 100,000 boys would enrol in the first 12 months. In fact, it was 200,000 strong within six months. The 1942 planned expansion of Sea Cadet Corps from 120 to 400 units, providing for 50,000 cadets, led again to a rush to join, exceeding the number of places available.[38]

We quote here from the many descriptions of pre-military training for boys in school histories. In the history of Wheelwright Grammar Schools, Dewsbury, we read that from 1942 large camps run by the military were held annually for school groups of the Army Cadet Force and boys also took part in training at school each weekday:

Mondays signalling; Tuesdays shooting (an hour and a half on the miniature range); Wednesdays Certificate A Class for map reading and weapon training; Thursdays Band practice; Fridays Company parade besides Certificate A training. A number of boys who passed Certificate A went on to Officer Cadet Training and gained commissions in both the British and Indian armies.

(p. 70)

The history of Wellingborough School reported on pre-service training, which was 'a major activity for the boys':

The Officers' Training Corps, renamed the Junior Training Corps (JTC) in 1941 was run by Lt. Col. Allsopp, parallel with the Air Section, under Flight-Lieutenant Witham, which in turn was renamed the ATC. Wellingborough was one of the first Public

Schools to set up its own Sea Scout Troop in 1944, an activity which was derided by some as amounting to nothing except playing with boats on the River Nene once a week. These units paraded each Thursday afternoon, and continued to hold field days at least twice a year, often on the estate of Lord Brooke of Oakley, Chairman of the Governors.

(p. 94)

That their lives were to be directly affected by serving their country was not lost on older boys in these schools. At Wellingborough, one later recalled at the end-of-term service 'looking about the Chapel and realising that he might never again see some of the sixth formers there, as they awaited their call-up papers' (p. 96). And the history includes a photo of the war memorial set up in 1948.

A similar story is told at Marling Grammar School, Gloucestershire, where 'most of the boys between sixteen and eighteen years of age' joined the Marling School Flight, whose officers were teachers at the school. Courses of instruction were organised twice a week, led by teachers. The school also had an Army Cadet Force (from June 1942) with about 70 cadets. The history records that about 1,000 old boys were of military age at some stage in the war and, for instance, the school magazine in May 1943 listed 470 old boys then serving in one or other of the services. Military awards were also listed in the magazine, including six Distinguished Flying Crosses; the history notes that of the 50 old boys who died in the war, 30 were RAF men (pp. 80–2).

Adverse comment on pre-military training is hardly to be found in the school histories. But this ex-student of Charterhouse, reminiscing soon after the war ended, reported that he had found parades and 'playing at soldiers' irritating. It may be that he represents a sceptical view shared by some others:

Quite the worst thing the War did to us was to get us on parade three times, including two afternoons, a week, playing at soldiers. The whole thing seemed rather futile, seeing that however much one learned in the Corps, the Army, when it got hold of you, assumed you had learned nothing and put you through it all over again.

(pp. 94–7)

He notes that the war seemed far away, and that the boys accepted it as a normal background to their school experience. However, he found the Home Guard 'more realistic' since it was 'more adult' and it brought the war closer to home. He also notes that he and his contemporaries did take an interest in the war; they spotted and identified aircraft and followed the course of the war: 'Eagerly we moved our flags across the *Daily Telegraph* maps of the Eastern Front, Tunisia and Normandy' (pp. 94–7).

Another kind of criticism came from a boy who thought that compulsion (by the headmaster) to attend weekly parades of the school cadet corps was ill-judged; the time would have been more profitably spent in study or waste paper collection.[39]

Girls

Official ideas about girls differed from those about boys. The Board of Education responded to the perceived wish of girls to join in, arguing in a 1942 circular that 'girls have an innate desire to serve and a sense of devotion to a cause. The hour of our destiny has not failed to inspire them with an urge to be up and doing.'[40] And the history of Merchant Taylors' School, Liverpool, echoes the point.

> *A new movement, the Girls' Training Corps, was also founded in 1942 (for girls aged 16 plus). This was a national association, supported by the government, supplying a demand among girls 'for some sort of practical training which would enable them to feel better equipped to serve their country in time of crisis, and also to prepare them to enter the Women's Services'.*
>
> (p. 117)

A handbook, *Training and Service for Girls*, was issued by the Board of Education in March 1942; this accompanied the compulsory registration of girls aged 16–18. It reiterates girls' wish to serve, and notes that opportunities for them to do so 'are less obvious and perhaps less attractive than those open to boys'.[41] It says that fewer than a tenth of 16–18-year-old girls were in full-time education; many were working long hours in war industry and on the land, but those not in full-time war-work should be encouraged to do training and various forms of direct work (paras 4–5). The handbook then sets out some suggestions, and in so doing indicates some points in the character of the civil servants' understandings of what girls can and should do.

Girls should engage in general training which develops qualities of character and of mind – a trained sense of responsibility, the power to carry on cheerfully, and to face new situations 'without losing one's head'. They should also pay attention to personal hygiene and to attaining high standards of physical fitness (paras 7–9). Training for entry to the women's auxiliary services should include skills such as clerical, technical and mechanical, medical orderly work, cookery and catering, household hygiene and management (paras 14–21). Other avenues are in pre-nursing and first aid courses with the St John Ambulance or the Red Cross Society, and in wartime nursery service. Alternatively, these girls may opt to work in the Land Army (paras 25–41) (see below), or they may choose to work voluntarily with the WVS or the Women's Institutes (paras 43–7).

An example of a school's response is provided by Luton Girls' High School. The history draws on editions of the school magazine at the time (pp. 161–5). The headmistress noted in 1944 that during the war years the girls were taking 'increased interest in the world outside the school, in the peoples of other lands and in home and home life'. She put stress on Christianity as guiding our actions 'all day and every day', and she said that 'her pride in the School rested chiefly on the good wives and mothers it produced'. The school established a 'Company of Service' in 1944, which trained the girls, from juniors upwards (11–18), in health and hygiene, in domestic work, in mothercraft, home nursing and 'food values'; the girls also helped in the school kitchen, visited the local hospital and discussed their responsibilities and their future leadership of youth movements. Senior girls took first aid exams, learned to manage household budgets and how to care for rabbits and chickens. They heard lectures on prenatal clinics, maternity hospitals and childcare. They also learned about civics and careers, discussed ethical issues and visited local industries and the police courts. For practical work they acted as messengers, worked in nursery and infant schools, war centres and play centres and sold flags for Army and Navy days.

Reproduced by kind permission of the family and estate of C.K. Bird.

A Fougasse poster.

Some of the Luton High School girls also joined the town's Girls' Training Corps, which was run mainly by school staff. It promoted much the same activities and also held parades, and included training in Morse code, air raid precautions and aircraft recognition. Six girls represented Luton High School on the Luton Youth Council and took part in a Youth Month in March 1944 which aimed to make the public aware of youth activities.

Clearly, the main kinds of training and work proposed are the varied and diffuse auxiliary tasks included under the heading 'women's work' – providing the back-up which helped men carry out their own war-work, and building on traditional women's work of nursing and caring. The exception is Land Army work, where the gendered understandings of girls and women give way to the dire necessities of substituting for men on the land.

We add here a brief note on the Land Army.[42] The handbook *Training and Service for Girls* suggested that girls could attend short preparatory courses organised by the County Council or by the agricultural department of a university, but we do not know the availability or character of such courses. Girls could join the Land Army at 17, but it was easy to get accepted, and some joined at 16, having lied about their age (Tyler, 1996: 24). Girls were given a medical examination, but it seems this was cursory in some cases. One girl who wore glasses and failed an eye test was nevertheless passed for service since 'the doctor said, "Never mind, I suspect you'd see a charging bull"'.[43]

As with harvest work, Land Army work inspired poetry, for example that published in the Luton Girls' High School magazine during the war. One poem is titled *The Land Girl*:

> *Picture if you can a Land girl,*
> *In November's icy freeze,*
> *Making whoopee with the carrots,*
> *Learning why the chickens sneeze.*
> *Seven days a week she's working*
> *Thirty cows to milk each day,*
> *Muddy clothes and boots too heavy,*
> *On her back she carries hay.*[44]

And so on. The long hours and very hard work carried out by land girls is documented in Shirley Joseph's 1946 book, an 'unofficial account', tellingly entitled *If Their Mothers Only Knew* (cited in Cadogan and Craig, 1978: 169).

Discussion

Young people as a national asset?

It seems that official understandings of working-class young people as a problem, to some extent changed as the war proceeded, to a belief that young people are a national asset. The Youth Advisory Council report of 1945 looked back to 1939 and noted that the government's 1939 campaign to promote young people's membership of organisations had been 'preventative and palliative' and was 'frankly and openly a "first aid" policy, with the aim of keeping young people off the street and out of trouble'.[45] As time went on, the official emphasis shifts to the contributions to the war effort that young people could make – and were indeed making. The Council noted the 'splendid response' of young people to the demands on them to serve their country in various ways.[46] However, the Council envisaged more social and psychological difficulties ahead for young people after the war, during a reconstruction phase, and so suggested that a youth service should be promoted.

And, notably, as we discussed in Chapter 4, a decent education service for all was seen to be required; this would constitute, as one commentator argued, a 'sociological influence without which there could be no betterment of human life and affairs'.[47] Legislation to provide a better education service was enacted in the 1944 Education Act; however, while some commentators applauded it, others noted it was 'the old order in a new disguise'.[48] Legislation for part-time education for 14–18s (or 'day-release') was proposed in the 1941 Green Paper (Barber, 1994: 28) and promised in the 1943 White Paper:

> *All young persons from 15 to 18 will be required to attend an appropriate centre part-time unless they are in full-time attendance at school.*[49]

In the event, while the 1944 Act included provisions for compulsory part-time education at 'county colleges' (Section 43), these were not implemented (Chapter 4, page 98). However, it has been noted that while in 1939 only 43,000 young people in paid work attended some part-time education, this had risen to 169,000 in 1946–7.[50] This increase presumably relates to wartime demands for more skilled labour. It is also worth noting that the county college scheme did not die without a bit of a fight. A Ministry of Education pamphlet in 1946 – *Youth's Opportunity* – took up the cause. It paid tribute to the 'steadfastness, the enthusiasm and the courage' of young people during the war (para. 3); it outlined the history of failure to implement the day continuation school scheme in the 1918 Education Act in the inter-war years (paras 5–11); and it argued that many employers had been against part-time education for their employees and that the public more generally had little sense that to 'cut off' from schooling at 14 the vast majority of the population was to 'waste human material and to nullify much of the work of the elementary schools' (para. 12). Then it set out for local education authorities its suggestions about planning, staffing and the curriculum.[51]

It is interesting therefore that the Youth Advisory Council, asked in 1942 (when the proposals for the 1944 Education Act were under discussion) to propose developments in youth services for the post-war years, was told it could assume: (1) that the school-leaving age would be raised to 15 without exemption (it was); (2) that the period from 15 to 18 would be treated as, in part an educational period, 'in the sense that adolescents will be regarded as remaining the concern of the education service' (only in some senses did this happen); and (3) that 'a system of compulsory part-time education during working hours will be established for all young persons after they have ceased full-time schooling, up to the age of 18' (which was not implemented).[52]

Patriotism

The appeal to serve their country is seen most overtly in the recruitment of young people to pre-military organisations, leading on to full military service. But appeals rested on a particular basis: the war, young people were told, was fought so that the democratic values of the country would prevail. This point is reiterated in countless reports. For instance the Youth Advisory Council (YAC) made clear its values in its 1943 report on post-war services for young people:

> *We neither expect nor wish all young people to grow up holding the same views, for if they did both they and the body politic would*

be the poorer. We want each one of them to come to see that the fullest life, both for himself and his community, demands that he should recognise duties and responsibilities as well as enjoy rights and benefits. We want to see them all grounded in the principal loyalties of a sound civilisation: their loyalty to God, to King and Country, to their family, to their neighbour and to their unit of livelihood. We believe that bringing up our young people to practise these loyalties will give disciplined freedom to society and yield what is due to both the individual and the community.[53]

Here we have reference to the democratic principle that people should have some self-determination, and reference to young people's rights as well as their responsibilities. But young people were to understand these principles within wider patriotic loyalties to the 'sound civilisation' of Britain. The notion of 'disciplined freedom' is key to these propositions. This YAC committee was chaired by the Headmaster first of Uppingham School and later of Shrewsbury School – private boys' schools. And as we have noted in quotations from the school histories, both private and state schools encouraged Christianity and patriotism through, for instance, school assemblies, celebrations of Empire Day and remembrance of Armistice Day.

Just as youth organisations stressed the ethic of service and patriotism, so too did schools. We gave earlier the example of Luton Girls' High School. According to the history of Barrow Grammar School, the Headmaster was clear about promoting the ethos of service, and, responding to the demands of war, he introduced pre-service groups, in the teeth of opposition (presumably from some staff?). For him:

the school meant training for citizenship and citizenship meant service. Pre-service units, therefore, of the Cadets and ATC should be introduced to this end. His battle lasted over a year, but he won with their setting up in 1942.

(p. 116)

The Headmaster of Stowe School – a private boys' school – wrote in the school magazine during the war about the changes that had come to England during the war and the need to develop new forms of service:

We have a new dream now. It is a dream of a changed England and a changed Stowe, and in the new dream as in the old the School is seen to be serving the country to the best of its power. What form that service can take we do not yet fully know. But when we see more clearly what the country requires of us we shall be ready and able to provide it. We were not founded to face a future of upheaval and impoverishment. But we shall face it if need be, and we hope that we shall face it not ignobly.

(p. 128)

He was right that the private schools survived to face the future!

Notes

1   For valuable studies of organisations established for children and young people from the late nineteenth century onwards, see papers in Gilchrist *et al.*, eds (2001), especially the Introduction (by Davies, 2001), ch. 7 on girls' clubs (Turnbull, 2001), ch. 8 on youth work in Sunderland (Spence, 2001) and ch. 9 on work in the Girl Guide movement in the interwar years (Oldfield, 2001).

2   For discussion, see Humphries, 1981; Pearson, 1983.

3   For instance Macalister Brew, 1943: ch. 2.

4   See, for increased rates of delinquency, Titmuss, 1976: 148.

5   Ministry of Education, 1945: para. 2. For an overview of the wartime history of youth work, see Macalister Brew, 1957: 91–8.

6   Gosden, 1976: 228; Bunt and Gargrave, 1980: 112.

7   This information is given in the appendix to the Board of Education November 1939 Circular 1486, 'The Service of Youth'.

8   The website information is excerpted from McFarlan, 1982. See also, for valuable notes on the work of religious organisations to control children and to offer them health-giving opportunities, Cranwell, 2003.

9   Membership figures for the Boys' Brigade are given by Springhall, 1977: Table 1.5.

10   Springhall, 1977: 130–1 gives a brief account of the movement.

11   This information comes from general notes about the Red Cross, available at <http://www.redcross.org.uk> (accessed 20 November 2009). However, no information on membership numbers for younger children is available.

12   The *Junior Red Cross Journal* for the war years is held in the archives of the Red Cross main UK office (44 Moorfields, London EC1).

13   'Lavender ladies' are sachets stuffed with lavender, to be stored with clothes.

14   *Junior Red Cross Journal* December 1942, Issue No. 75.

15   *Junior Red Cross Journal* June 1941, Issue No. 69, p. 735.

16   The logbook of Boughton Monchelsea has no page numbers.

17 We have been unable to ascertain what numbers of children 'belonged' to the Red Cross during the war – the Information Assistant at the London headquarters, Emily Oldfield, says this information is not available. However, perhaps more relevant is that the work done was done not just by members, but by schools and local groups, especially in fundraising.

18 Unfortunately Anderson (2008) gives no sources for the information in her book.

19 See, for discussion of German youth movements, Stargardt, 2005: 32.

20 Membership of the Guides in the UK was about 600,000 in 1937 and declined thereafter. Membership of Scouts in 1939 was 500,000 and this dropped during the war but recovered by 1945 (Saunders, 1949: 37; Reynolds, 1950: 197).

21 Liddell, 1976: 15; Stewart Brown, 1966: 26–7.

22 Saunders, 1949; Reynolds, 1950.

23 Springhall, 1977, Appendix 2. Numbers decreased after the outbreak of war.

24 For instance, the *Scouter* editorial on 16 September 1939 (p. 135) was titled 'How You Can Serve', and ended with the list of helping work quoted.

25 The *Scouter*, March 1941, p. 59.

26 The *Scouter*, 29 June 1940 (p. 809) on 'farmping'; on 13 July 1940 (p. 846) on digging for victory.

27 This information is given in detail in Saunders, 1949: ch. III. A comprehensive and detailed list of work carried out is given in his Appendix 1.

28 This story is given in a pamphlet published by the Boy Scouts Association in 1941, p. 12.

29 This memory is quoted in Smith, 2008: 231.

30 For an account of national and international work during the war, see Scott-Davies, 2010.

31 For a study of Guiding through the war years, see Hampton, 2010.

32 The *Guider* journals are held at the Girl Guide Association headquarters, 17–19 Buckingham Palace Road, London, SW1.

33 Wartime memories written by Eileen Mary Rashleigh, held in the Girl Guides Association archives.

34 In 1941 there were 400,000 Brownies, Guides and Rangers; and, as with the Scouts, these numbers had decreased since 1939 owing to the disruptions of war. This information was kindly provided by the archivist of the Girl Guides Association, Karen Stapley.

35 For study of other socialist children's and young people's organisations, see Kean 1990: 58–66.

36 <http://www.fsc.org.uk/about.htm> (accessed 4 March 2010).

37 This information comes from Springhall, 1977: Appendix 2, Tables 1.5 and 7.1, p. 131; also on Guides from the archivist at the Girl Guides Association, Karen Stapley.

38 Dent, 1944a: 111–13; Gosden, 1976: 226–7.

39 This story is told by Gosden, 1976: 221.

40 Board of Education Circular 1585 (6 March 1942). quoted in Gosden, 1976: 227.

41   Board of Education and Scottish Education Department 1942: para. 1. *Training and Service for Girls*. London: HMSO.

42   For a history of the Land Army, see Tyler, 1996.

43   BBC website on Women's Land Army, available at <http://bbc.co.uk?dna/h2g2/A2116478> (accessed 18 November 2009).

44   Poem printed in Luton Girls' High School magazine (see school history, p. 162).

45   Ministry of Education 1945: para. 5.

46   Ministry of Education 1945: para. 2.

47   Richmond, 1945: 143; see also Dent, 1944a : ch. IV.

48   For this quote and for discussion of the merits and demerits of the 1944 Act, see Simon, 1986. Among those who applauded the Act at the time were Dent, 1944b: 3; and Barnard, 1968 [1947]: 296.

49   Board of Education, 1943b: 19.

50   Dent, 1949b: 57.

51   Ministry of Education, 1946 (reprinted 1959).

52   Board of Education, 1943c: para. 1 (p. 5).

53   Board of Education, 1943c: para. 5 (p. 6).

Chapter9

Closing points

...and I would say to the coming generation – the boys and girls of to-day, the men and women of to-morrow – train yourselves in body, mind and spirit so as to be ready for whatever part you may be called upon to play, and for the tasks which await you as citizens of the Empire when the war is over...Make yourselves ready...to give and to offer your very best.

(His Majesty the King, Christmas Day, 1941)[1]

This book has addressed a relatively neglected topic in the history of the Second World War on the home front and in the history of English childhood. We have forefronted children's contributions to the war effort. We became interested in this topic because it focuses on children as agents, who make a difference to social welfare, in contrast to the dominant narratives which describe evacuation and bombing and the consequent traumas suffered by children. While these descriptions often portray children as victims and as powerless in the face of social policies and practices implemented by adults who gave scant consideration to the adverse impacts of war on children, we have aimed to present another set of accounts of how childhoods were lived and experienced at the time. In so doing, we do not deny the hard times of childhood – which indeed evidence from our interviews and school histories describes – but we have aimed to complement the dominant narratives, and thereby to help fill out a more rounded account of childhood at the time.

Children as earners or learners in the war years – a summary

If children could at the time be conceptualised as, among other things, agents, then that raises the question of what social conditions were in place at the time that allowed for such conceptualisation. In Chapters 2 and 3 we examined the social conditions in which children experienced childhood in the years leading up to the war, and through which childhoods were constructed. One outstanding factor in the documents we have consulted, and especially in those written at the time, is social class as a major force that constructed childhoods. The vast majority of English children did socially useful work as soon as they could and were destined to be workers in the public domain (boys and girls) and the private domain (girls). For many adult commentators, it followed that their schooling should do no more than prepare them, for a few short years, for such work. Many onlookers found it difficult to contemplate the idea that perhaps high intelligence was not confined to the upper classes. A circular argument, though generally implicit rather than expressed, proposed that people rose to the top or sank to the bottom of society because they varied in intelligence. Challenges to that argument formed part of the movement to extend schooling and to promote a curriculum that offered better education to the mass of the people. Cross-cutting social class were gendered conceptions of girls and boys. A deterministic argument consigned girls' futures to housewifery and child-rearing, though servants would take on some of the tasks in wealthy households. So schooling should include training for girls' futures, even if that might mean that they took school matriculation exams a year after boys. Boys would grow up to be breadwinners, supporting wife and family, and so the paucity of education and training available for boys was deplored.

The long slow march towards confirming working-class children principally as learners, through a series of education acts, was certainly not over by 1939. Most children as contributors to the domestic economy were mainly earners, from as young as they could earn, and most were also unpaid workers at home. Work therefore was an accepted part of childhood and children contributed to the division of labour. School had not been established as the proper place for the generality of under-18s; rather, schooling was interspersed with work, and schooling itself was a short preparation for life. However, we have also drawn attention to ways in which working-class children were schooled in loyalty to Christianity, to

King and to Country, through school assemblies, celebrations and recognition of key dates (e.g. Armistice). The mass of children were understood and encouraged to understand themselves as part of the Christian nation – to be called upon to help, when the democratic, Christian way of life was threatened.

We have argued that the conceptualisation of most English children as working class – that is, those who attended elementary schools – up to the war years may have facilitated adult encouragement to those children to participate in the war effort. Their schooling was a relatively minor matter, fitting them for their future working lives. So it was perhaps not a great shift for adults to accept that war-work should take up some of their school time. But it seems that other longstanding traditions, the appeal to patriotism and to Christianity in all (but a few) schools, together with similar traditions in youth groups, allowed for ready acceptance by adults and children alike that these children could be called upon to serve their country, through a wide range of activities.[2] If that meant academic standards suffered, then that price had to be paid, however unwilling some adults (and some students, perhaps) were.

For the minority who attended private and grammar schools, school, while also providing education appropriate for university entrance, was – overtly – preparation for 'service'. School prepared young men (and a few young women) to serve God, King and Empire, through work in leadership jobs. Girls were to carry forward the morale of the nation as wives and mothers. Probably paid work and domestic work featured less in the lives of these children, since many families would have had servants, children had homework, and boarding school children were away from home for most of the year.

We noted early on that we were interested in why children were asked to help during the war. The indoctrination children of all kinds received at school (as noted above) provides one clue. But viewed in the context of how most childhoods were lived – children as earners – and how they were perceived, it seems unsurprising that children were, from the outset of war, urged to do their bit. Shortages of manpower, shortages of goods and the need for money from private sources all provided incentives for government to encourage children, as well as adults, to do what they could. Yet there were many voices during the war years expressing reservations at the notion and practice of children as war-workers. Some argued that children should not deprive adult workers of their jobs (especially in agriculture); others that school work suffered where war-work took precedence; still others that some kinds of war-work might damage children's chances of healthy growth. But commentators also noted: (1) that there were not enough adults available to do all the jobs; (2) that in time of crisis school work should rightly take second place; (3) that most of the work was not damaging to health; and (4) that children enjoyed and valued participation. Furthermore, we noted that children themselves had views on these matters; voices that speak from the past, and voices of those telling us their memories. Our quotations indicate that children held a range of views and had varying experiences during the war. Some record exhilaration and exhaustion in equal measure; some enjoyed learning new skills, and collaborating with adults; others were bored or irritated by adult expectations that they would dig for victory or line up on a parade ground; some felt they had to bear heavy loads. But an important theme running through these accounts is that the work was there to be done, and everyone should do what they could. Of course we are not arguing that all children worked all the time, or that their contributions were as great as those of adults: only that they were urged to help, and that many did.

In Chapters 5, 6, 7 and 8 we described and exemplified a wide range of work carried out by children during the war. It is perhaps time to return to consideration of what we mean by 'work'. As we noted in Chapter 1 (page 10), we include under 'work' socially useful activities, and it is a major aim in our sociological approach to childhood to consider how far it is appropriate to argue that children did indeed carry out socially useful activities during the war. Though it can be argued that nowadays children's main contribution is through their school work, we think it is fair to suggest that during the war years many children's work comprised a wide range of useful activities. Thus, at home they worked unpaid in family enterprises, including both domestic work and household businesses. Out of the home, in their neighbourhoods, many engaged in activities that promoted social welfare; by the age of 12 or 14 most also did paid work. At school, both traditional learning and more 'progressive' active learning were taking place and these were balanced by tasks specifically related to winning the war: food production, salvage, fire watching and substituting for adults called up to the services.

In the chapters detailing what children contributed to the war effort, we have noted interconnections between 'work' and 'education'. The war years encouraged people to reconsider these connections. Children learned not only at school, but also in their daily lives and while helping to win the war. Indeed it can be said that 'work' includes 'education', for the socially useful activities people do, in whatever setting, include the tasks of formal learning. Furthermore, 'education' includes 'work', for people learn, whether at a school desk or while out collecting salvage or while collaborating with their teachers on the allotment: for example, children who worked in the fields learned that agriculture was an important and complex occupation. However, the proposals in the inter-war years to increase the time all children spent in school, and in education (for instance in 'continuation classes'), served to sharpen distinctions between 'education' and 'work' and to emphasise the importance of what takes place in school over the learning that takes place in all the transactions and interrelations of daily life.

The visibility of young people during the war

One of the main points to emerge from our accounts of children's work during the war is the sheer visibility of children. There are at least two features of this. Firstly, children simply were out and about, doing useful tasks in the local area, as well as attending school and living in domestic environments. Furthermore, in many cases they were working alongside adults, for instance working in the fields and gardens, helping in canteens, rescuing people trapped in air raids, collecting money for the many good causes and for the annual 'Weeks' (such as War Weapons Week). Secondly, our quotations from adults show that they understood children as rightfully visible – as rightfully active in the locality, making their contribution. As some quotations indicate, some adults expressed the view that rather than protect children from the large events taking place, they should be encouraged to know not only about the progress of the war, but about the very hard times many people were going through. This perception included the idea, well expressed in several quotes, that it was better for children to be part of the war effort than protected from it, and that if that meant they had to endure more than usual amounts of hard work, then that was better than letting them feel there was nothing they could do to help (pages 167–8 and 188–9). This visibility is in sharp contrast to children's status today – shut inside homes and schools.

The place of work in children's lives today

As we noted in Chapter 1, the history of childhood in 'Western' industrialised societies is the history of the movement of childhood from production to preparation. Where formerly children participated directly in the division of labour, as workers in homes, fields and factories, they were gradually removed from such participatory work and sited in schools. While their activities there can be defined as work, it is common for commentators nowadays – including government agents – to see school as preparation. And as we have also noted (page 11), while masses of official information is collected about children as schoolchildren, there is virtually none on children's other work, even though children do continue to work in the spaces allowed them outside school. This gap in official data collection is indicative of how officials understand what matters about childhood.

Studies of children's paid employment in developed countries across the twentieth century indicate that substantial proportions of children worked in tandem with attending school, and that many children still do.[3] Studies show that children value work for a range of reasons (Morrow, 1994; Mizen et al., 2001). It brings in money for their own use and for indirectly contributing to the household budget. It gives experience of the working world – which differs from the world of school. It gives young people a sense that they can do something worthwhile, that they can contribute to social welfare. In countries where schooling is not free, children work partly to raise the money for fees, uniforms, books and food (e.g.

Invernizzi, 2001). These are important points, and they provide messages for schools and for schooling. Participation, contribution and engagement with the world outside home and school — these are values we think should be promoted in schools too. There are both ethical and practical reasons for such promotion. It is right that children's wish to participate be respected, and only if their participation rights are respected are they likely to be willing to derive benefit from the education that schools offer.

As we noted above, under-13s do not have the right to work in paid employment in the UK; older children do, under a complex of laws dating back to the 1930s (Cunningham, 1999; Leonard, 1999). But there is an international consensus that 'education' — which tends to mean 'schooling' — should take priority in the lives of children. Thus, the UN Convention on the Rights of the Child (UNCRC) is clear that children have the right to be 'protected from economic exploitation and from performing any work that its likely to be hazardous or to interfere with the child's education, or to be harmful to the child's health or physical, mental, spiritual, moral or social development' (UN, 1989: Article 32). It is not clear how far this statement reflects a view that, in principle, all 'work' is inappropriate for children, but that, in practice, given the worldwide engagement of children in work, child work has to be accepted until such time as nations have lifted their populations out of poverty. However, it seems that the thinking behind Article 32 is that work does not include education, and that education takes place in school.

One way to respect children's rights, both as workers and learners, would be to bring politics into schools, in order to make it clear to children that their views on political questions matter and that adults respect their views. A proposal which seems to be gaining consensus is that the voting age should be reduced to 16; this was set out in Labour and Liberal Democrat election manifestos in 2010. It would send the clear message that children at school have the right to engage with politics, and it would, perhaps more importantly, allow for fundamental questions to permeate politics, questions such as what childhood should consist of, what education consists of and what schools are for. Children's own views on the schools that they would like to see and on appropriate uses of their time – at school and elsewhere – might at last be represented in Parliament.[4]

Schools today

Commentators' visions of school and education in the 1920s and onwards have to some extent been realised; however, writing in summer 2010, we have yet to see what the coalition government will do in response to the initiatives of the Labour government (1997–2010), which gave 'education' priority. It provided for free schooling to age 18. Children have been exhorted to stay at school, and moves are in train to make their participation in education and/ or training compulsory; thus, the Education and Skills Act 2008 proposes that the school-leaving age will be raised to 18, from 2013. There are many more places for pre-school children, though most of the expansion since 1997 has been in the private sector and is of varying (and often low) quality. It is also expensive for parents (for a review, see Mayall, 2007). Apprenticeships are being revived:[5] in 1997–8 there were 60,000 apprenticeships; in 2003–4 there were 193,600 and in 2008–9 there were 239,000; all training costs are government-funded for 16–18 year olds. And while in 2000 only 25 per cent completed their apprenticeships, that figure rose to 71 per cent in 2009.[6] Other kinds of vocational training are being developed – for instance, schemes led by schools and colleges in collaboration with individual businesses.[7] Furthermore, the welfare functions of schooling have been extended, so that breakfast clubs and after-school clubs provide care, food and entertainment for children – though at a price, so some parents who want this help cannot afford it. In these many ways, the inter-war vision of keeping children under the umbrella of education has to some extent been realised.

However, there is more than one view of these moves. They may be greeted with enthusiasm: the vision of childhood as a period of learning is being implemented, and if some children do not seem to wish to take advantage of these opportunities, then policies are also providing a range of routes whereby they may learn skills for their future, socially useful, adult lives. Clearly there has been a huge widening of educational opportunity for children, with more years of free education on offer, with hugely increased resources (such as science blocks and drama studios), and with more solid ladders onwards and upwards to training and to further and higher education. However, less enthusiastic views are also in evidence. Social control over young people can be regarded as increasing and undesirable (James and James, 2001; Hendrick, 2008, 2010); it contravenes their rights to self-determination. Furthermore, emphasis on childhood as learning, as preparation, devalues the active participation of children in other socially useful activities: their unpaid and paid work in households and families, and their work outside the home. Children's work, it can be argued, is thereby rendered invisible, of little importance and of low status.

The increasing time spent by children in schools and the notion that school is what matters most in the lives of children have been referred to as the 'scholarisation' of childhood, whereby learning is prioritised over acting, and all children are to be turned out from a common mould. It can be argued that over the last 60 years, schools have increasingly been conceptualised as the principal places where education takes place (Whitney, 1999). Yet it has been demonstrated that children learn many important, indeed critical, things outside school. Thus they learn basic morality at home, in interactions with parents, brothers and sisters and friends (Dunn, 1988). In daily lives around the neighbourhood, they learn about social relations more generally, and it is through their conversations with caregivers that they learn to speak, to discuss, to reflect (Tizard and Hughes, 1984). A large-scale study of young children at home and at pre-school found that good-quality home environments promoted children's intellectual and social development (Sylva *et al.*, 2003, 2004). Through their engagement with new technologies, children learn how to use them, and, in particular, media literacy is an essential tool for much paid work nowadays (Buckingham, 2005; Buckingham *et al.*, 2005).[8]

One most important change has not taken place. In the 1930s and 1940s some commentators wished to see the private schools either abolished or thrown open to everyone on merit.

For instance, in the inter-war years the headteacher of Rendcomb College (a school for paying and non-paying children) said he looked forward to the day when all boys and girls would go to the same secondary schools (Simpson, 1936: 79). It is a measure of the social power of private school products that they have blocked any attempt to reduce or abolish their hold on social institutions. In practice, much the same small proportion of children now as then (about 6 per cent) go to private schools,[9] but they continue to consolidate and perpetuate the class system in England, through the privileges conferred by Oxbridge and through their subsequent access to careers in influential arenas.

However, while the power of the private school to structure social institutions and policies continues to hinder moves towards equality of opportunity, we can point to other messages that continue to work their way through our education system. For instance, the wartime proposal that working-class adults be offered residential courses, on the lines of the Danish Folk High School (Livingstone, 1941), finds resonance in the much wider opportunities nowadays for people to return to education, at colleges as well as universities. People who have reared children, who have worked in a range of careers and jobs, are able to go back and pick up on their education, bringing with them knowledge and experience which can feed into their studies.

Childhood and child–adult relations

These general points about children and the war effort lead on to a reconsideration of the character of childhood in the first half of the twentieth century and the part played by ideas about child–adult relations in shaping childhood. We point here to some key themes. Our interviewees, like those in other studies, emphasise that children occupied clearly delineated subordinate positions in relation to adults. Children had to do what they were told, without question; parents, teachers and employers asserted their authority. Yet in some respects children's lives were closer to those of adults than they are nowadays, since many of them worked alongside adults. And adult control was counterbalanced by children's greater physical freedom in those days:

they were able to escape from adult control into spaces and times of their own choosing. Roaming the streets and countryside was a valued component of childhood, as people reminiscing relate. Young workers could pay for entertainment in pubs and dance halls. But while children had greater physical freedom, they had less psychological freedom. Many adults prevented their knowledge about important family matters, including knowledge about sex. For some children, the war changed aspects of these child–adult relations; children endured bombing and shortages, worked hard and enjoyed what pleasures could be found, in company with adults. Both the air raid shelter and the cinema could be joint experiences. Some children also entered the worlds of the war that adults were fighting, through engaging in war-work such as fire-fighting, through hearing stories about the fate of relatives and through following the course of the war. In some accounts, children's relations with their teachers became closer, as teachers had to look after evacuated children, had to provide social services in schools for children, and worked alongside them in school gardens and harvest camps (Cunningham and Gardner, 1999).

Secondly, we note the story of psychological and welfarist thinking and the varying influences on childhoods of these ideas which developed especially in the inter-war years. The notion that all children went through a series of developmental stages, the notion that children were active learners, and the notion, promoted by women's groups, in the name of national efficiency, through the eugenics movement and the labour movement, that the state bore some responsibility for the health and education of all children – these were ideas challenging to the status quo. For if there was commonality between children, if all children required – or could benefit from – similar educational and health environments, then the current education and health systems were totally inadequate. They were divisive, unfair and based on inadequate theory (or on no theory except adherence to social-class distinctions). As we have described, however, social forces proved stronger than theory; and change in the education system was slow to happen and piecemeal. The radical change in health services took place after the war. The childhoods of the wealthy may have been affected by new psychological theory – in homes and nursery schools – but the childhoods of the vast majority were barely touched. Yet it seems that some filtering down of new ideas did take place in some schools, and schools also responded to the development of secondary elementary schooling for 11–14s by providing more appropriate curricula; wartime conditions helped to raise the profile of life-related activities; and government took increasing responsibility for feeding and clothing the children and, indeed, the whole population.

Thirdly, debates continued throughout the period on how adults should deal with young people. From the standpoint of middle-class adult commentators, educated in private schools and grammar schools, most young people aged 14–18 or 20 constituted – or threatened to constitute – a social problem. They were liable to hang about in pubs and at street corners, to engage in antisocial practices, even crime, to amuse themselves with the crudest kinds of entertainments – dancing, magazines, music halls, cinema. Girls were especially at risk of moral degradation. Commentators asked how young people could be taught middle-class morality and trained in responsible citizenship.[10] One common vision was that, without going to the expense of state-funded full-time education to 18, somehow or other, young people should come under the umbrella of education. This might be through part-time day release and/or by raising the school-leaving age to 15 (1918 Fisher Act), or through encouraging them to join worthy organisations such as the Scouts. Through whichever means, the argument was that adults had a key function in guiding young people, even in controlling them; in particular, moral guidance was key to rearing well-thinking young people and adults. Preparation for citizenship was a key theme in guidance for young people; an Association for Education in Citizenship, led by Ernest Simon and Eva Hubback (1935), argued that schools should promote children's understanding of their civic responsibilities, both through developing a school ethos with high social ideals and through teaching, especially in history and geography, and also via courses in social studies as well as cross-curricular work. They identified the age-group 14–18 as a key group for this enterprise and endorsed the expansion of educational opportunities for them, both in formal educational establishments and in youth clubs.[11] One proposal was for a year of community service, at, say 18 or 19.[12] As ever, these ideas focused mainly on the mass of young people, viewed through the eyes of the adult minority; commentators did not conceptualise privately educated young people as a social problem, and significantly, they were more firmly under adult supervision in schools which promoted an ethos of service to the society.

We suggest that, during the war years, the valuation of childhood by adults changed, at least for the duration. We contend that children were understood to constitute a population group on whom it was legitimate to draw in times of national crisis brought about by the war. While children had to do what adults said, and submit to adult control, children could be expected to participate; the concept of service – people's duty to take part – was invoked to reinforce demands on children. Participation expectations were built, perhaps, on a tougher vision of childhood than the ones people hold today, as well as on the exigencies of war conditions. Towards the end of the war, we find adult commentators expressing not only gratitude for children's contributions, but surprise that they, especially teenagers, had responded so fully to the call to help. Children themselves contributed to changes in adult understandings of childhood; through demonstrating their willingness to help out, children and young people showed that they were not (all) disaffected, uncommitted and superficial people. Both by joining youth groups and pre-military organisations, by making munitions, by working in agriculture and by the less formally organised activities of salvage collecting, gardening and engaging in saving schemes, under-18s showed that they could be taken seriously as members of the community. In some cases, it can be asserted that children stepped outside the normal parameters of childhood; for while childhood then (as now) could be, at least in part, conceptualised as preparation, some children engaged directly in war-work: rescuing people from bombed houses, repairing damaged school premises, patrolling school premises, reading letters to the wounded, even capturing enemy soldiers. However, we also have to reiterate that some adults valued shielding children from knowledge and from war-related stress, while others thought it important to keep them informed.

Children, parents and the state

One important set of changes that has been taking place over the last century is in the relative responsibilities of the state and parents for childhood. Across the domains of education, health and welfare, the state has taken on increased responsibilities. This process accelerated in the 1930s and 1940s. Over the subsequent 60 years, increased state responsibility was shown in raising the school-leaving age to 16 and then to 18, increasing numbers of further and higher education places, and intervening directly in the work of schools by putting in place a national curriculum and testing. The health of children from birth to 18 has come under the National Health Service since its inception in 1948, while there has been increased attention to welfare through, for instance, school dinners (with a blip in the 1980s when standards were abandoned in favour of the market); family allowances and tax credits have provided financial help to parents. All this means that parents have more help with raising children but it also means that they have less choice in *how* they raise their children; for, through interventions by health, welfare and education workers, parents are regarded as responsible for complying with state agendas. Furthermore, the existence of state help for parents leaves the door wide open to blame those who are perceived as doing poorly in child-rearing.

The advance of state intervention in the lives of children and their families has been in some respects universalist, and writings contemporary with the war years tend to point to wartime as both requiring universalism and as teaching people to value the benefits of universalism (e.g. Titmuss, 1976). However, universalism has never gained full acceptance and continues to be debated; targeted benefits continue, together with judgements about poorer people, based on assumptions about relative moral worth. Thereby, the UK remains at the more 'neo-liberal' end of welfare states, in contrast to, for instance, the social-democratic Nordic states (Pringle, 1998) and looks likely to become more so under the 2010 coalition government.

The social status of children in present-day England is many-faceted. 'Childhood as learning' has expanded to include all children, and it is longer now than during the war. Children continue to be understood as inhabiting a preparatory state, where they learn what is needed for adulthood. It is notable that the UK has been very unwilling to recognise children's agency, including their moral agency, within the education system (e.g. Jeffs, 2002). Yet psychological theory firmly espouses children as active learners – notably through Piaget and later (once his work was translated) through Vygotsky. The ideas that children learn through exploring and that the less knowledgeable will learn through interaction with the more knowledgeable are promoted through teacher training. These theories, which filtered into classrooms in the second half of the twentieth century, received a setback under the 1988 Education Act (National Curriculum and testing) and are again up for discussion under the Coalition Government. Nursery schools have always implemented active exploratory learning, but downward pressure from the National Curriculum threatens this value. Children's learning through new technologies has acquired new characteristics, such as individual access to wide ranges of knowledge and fun. Children's technical competence is displayed in their engagement with new technologies, and it is possible that this competence may help to modify ideas about childhood capacities more generally and how, accordingly, child–adult relations might be better envisaged.

Childhood in England nowadays has another important set of characteristics. Whereas some children in the war years engaged during their war-work in risky and downright dangerous activities, as some of those looking back remarked, children now are presented as vulnerable, and so, in a climate imbued with health and safety considerations, adults are ascribed increased responsibilities for protecting and providing for children. 'Health and safety' has become a byword for restricting children's activities. It is probable that if evacuation were contemplated today, for whatever reason, appeal would immediately be made to the inevitable damage to be caused to children's psychological welfare. Of course, psychological concerns were voiced in 1939 and studies were immediately undertaken to consider damage, but on the other hand, officials thought parents would be willing to send their children away, and so they closed the schools and school medical services in evacuation areas, since such services would not be needed. The huge growth of concern about child abuse, fuelled by the media, which has swept the country since the 1980s and has led to social service concentration on this one problem, is another instance of the conceptualisation of childhood as a vulnerable period, and, in its wake, has led to the development of increased responsibility for the state – to keep children safe.

One continuity in adult thinking about childhood is that young people continue to be regarded as a social problem, or as threatening to become a social problem. The focus has changed, though. Children who 'truant' from school, who do not conform to social norms handed down by their betters, who form gangs and commit crimes: these are well-worn themes, which seem part of English culture over centuries (Pearson, 1983). Nowadays, children as social problems have, however, a slightly different or new character; the bad child is one who does not conform to the kinds of childhood laid out through the education system and the moral order encoded there. An example was provided in 2003 by children who walked out of school to take part in anti-Iraq war marches; they were described by some onlookers as 'truants' for they were stepping out of the proper pre-political arena of childhood (e.g. Weller, 2007: 58).[13]

Children as citizens

As we have indicated (Chapters 5, 6, 7 and 8), children and young people during the war years were regarded as preparing for citizenship. Those attending state elementary schools were taught loyalty to God, King and Country. The ethos of private and grammar schools valued preparation for service, and a central goal of organisations such as the Scouts and the Guides was inculcating young people with a sense of responsibility towards their communities, not as full citizens, but as people learning to be citizens. At the present day, 'education for citizenship' in schools follows these traditions, and regards children as learners, not as citizens.

This viewpoint found support from Lea Shamgar-Handelman (1994: 264) who strongly argued that childhood and children will always be subservient to adulthood and adults. She asked, can it be any other way? And she replied: 'As long as a child is defined as not (yet) an adult, and being so defined is therefore excluded from the right and responsibility of full social participation, I think the answer to this question has to be negative.' Her argument rests on the societal assumption that the family is the social unit for bearing and rearing children, that there is an ongoing process about the working contract between the state and the family for relative responsibilities for children, and that children are excluded from controlling their own lives and engaging in productive work. In other words, children can be understood as used by parents and by the state for their own respective purposes.

This argument is discussed by the sociologist Paul Close (2009), who points out that children are denied full citizenship rights. Thus, under-13s do not have the right to do paid work; on the contrary, they are required to engage in activities (schooling) which are not regarded by adults as productive labour. He argues that children's dependency on adults is constructed in the UNCRC as natural (as indeed the Preamble to the UNCRC states), and that the exclusion (in adults' constructions) of children from productive labour is combined with these dependencies to constitute children as non-citizens, under the control of adults.

These arguments are countered by another view, which is that the ratification of the UNCRC has changed the social status of childhood. Whereas the earlier Declaration of Children's Rights (1959) was not legally binding, ratification of the UNCRC, carried out by the UK in 1991, carries with it a commitment to ensure that the articles of the UNCRC are inserted into national law. Osler and Starkey (2005: ch. 3) argue that this commitment marks a major step forward in children's social position. In particular, they state that while children have special claims on adults for protection and provision, the UNCRC emphasis on children's participation rights is critical. Participation rights enable children to take part in decisions affecting their own lives and their futures; so, they argue, children are no longer to be perceived as *objects* of protection and provision, but should be understood as *subjects*, bearers of human rights like adults. While, therefore, progress may be slow, because adults will resist change, ratification of the UNCRC provides a framework for change.[14]

Further interesting discussions on citizenship are taking place within feminist traditions that challenge male assumptions. Feminists propose replacing sharp distinctions between being and not being a citizen – included or excluded – with more inclusive, multi-layered concepts which pay attention to the variations between groups of people in their power to participate and at what levels – including both the 'public' and 'private' domains (Lister, 2007). While many concepts of citizenship include notions of duty – often understood as meaning duty to contribute economically to society – Lister argues that less powerful people (among whom many are women) can be understood as citizens by virtue of their rights. Further, she extends the activities of citizens into the 'private domain', arguing that women's care work can constitute their contribution as citizens to social welfare. We would add that, as discussed elsewhere (Mayall, 2002: ch. 6), children too carry out caring or 'people work' and thus may lay claim, in this argument, to citizenship.[15] In an earlier paper, Lister and colleagues (2003) draw on their study of young people's views on citizenship. They found that young people espoused the idea (promoted by New Labour) that as citizens they had social responsibilities, so some stressed social participation in the community, but most prominent in their comments was a less active notion: that a citizen is a member of the community or nation. Susie Weller carried out a study of teenagers' citizen-like activities in one area of England, and concludes that their citizenship can be expressed through a range of activities, from more conventional community or political participation to 'micro-participation' – such as reshaping local spaces to make them more user-friendly for teenagers and other young people (Weller, 2007: 130–1). This argument is reminiscent of the wartime proposal to engage young people with a year of community work. Similarly we argue that younger children can and do contribute within their own homes and families, as well as within schools and in neighbourhoods, to constructing and maintaining physical and social spaces for interaction (Mayall, 2002: ch. 6).

The sociology of childhood

We hope we have demonstrated in this book that the sociology of childhood is a useful tool for understanding childhoods and child–adult relations. A first point is that the special case of childhood is that it is practised by people who are under the control of the other major social group – adults – and this control (which includes care and responsibility) allows for adults to shape and direct childhood and the children who inhabit childhood. Thus, the character of child–adult relations is crucial for the character of childhood itself. What seems to have happened during the Second World War is that prevalent concepts of children as people who worked, or, in the case of the privileged minority, as people being trained for leadership, formed a basis for enlisting children in the war effort. This meant that for the duration schooling might have to coexist with children's contributions, and some teachers reflected on this point, noting whether or not academic achievement did suffer. Children themselves varied in how much they did and they had varying views on war-work. But one important theme in their comments is that war-work altered child–adult relations. There were several components of this change: teachers had to work as welfare officers, caring for children separated from their families; and teachers and children worked together on projects, so child–adult relations were in some cases experienced as more equal than before. Teachers could and did bring the world into the classroom and take the children out of the classroom, to engage with real-life topics and events. These included, for instance, following the progress of the war, learning about the histories and cultures of the allied countries, learning gardening techniques and turning mathematics lessons into practical calculations about the costs and benefits of running an allotment.

A second point that we learn via sociology (and also from current psychology) is the relevance of focusing on children as social agents. Sociology draws attention to how varying social groups contribute to the division of labour in society. The many examples we give point to children as contributors. Probably there is a gap here between adults' understanding of this work then and now. It was then clear that children could make active contributions, through housework, food preparation, running errands, acting as messengers or childcare. In many families they were required not just to help but to take responsibility for some tasks. Nowadays, because we adults are less used to seeing children as contributors, we look back with surprise at some of the things children were asked to do, or volunteered to do. Some of these tasks involved hard work, dangerous work and work that brought children very close to the harsh events of the war. We have to set aside our own preconceptions in order to consider how far it was the demands of war on the home front, and how far these fitted with current ideas about childhood, which allowed children to be asked to participate in these ways.

But what does come down to us from the study of wartime is a third point: the importance of recognising the possible contributions of all social groups, including children, to promoting social welfare. Children can be understood as contributing to the division of labour, doing their bit, working for victory. Nowadays, we have made it hard for children to help promote welfare, and still harder for adults to recognise what children do. But there is some scope in the character and functions of schools. It is widely recognised that schools are an important social resource; in some versions they are the hub of the community; in others they are urged to make contact with the community; children themselves say they want schools to engage with the real world (Alexander, 2010: ch. 5). Schoolchildren do carry out various kinds of community work – for example, working in residential homes for older people or sitting on committees to consider neighbourhood regeneration. Within schools, the environmental movement has led to children engaging with the large-scale issues, as well as with the more local activities of gardening and recycling, or working with teachers to improve the school environment. There is scope for much closer interactions between children, their schools and local people and groups.

But the demands made on children to follow curricula laid down centrally and to pass tests and exams has undoubtedly meant that what goes on in schools is narrow, compared to what it could be. Crucially, we should like to see fuller recognition of children's rights to engage with life beyond the school gates. We also agree with those who say that hours spent in institutions are too long, if they mean that children cannot carry out the learning and the work that take place outside school. Furthermore, children's rights to engage with the culture and arts of their society could be respected much more fully than at present – both at school and in their free time (Mayall, 2007). And, finally, children's rights to leisure and social activities could move higher up adults' agenda.

Further studies

As we have suggested at various points, our study has made only a start in tackling a large field. We know that there is much more to be done. Our main priority was to make available the research we did do. We make a few suggestions here for research that would improve understanding of childhoods in the years up to, through and immediately after the Second World War.

There is scope for complementing the many studies of women's work during wartime with study of young people's work (we have found little information on this).

Our look across England could be complemented with a case study of children's contributions to the war effort in one area, or in two (perhaps rural and city) – to consider possible differences. This could provide satisfying information on the range of agencies involved, and in the particular local social conditions that prevailed and structured children's activities.

Further research could give detailed consideration to the work of teachers who were not evacuated, and who accompanied children to harvest camps, or facilitated children's contributions in other ways. Of particular interest here are the relationships between children and teachers.

There is scope for investigating children's experiences of youth organisations in the war years; we have touched on only a few and given only a flavour of the huge amount of material in archives.

Much work remains to be done on the BBC's work with and for children during the war years, and on the widening remits the staff took on. BBC links with academia and the development of programmes for older children, hosted by professors (such as Mannheim) remain to be explored.

A detailed study of propaganda and notably Ministry of Information efforts to target specifically children would also be useful.

Concluding remarks

Looking back on our work, we suggest we are presenting a revised account of childhoods in the Second World War. It is complementary to the dominant one – the powerful narrative of evacuation which dominates people's thinking about English childhood at that time. In its view of children as subjects rather than objects, our account lays claim to difference from the evacuation studies. One theme we have tried to pursue is variation in childhoods – the experiences of evacuated and non-evacuated children in doing their bit, in cities and villages, in schools and out of schools. We have drawn attention to the contributions of younger children in elementary schools, to school leavers out at work and to children in grammar and private schools. And we have aimed to give due attention to those who did a lot and those who did very little, as well as to their interpretation of their wartime experiences.

Thinking about English childhoods nowadays, we wonder whether it is possible today to think of children as a reserve army of labour, who could contribute to social welfare. Would they be called on in times of crisis? In the protectionist climate we adults have constructed, probably not. But over the last 20 years the rights of children to participate have moved slightly higher up English agendas, and offering children opportunities to help might be acceptable to at least some adults. Indeed, there are currently moves to engage young people with community service. Whether or not English society is in crisis, we should like to see children being offered the chance to make a difference and being given something serious to do. An important part of this is being offered opportunities to think that they are a part of the community locally, nationally and internationally (Holdsworth, 2005). We say, 'offering the chance' and 'being given something serious to do' because it is adults who control children and childhood, so it is up to adults to enable children's participation. But not altogether: we also pay tribute here to the work that children themselves instigate nowadays, as in the case of their participation in the anti-Iraq war marches. Recent studies, notably in the USA, have focused on the work that immigrant children do as a matter of course, in helping their parents settle in the new country, in acting as interpreters for their parents and in caring for family members.[16] A UK example of native children working to help immigrant children is given in a recent study – where classes of children campaigned, with their teacher, to prevent the forcible detention and removal from the UK of immigrant children who had become settled at school and made friendships there (Pinson *et al.*, 2010: ch. 10).

We endorse the idea that children can combine school activity with some socially useful work; this could include community development work. Some of the modest schemes currently being enacted by schools could be developed; we might move to an agreement that, say, a day or half-a-day a week might be given over to a range of activities that linked children into local, national and international work. A recent proposal is that 30 per cent of primary school weekly teaching hours should be given to a 'community curriculum': to community-related work, to projects worked up with local people, groups and agencies.[17] The notion of the school as hub of the community underpins this proposal. These activities would be an important means of honouring important articles in the UNCRC. Thus children should (1) be offered opportunities to express their views and have them taken fully into consideration (Article 12); (2) have opportunities to access information from a range of national and international sources, especially those aimed at the promotion of their social, spiritual and moral well-being and physical and mental health (Article 17); (3) be offered opportunities to participate in the 'cultural and artistic life' of their communities and societies (Article 31); and (4) be given full information about their rights (Article 42). We envisage a mixture (to be offered as choices to children) of: (1) community work; (2) expeditions to take part in the cultural and artistic life of the society, as well as taking part in artistic and cultural events at school; (3) time to engage with information available through internet connections; and (4) engagement with a wide range of sports facilities beyond the school gate.

Notes

1   Quoted in Board of Education, 1942: frontispiece. © Crown copyright.

2   The historian of Charterhouse school notes (p. 22) that Baden-Powell, founder of the Scouts, was a student at the school, and used its school motto as a basis for the scouting movement's motto: *Deo Dante Dedi* (By serving I serve God).

3   Cunningham, 1999; Leonard, 1999; Mizen *et al.*, 2001; Howieson *et al.*, 2006 for Scotland.

4   An enquiry among schoolchildren in 2001 about the characteristics of the school they would like is described by Burke and Grosvenor, 2003. It replicates the study carried out in 1967 by Edward Blishen (1969).

5   Support for apprenticeships was set out in the election manifestos of the Conservatives, Labour and Liberal Democrats in 2010.

6   These figures are given in an advertising insert by Mediaplanet in the *Guardian,* 26 March 2010, p. 12.

7   Report on vocational training is given in a paper by Peter Jones in the *Guardian (Education)*, 20 April 2010, p. 8.

8   'Media literacy' refers to the learned ability to engage critically and constructively with a range of modern technologies.

9   Percentage quoted in the *Guardian* (pull-out on education), 27 February 2010.

10 Jephcott (1942) and Macalister Brew (1943) argue that the basic function of youth clubs was to train young people for future citizenship.

11 Simon and Hubback (1935) list a range of educational settings (which at the time reached few young people): technical schools, day continuation schools, evening classes and youth clubs.

12 For discussion, see Macalister Brew, 1943: 275 and Simon and Hubback's 1935 book, *Training for Citizenship.*

13 In 2010–11, school and university students protested against the abolition of the Education Maintenance Allowance and increases in university tuition fees.

14 For a useful summary of progress in implementing the UNCRC in England, see Franklin's (2002) Introduction to *The New Handbook of Children's Rights* (2002a, b). And Michael Freeman's paper in the same book details how far we have to go.

15 See Invernizzi and Williams, 2008.

16 For instance, Levison, 2000; Orellana *et al.*, 2001; Zelizer, 2005.

17 See, for discussion Alexander, 2010, especially chs 12, 14 and 18.

Appendix

This appendix gives some information from studies at the time – two studies of evacuation as it affected children and one study of children's leisure activities. The initial evacuation in September 1939 was of nearly two million people – schoolchildren, mothers and their under-5s and teachers; but over 80% of the mothers and young children, and 43% of the schoolchildren returned home by January 1940 (Padley and Cole, 1940: 42).

The Cambridge Evacuation Survey

The Cambridge Evacuation Survey, edited by S. Isaacs, was published in London by Methuen, in 1941. The fieldwork for this study took place in Cambridge in summer 1940; 304 children from Tottenham and 352 children from Islington were studied, aged 5–16. The study focuses on the organisation of the evacuation from September 1939, the difficulties and chaotic conditions and the adjustments that were made, and voluntary efforts to help; it considered all this from the point of view of mothers and children, and also of foster parents and teachers. It included a survey of children's views (ch. 5, Tottenham children only); they were asked to write about what they liked about Cambridge life and what they missed most in Cambridge (which could have had both negative and positive connotations). Children liked the open spaces in Cambridge, and good relations with foster parents came high on their lists. Notably, boys and girls missed parents, relatives and friends, home activities and life at the London school.

There is a chapter on children's leisure activities, which notes the efforts made by the WVS, the local education authority, foster parents, groups of undergraduates and the children's teachers to arrange activities, and also the work of the Scouts,

Guides and other youth organisations to absorb the evacuated children into local troops. There is no mention of children's participation in the war effort, or of work/employment. No doubt this is partly because these were early days, before children were fully settled into this new environment, but it partly reflects the interests of the researchers (who were psychologists and social workers) – in change, adjustment, difficulties and benefits of the evacuation process. The researchers also canvassed the views of teachers who accompanied the children; about 50 (of 85 – see p. 35) filled in a questionnaire, on changes due to evacuation, difficulties experienced and their comments more generally (ch. 10). Among the many points that teachers made were: children's health had improved and they had become more self-reliant, with broader interests and better relations with their peers, but their concentration and progress at school had declined. There was a closer bond of sympathy and understanding between children and their teachers, since teachers took responsibility for caring for the children (p. 186). Relations with teachers had become more intimate, trustful and confident (p. 9).

London Children in War-time Oxford

London Children in War-time Oxford, produced by the Barnett House Study Group, was published in London by Oxford University Press in 1947. This study built on the Cambridge study; it was carried out with children, teachers and parents, in 1942–3. It aimed to consider how far children were 'successful' in school work, out-of-school activities, relations with other children, and behaviour, and it set measures of these successes against a range of factors. However, for us the interest of the study is in its accounts of children's daily lives and of their perspectives on those lives.

The study's main sample was 319 children evacuated from London (mainly the East End) to the city of Oxford and surrounding areas (a small town and villages). They were aged 11–15 and were randomly chosen from 18 schools they were attending in the reception area. Control groups were included: 120 local children (from the same schools) and 64 London children (living in the same areas from which the sample children had been evacuated). The main sample children had been out of their London homes for two or more years (pp. 2–3).

Of the 319 children, 217 were unaccompanied (no parent lived with or near them) and, of these, 81% lived in foster families, 4% with relatives and 15% in hostels or a camp school. Among the 102 children who were accompanied by a parent, 56% lived in the parental household, 27% lived with a parent in a foster family household and 17% had a parents living nearby their billet (pp. 17–18).

Contact with parents: Of the 217 unaccompanied children, 39% received two or more letters per week and/or one visit or more per month, 48% received one letter per week and/or a visit per quarter and 13% received fewer than this (pp. 38–9).

School life: in contrast to the unsettled experiences of children in evacuation areas, most of these children had 'continuous and adequate' schooling, although the drift of children back and forth from evacuation to reception areas made for some problems. Some specialised practical subjects had to be abandoned because technical equipment was lacking, but nature study, biology, weather observation and geographical excursions took their place. Organised sport and recreation were hard to provide; children evacuated from London missed libraries. However, one advantage of the moves was smaller classes (down from over 40 to, in some cases, under 20). Teachers and children were 'unanimous' in their praise for this: more friendly teacher–child relations and individual attention. Most schools were active in selecting billets and keeping in touch with 'billetors' (pp. 52–3).

Some schools provided **meals**, but demand varied: in one school 58% and in another 22% took meals at school. In one school where the boys grew vegetables in the school garden, almost all boys had school dinner. **Repairs to shoes and clothes** were another issue – and both teachers and boys undertook repairs (p. 54).

Self-government: Several evacuated schools experimented in entrusting children with responsibilities, such as membership of school committees, which discussed, for instance, how to solve problems of evacuation. Children and teachers thought these initiatives increased children's loyalty to school, self-confidence and feelings of security (p. 54).

Paid employment: Of the 319 evacuated children, 30% (42% boys and 16% girls) did some paid work. In contrast only 14% of the local children and 8% of the London children did paid work. This work included: chopping wood, fetching groceries, minding the baby – these are described as 'natural occupations at home' (p. 78). Children also worked at: newspaper deliveries (boys), potato-picking, other farm work, running errands, shop work, canteen work, fetching coal and pumping water.

Of the 88 children who did paid work, 56 specified their earnings: 7 earned 9–15 shillings per week, 18 earned 6–8 shillings, 8 earned 2–5 shillings, 12 earned 1–2 shillings and 11 less than 1 shilling. An example is given of a 16 year old who earned 10s6d; he saved 6 shillings, gave 1 shilling each to his two sisters, and kept 2s.6d for clothes and personal expenses (p. 79).

Leisure activities: Children were asked how they spent their leisure time, apart from paid work (pp. 69–74). Their responses are reproduced in Table A.1. A number of points can be made about this information. Cinema-going was clearly important. Macalister Brew (1943: 246) also notes the prevalence of cinema-going among the older age-group (16–18s) interviewed in 1942 (see below). Presumably 'organised games' were organised to help encourage group membership and healthy physical activity, aims which may have been more important to those helping evacuees than to those who were caring for local children. 'Gardening and farm work' was easier to arrange and more prevalent in Oxford/shire than in London, and easier/more prevalent in the country districts than in the city. 'Reading' was high on the list of leisure activities. Among boys, adventure stories were the most popular; also technical books – which, in practice, means books about aircraft, and among sample group boys, books on history, geography and politics were mentioned – presumably in relation to the war. Girls preferred school stories, the Oxford control group liked fairy tales and adventure stories, and evacuees in Oxford liked 'the classics' (pp. 72–3).

Table A.1 Percentage who mentioned the following as one of their spare-time activities

	Reading	Cinema	Clubs	Gardening/ Pets/Farm work	Constructive	Organised games	n
Evacuated children in Oxford	52	44	30	22	21	18	188
Controls in Oxford	82	33	53	8	43	10	no inf.
Evacuated children in villages	22	21	11	32	15	33	131
Controls in villages	67	60	27	27	45	5	no inf.
All sample children	40	35	23	26	19	24	319
Controls in London	73	39	42	11	20	2	64

Notes: 'Constructive' includes woodwork and metalwork, needlework, cooking. 'Gardening/Pets/Farm work' refers to non-paid activities. If all gardening and farm work, paid or unpaid is included, then 28% of the evacuees took part, compared to 13% of the control group in Oxford/shire (p. 66). Note too, that the complexities of the sample (and perceived need to be reasonably brief?) result in some lack of clarity in the reporting.

The authors of the Oxford study made a number of recommendations for education after the war, drawing on the findings of their survey:

- that the scope of education be widened to include knowledge and experience of the countryside; time spent in rural schools ('country terms'), so that children could learn about the countryside, would be good for all children. (A widening of school environments was suggested in the 1943 White Paper, section 76, building on the experiences of children and teachers in the camp schools established in 1939 (see page 84));
- that boarding schools (valued by parents, teachers and children) could be part of the state system (this was recommended in the 1943 White Paper, section 33);
- that non-academic subjects, such as gardening, games and swimming should be part of all schools curriculum;
- that small classes had been shown to be beneficial;
- that boarding-out with foster parents could be beneficial to some children and could be used during 'country terms';
- that cooperation by schools with parents was beneficial to children's development;
- that delinquent children could best be fostered or placed in hostels, rather than in custodial institutions.

Some points in the above relate to points made in our analysis:

- Relations between teachers and children in reception areas: where a whole school, or whole classes were together in the new environment, teachers said that children found that school was familiar and stable, unlike other aspects of their experience. They turned to teachers for sympathy, and relations with teachers were more intimate; they valued school (pp. 180–1).
- Teachers had to take on new responsibilities: (1) keeping an eye on children, as requested by parents; (2) helping children through difficult events; (3) escorting children home in the blackout; (4) negotiating with foster-families; and (5) accompanying children to social events laid on locally (pp. 180–1).

- Children were thought by teachers to have gained in self-reliance and independence; they have gained wider experiences and in consequence a broader and more mature outlook on life (p. 181).

What do Boys and Girls Read?

What do Boys and Girls Read? (Jenkinson, 1946) first published in 1940, was written by an experienced English teacher who was concerned with the kinds of English literature teaching he observed in the new senior schools. These schools, established during the 1930s in the wake of the Hadow Report of 1926 (see page 76), did not have sixth forms, and the children did not take School Certificate, because they left at 14 or 15. The pedagogical problem he identified was what teachers should do with the freedom from these more scholarly traditional regimes, working with these children who could now be offered a syllabus different from that in the elementary schools. He carried out a survey of children's reading, including a large sample (1,570 boys and 1,330 girls) of children attending the senior schools and those at the more traditional grammar – or 'secondary' – schools. (Unfortunately, he does not give the date of the survey but presumably it was carried out in 1938 or 1939.) He found that both boys and girls read light fiction, though some classics, and also cheap magazines (known as 'bloods'). He also surveyed teachers and, using this information and his experience of teacher training, he found that teachers aimed to teach children to read what they should read – the classics, essays and poetry. Instead, Jenkinson argued that teachers should be *responsive* – they should work with what children did read; so, for instance, since Richmal Crompton's 'Just William' stories were hugely popular among boys, the teacher should work with these (chs 14 and 28).

Jenkinson also explored cinema-going habits among the children, and like the Oxford researchers, he found high rates (by modern-day standards). Among both boys and girls, aged 12–15, 30–39% attended the cinema at least once a week, but fewer of the children attending the secondary (i.e. grammar) schools than of those attending senior schools went more than once a week. In this connection, it is interesting that Macalister Brew, who interviewed 16–18 year olds when compulsory registration and voluntary interviews were introduced in 1942, found that the young people were very knowledgeable about the cinema as a medium – they could talk about the production and technique of film, about sets, cuts and angles, as well as about their favourite film stars (1943: 246). She argues (p. 236) that the cinema – 'the greatest artistic and sociological experiment of the century' – could be harnessed as educational material:

> *If one can once discuss with these young things the sociological significance of the* Dead End Kids *or the implications of* 49th Parallel, *one is surprised at the response and the interest.*

Unlike many commentators at the time, she found (during evening visits to 100 pubs) that the young people were intelligent and interested in discussing issues of the day. They had been badly treated by the education system, and that was why a youth service was so badly needed (rather than raising the school-leaving age).

Thus she supports Jenkinson's argument, that education could and should start from what children know about and are interested in – a view that became more popular in the post-war period.

School histories

Listed here by school name are the school histories to which we refer. We give page references to the histories in the text. We have given the city/town or county where the school is sited. For some schools, we refer to the summaries given in Stranack's (2005) *Schools at War*. Where the school title or book title does not indicate what sort of school it was, we have noted – where possible – whether the school was private, whether it was a grammar or other non-grammar secondary school ('modern', 'senior' or 'central'), and whether it was for boys, for girls or for both. In the case of private schools, we do not always know which age range attended, so have not given age-ranges. 'Elementary', 'parochial' and 'village' schools were state schools for boys and girls aged 5–14. Note too that histories often give their status or type at the time of writing, and this may have changed since the war years. We apologise to any school whose details we have misread.

Amberley Parochial School, Minchinhampton, Gloucestershire
No author (1988) *Amberley Parochial School: The history of a village school, a source book*. Published by Amberley Parochial School Governors.

Badsey Schools, Evesham (elementary)
Spinks, M. (no date) *Badsey Schools*. No publisher.

Barnard Castle School, County Durham (private, boys)
Stranack, 2005: 2.

Barrow Grammar School for Boys, Lancashire
Chadderton, J.F. (no date) *Barrow Grammar School for Boys 1880–1960*. Published by James Milner (Barrow) Ltd.

Barr's Hill House, Coventry (private, girls)
Adams, K. (no date) *The Chronicles of Barr's Hill House*. Published by the school.

Beaudesert School, Leighton Buzzard (elementary)
Aldridge, P. and Kitelley, R.C. (1958)
Beaudesert. Published by the school.

Beaumont College, Windsor (private, boys)
Levi, P. (1961) *Beaumont 1861–1961*.
London: Andre Deutsch.

Bedford Girls Modern School (private)
Broadway, C.M. (1982) *The History of the School: Bedford Girls Modern School 1882–1982*. Published by the school.

Bishop's Stortford College, Hertfordshire (grammar, boys)
Morley, J. and Monk-Jones, N. (1969) *Bishop's Stortford College 1868–1968*. London: J.M. Dent.

Bolton School, Bolton, Lancashire (grammar, boys' and girls' sections)
Brown and Foskitt (1976) *The History of Bolton School*. Published by the school.

Boughton Monchelsea School, Kent (elementary)
Tye, D.F. (ed.) (1976) *Boughton Monchelsea School*. Published by the school.

Bruton School for Girls, Somerset (private)
Stranack 2005: 8.

Charterhouse, Godalming, Surrey (private, boys)
Holden, W.H. (1950) *The Charterhouse We Knew*.
London: British Technical and General Press.

Cheltenham College (private, boys)
Pearce, T. (1991) *Then and Now: Cheltenham*.
Published by the Cheltonian Society.

Coatham Road School, Redcar, Yorkshire (grammar, boys)
Elliott, H. (1983) *Sir William Turner and his School*.
Published by Old Coathamians Association, Redcar.

Earl's Colne Grammar School, Essex (boys)
Merson, A.D. (1976) *Earl's Colne Grammar School*. Published by the school.

Friary School, Lichfield (private, girls)
Bird, J. (1995) *Hyacinths and Haricot Beans: Friary School memories 1892–1992*. Lichfield: Lichfield Press.

Gamston Elementary School, Nottinghamshire
Sutton, K. (ed.) (2005) *Gamston Elementary School*. Published by the school.

George Dixon School, Birmingham (grammar, girls and boys)
Reading, L. (2006) *100 Years at City Road*. Published by the George Dixon International School, Birmingham.

Great Rissington School, Gloucestershire (elementary)
Boyes, M. (1997) *A Cotswold Village School from Victorian Times*. Published by Rissington's Local History Society.

Hackney Downs School, London (grammar, boys)
Alderman, G. (1972) *History of Hackney Downs School*. London: Clove Club.

Hollies FCJ Convent School, Manchester (grammar, girls)
Harris, P. (2002) *Against the Odds*. Published by Fosse Data Systems Ltd.

Hurstpierpoint College, Sussex (private, boys)
King, P. (1997) *Hurstpierpoint College 1849–1995*. London: Phillimore.

John Mattocke School, Hitchin, Hertfordshire (grammar, boys)
Donald, J. (1990) *The John Mattocke School*. Published by J. Donald.

Kingston High School, Hull (grammar, boys and girls)
Conyers, S. and Plater, M. (eds) (1990) *Backward Glances: Kingston High School*. Published by the school.

Leedstown School, Cornwall (elementary)
Jenkin, A.T. (1978) *Leedstown School 1878–1978*. Published by the author.

Leighton Park School, Reading (private, boys and girls)
Stranack, 2005: 41.

Lord Wandsworth College, Hampshire (private, boys and girls)
Stranack, 2005: 43.

Loughborough College School (grammar and technical, boys)
Elliott, B. (1971) *The History of Loughborough College School*. Published by the school.

Luton Girls' High School (grammar)
Allsop, A. (2004) *Crimson and Gold*. Dunstable: Book Castle.

Luton Modern School (grammar, boys)
Dyer, J. (2004) *Rhubarb and Custard*. Dunstable: Book Press.

Malvern College, Worcestershire (private, boys)
Blumenau, R. (1965) *A History of Malvern College 1865–1965*. London: Macmillan.

Marling School, Stroud, Gloucestershire (grammar, boys)
Wicks, W.O. (1986) *Marling School 1887–1987*. Published by the author.

Merchant Taylors' School for Girls, Liverpool (grammar)
Harrop, S. (1988) *Merchant Taylors' School for Girls: 100 years of achievement 1888–1988*. Liverpool: Liverpool University Press.

Merton Court School, Kent (private preparatory, boys)
Evans, G. (1999) *A Centenary in the Life of Merton Court School, Sidcup 1899–1999*. Stafford: Stowefields Publications.

Nash Mills School, Watford (elementary)
Ward, A.J. (1987) *Nash Mills School: A history of the school 1847–1987*. Published by Nash Mills governors.

Oundle School, Northamptonshire (private, boys)
Walker, G.W. (1956) *A History of the Oundle Schools*. Published by the school.

Piggott School, Wargrave, Berkshire (secondary to age 14, with some staying to 18)
Haseltine, P. (1986) *The Piggott School, Wargrave: A profile*. Published by the school.

Powell Corderoy School, Dorking, Surrey (elementary)
Sykes, E. (1989) *The Story of Powell Corderoy School*. Published by the Dorking History Group.

Queen Mary's Clitheroe, Lancashire (grammar, boys)
Green, D. and Harwood, K. (1983) *Queen Mary's Clitheroe*. Chorley: Countryside.

Reading School (private, boys)
Oakes, J. (2005) *Reading School: The first 800 years*. Published by DSM for Reading School.

Rendcomb College, Cirencester (state and private boarding school for boys and girls)
Osborne, C.H.C. (1976) *A History of Rendcomb College*. Published by the college.

Repton School, Derbyshire (private, boys)
Thomas, B. (1957) *Repton 1557–1957*. No publisher.

Royal Grammar School, Worcester (boys)
Wheeler, R.A. (1990) *The Royal Grammar School, Worcester 1950–1991, with a retrospect to 1291*. Published by the school.

Royal Hospital School, Holbrook, near Ipswich (boys training school for the navy)
Turner, H.D.T. (1990) *The Cradle of the Navy: The story of the Royal Hospital School at Greenwich and Holbrook 1694–1988*. Published by William Sessions.

Royal Latin School, Buckinghamshire (grammar, boys and girls)
Poonan, P.K. (2001) *Royal Latin School, Buckinghamshire*. Buckingham: Dusty Old Books.

St Clare, Penzance (grammar, girls)
Laws, P. (1989) *The Centenary Book of the School of St Clare, Penzance, 1889–1989*. Published by Woodward Schools (Western Division).

St Clement Dane's Holborn Estate Grammar School, London (boys)
Pooley, R.J.B. (1959) *The History of St Clement Dane's Holborn Estate Grammar School*. Published by the school.

St Edmund's College, Liverpool (grammar, girls)
Goodacre, K.A. (1991) *A History of St. Edmund's College, Liverpool*. Ormskirk: Lyster.

St George's School, Harpenden (private, boys and girls)
Weatherley, P. (1982) *A History of St Georges School, Harpenden*. Published by the school.

St James's School, Worcestershire (private, girls)
Stranack, 2005: 61.

St Lawrence College, Kent (private, boys)
Holmes, R.S. (1979) *Saint Lawrence College, Kent: The first 100 years*. No publisher.

St Mary's School, Wantage, Oxfordshire (private, girls)
Stranack, 2005: 63.

St Mary and St Giles Church of England Senior School, Stony Stratford (boys and girls)
No author (1987?) *St Mary and St Giles Church of England Middle School: Golden Jubilee 1937–1987*. Published by the school.

Sandown Grammar School, Isle of Wight (boys and girls)
Ayling, S.E. (no date) *Sandown Grammar School 1901–1951*. Newport: Isle of Wight County Press.

Shrewsbury School (private, boys)
Oldham, J.B. (1952) *History of Shrewsbury School*. Published by the school.

Stationers' Company School, Hornsey, London (grammar, boys)
Baynes, R. (1987) *A History of the Stationers' Company School 1858–1983*. Published by the Worshipful Company of Stationers and Newspaper Makers.

Steyning Grammar School, Sussex (boys)
Sleight, J.M. (1981) *A Very Exceptional Instance: Three centuries of education in Steyning, Sussex*. Published by the school/author.

Stoke Poges Elementary School, near Slough
Tarrant, J. (no date) *The Village School*. Published by the school.

Stowe School, Buckinghamshire (private, boys)
No author (no date) *Roxburgh of Stowe*. No publisher.

Tackley School, Oxfordshire (elementary)
Hardy, J.H. (1992) *The History of Tackley School 1840–1946*. Published by Tackley Local History Group.

Tedburn St Mary School, Devon (elementary)
Priestley, J.G. (1977) *Tedburn St Mary School, Devon*. Exeter: Heriz Studios.

Terra Nova School, Cheshire (private, boys)
Elleray, A. (2000) *Terra Nova School*. Published by Terra Nova School Trust.

Trewirgie Infants School, Redruth, Cornwall
Dyer, F. (1978?) *A Start in Life: The story of Trewirgie Infants School*. Redruth: Len Truran.

Trinity Grammar School, Wood Green, London (grammar, boys and girls)
Grammer, D. (1999) *Trinity – A school with a past*. Published by the author.

Twickenham County Grammar School for Girls, London
Hawkes, J. (1981) *Twickenham County Grammar School for Girls*. Richmond, Surrey: Puritan Litho.

Walkington Elementary School, Kent
Scrowston, R.M. (1976) *A Hundred Years of Education in Walkington 1876–1976*. Published by the Governors of Walkington County Primary School.

Wellingborough School, Northamptonshire (private, boys)
Lyon, N.B. (1988) *A History of Wellingborough*. Published by the school.

Wellington College, Crowthorne, Berkshire (private, boys)
Newsome, D. (1959) *A History of Wellington College*. London: John Murray.

Westminster City School, London (grammar, boys)
Carrington, R. (1983) *Westminster City School and its Origins*. Published by the school.

Weston-super-Mare Grammar School (boys and girls)
Kingsmill, A. (2005) *A School in the Forties.*
Published by Karanfil Press.

Wheelwright Grammar Schools, Dewsbury (boys and girls)
Pickles, W. (1973) *The History of the Wheelwright
Grammar Schools.* Published by the author.

Whitehills Schools, Buckinghamshire (grammar, boys)
Palmer, P. (1990) *Whitehills Schools.* Published by
Chess Valley Archaeological and History Society.

William Ellis Grammar School, Camden, London (boys)
Wickenden, T.D. (no date) *William
Ellis.* London: Moore Bartley.

Wisborough Green School, Sussex (elementary)
Sergeant, L. (1990) *A History of Wisborough Green
School 1850–1990.* Published by the school.

Wittersham Church of England School, Kent (elementary)
Barber, M.J. (2000) *A Handsome School: A history of
Wittersham Church of England Primary School from 1820
to 2000 AD.* Published by G. David Neame.

Woodroffe School, Lyme Regis (grammar, boys and girls)
Warr, G. (2007) *The School on the Hill: A history of the Woodroffe
School and its pupils.* Lyme Regis: Woodroffe Association.

Wrekin College, Shropshire (private, boys)
Johnson, B.C.W. (1965) *Wrekin.* Shrewsbury: Wilding & Son.

Bibliography

Adler, N. (1908) 'Child employment and juvenile delinquency'. In G.M. Tuckwell (ed.) *Women in Industry*. London: Duckworth.

Alanen, L. (1992) 'Modern childhood? Exploring the "child question" in sociology'. Research Report 50. Finland: University of Jyväskylä.

Alexander, R. (ed.) (2010) *Children, their World, their Education*. London: Routledge.

Anderson, J. (2008) *Children of the War Years: Childhood in Britain during 1939 to 1945*. London: Futura.

Armstrong, D. (1983) *The Political Anatomy of the Body*. Cambridge: Cambridge University Press.

-- (1995) 'The rise of surveillance medicine'. *Sociology of Health and Illness* 17(3), 393–504.

Bailey, V. (1987) *Delinquency and Citizenship: Reclaiming the young offender 1914–1948*. Oxford: Clarendon Press.

Bakewell, J. (2004) *The Centre of the Bed*. London: Sceptre.

Barber, M. (1994) *The Making of the 1944 Education Act*. London: Cassell.

Barker, R. (1972) *Education and Politics 1900–1951: A study of the Labour Party*. Oxford: Clarendon Press.

Barnard, H.C. (1968) *A History of English Education from 1760*. London: University of London Press. First published 1947.

Barnett House Study Group (1947) *London Children in War-time Oxford*. London: Oxford University Press.

Bathurst, M. (1944) 'Juvenile delinquency in Britain during the war'. *Journal of Criminal Law and Criminology* 34(5), 291–302.

Bertaux, D. and Thompson, P. (1993) *Between Generations*. Oxford: Oxford University Press.

Black, C. (1907) *Sweated Industry and the Minimum Wage*. London: Duckworth.

Blanchard, P. (1921) *The Care of the Adolescent Girl: A book for teachers, parents and guardians*. London: Kegan Paul.

Blewitt, T. (ed.) (1934) *The Modern Schools' Handbook*. London: Gollancz.

Blishen, E. (1969) *The School that I'd Like*. Harmondsworth: Penguin.

Board of Education (1916) 'Return of school attendance and employment of school children in agriculture'. 16 October. London: HMSO.

-- (1923) *Report of the Consultative Committee on Differentiation of the Curriculum for Boys and Girls Respectively in Secondary Education*. London: HMSO.

-- (1926) (Hadow Report) *Report of the Consultative Committee on the Education of the Adolescent*. London: HMSO.

-- (1931) *Report of the Consultative Committee on the Primary School*. London: HMSO.

-- (1933) *Report of the Consultative Committee on Infant and Nursery Schools*. London: HMSO.

-- (1937) (reprinted 1944) *Handbook of Suggestions for Teachers: For the consideration of teachers and others concerned in the work of public elementary schools*. London: HMSO.

-- (1938) (Spens Report) *Report of the Consultative Committee on Secondary Education with Special Reference to Grammar Schools and Technical High Schools*. London: HMSO.

-- (1939) 'The Service of Youth'. Circular 1486, November. London: HMSO.

-- (1940) 'The Challenge of Youth'. Circular 1516, June. London: HMSO.

-- (1941) *School Broadcasts and How We Use Them: By a number of teachers*. London: HMSO.

-- (and Scottish Education Department) (1942) *Training and Service for Girls*. London: HMSO.

-- (1943a) (Norwood Report) *Curriculum and Examinations in Secondary School*. London: HMSO.

-- (1943b) 'Educational Reconstruction'. Cmd 6458 (White Paper), London: HMSO.

-- (1943c) *The Youth Service after the War*. London: HMSO.

Bowlby, J. (1940) 'Psychological aspects'. In R. Padley and M. Cole (eds) *Evacuation Survey: A report to the Fabian Society*. London: Routledge.

Boy Scouts Association (1941) *They Were Prepared: Boy Scouts National Service*. London: Boy Scouts Association.

Boyd, W. (ed.) for the New Education Fellowship (NEF) (1930) *Towards a New Education: A record and synthesis of the discussions on the new psychology and the curriculum at the fifth World Conference of the NEF, held at Elsinore, August 1929*. London: Alfred A. Knopf.

Boyd, W. and Rawson, W. (1965) *The Story of the New Education*. London: Heinemann.

Brannen, J. (2004) 'Childhoods across the generations: Stories from women in four-generation English families'. *Childhood* 11(4), 409–28.

Bray, R.A. (1911) *Boy Labour and Apprenticeship*. London: Constable.

Briar, C. (1997) *Working for Women*. London: UCL Press.

Briggs, A. (1955) *Victorian People*. Harmondsworth: Penguin.

Bristow, A. (1999) *Pride and Some Prejudice: The story of the junior technical schools*. No place of publication cited: Imogen.

British Broadcasting Corporation (BBC) (1945) *BBC Handbook 1945*. London: BBC.

British Film Institute (BFI) (2007) *Land of Promise: The British documentary movement 1930–1950* (booklet and DVD). London: BFI.

Brown, M. (2009) *Wartime Childhood*. Oxford: Shire Publications.

Bruce, M. (1961) *The Coming of the Welfare State*. London: Batsford.

Bryder, L. (1992) 'Wonderlands of buttercup, clover and daisies: Tuberculosis and the open-air school movement in Britain 1907–1938'. In R. Cooter (ed.) *In the Name of the Child: Health and welfare 1880–1940*. London: Routledge.

Buckingham, D. (2005) *Schooling the Digital Generation: Popular culture, the new media and the future of education*. London: Institute of Education, University of London.

Buckingham, D. with contributions from Shaku Banaji, Andrew Burn, Diane Carr, Sue Cranmer and Rebekah Willett (2005) *The Media Literacy of Children and Young People: A review of the academic research*. London: Ofcom.

Bunt, S. and Gargrave, R. (1980) *The Politics of Youth Clubs*. Leicester: National Youth Bureau.

Burke, C. and Grosvenor, I. (2003) *The School I'd Like*. London: RoutledgeFalmer.

Burnett, J. (1994) *Destiny Obscure*. London: Routledge.

Burt, C. (1943) 'The education of the young adolescent: The psychological implications of the Norwood Report'. *British Journal of Educational Psychology* Nov. 1943, 131.

Butler, R.A. (1952) 'The 1944 Education Act seen against the pattern of the times'. In *Institute of Education Jubilee Lectures*. London: Evans Bros.

-- (1973) 'The politics of the 1944 Education Act'. In G. Fowler (ed.) *Decision-making in British Education*. London: Heinemann/Open University.

Buxton, D. and Fuller, E. (1931) *The White Flame: The story of the Save the Children Fund*. London: Longmans, Green.

Cadogan, M. and Craig, P. (1978) *Women and Children First: The fiction of two world wars*. London: Victor Gollancz.

Cain, J. and Wright, B. (1994) *In a Class of its Own: BBC Education 1924–1994*. London: BBC Education.

Central Advisory Council for Education (England) (1967) (Plowden Report) *Children and their Primary Schools.* London: HMSO.

Chamberlin, R. (1989) *Free Children and Democratic Schools: A philosophical study of liberty and education.* London: Falmer.

Chandra, V. (2001) 'Children's work in the family: A sociological study of Indian children in Coventry (UK) and Lucknow (India)'. Unpublished PhD thesis, University of Warwick.

Chapman, J. (1999) 'British cinema and "The people's war"'. In M. Hayes and J. Hill (eds) *Millions Like Us? British culture in the Second World War.* Liverpool: Liverpool University Press.

-- (2007) 'The British documentary movement in the Second World War', introductory notes to *Land of Promise: The British documentary movement 1930–1950* (booklet and DVD). London: British Film Institute.

Clarke, F. (1940) *Education and Social Change.* London: Sheldon.

Clarke, G. (2008) *The Women's Land Army: A portrait.* Bristol: Sansom.

Clegg, A.B. (ed.) (1972) *The Changing Primary School.* London: Chatto & Windus.

Cloete, J.G. (1904) 'The boy and his work'. In E.J. Urwick (ed.) *Studies of Boy Life in our Cities.* London: J.M. Dent.

Close, P. (2009) 'Making sense of child labour in modern society'. *Sociological Studies of Children and Youth* 52, 167–94.

Cole, M. (1940) 'Introduction'. In R. Padley and M. Cole (eds) *Evacuation Survey: A report to the Fabian Society.* London: Routledge.

Collier, D.J. (1918) *The Girl in Industry.* London: G. Bell & Sons.

Cooter, R. (ed.) (1992) *In the Name of the Child: Health and welfare 1880–1940.* London: Routledge.

Cranwell, K. (2003) 'Sunday schools, treats, day trips and country holidays: London (1880–1920)'. In R. Gilchrist, T. Jeffs and J. Spence (eds) *Architects of Change: Studies in the history of community and youth work.* Leicester: National Youth Agency.

Crawford, E. (2002) *Enterprising Women: The Garretts and their circle.* London: Francis Bootle.

Crompton, R. (1995) *William Does His Bit.* London: Newnes.

Cunningham, H. (1990) 'The employment and unemployment of children in England *c.*1688–1851'. *Past and Present* 126, 115–50.

-- (1991) *The Children of the Poor: Representations of childhood since the seventeenth century.* Oxford: Blackwell.

-- (1995) *Children and Childhood in Western Society since 1500.* London: Longman.

-- (2006) *The Invention of Childhood.* London: BBC Books.

Cunningham, P. (2002) 'Primary education'. In R. Aldrich (ed.) *A Century of Education.* London: RoutledgeFalmer.

Cunningham, P. and Gardner, P. (1999) 'Saving the nation's children: Teachers' wartime evacuation in England and Wales and the construction of national identity'. *History of Education* 28(3), 327–37.

Cunningham, S. (1999) 'The problem that doesn't exist? Child labour in Britain 1918–70'. In M. Lavalette (ed.) *A Thing of the Past? Child labour in Britain in the nineteenth and twentieth centuries.* Liverpool: Liverpool University Press.

Davies, B. (2001) 'Struggling through the past: Writing youth service history'. In R. Gilchrist, T. Jeffs and J. Spence (eds) *Architects of Change: Studies in the history of community and youth work.* Leicester: National Youth Agency.

Davin, A. (1990) 'When is a child not a child?'. In H. Corr and L. Jamieson (eds) *Politics of Everyday Life.* London: Macmillan.

Davis, M. (2000) *Fashioning a New World: A history of the Woodcraft Folk.* Loughborough: Holyoake Books.

Deem, R. (1981) 'State policy and ideology in the education of women 1944–1980'. *British Journal of the Sociology of Education* 2(2), 131–43.

Defence (Agricultural and Fisheries) Regulations (1942) No. 802: 105. London: HMSO.

Dent, H.C. (1942) *A New Order in English Education*. Bickley, Kent: University of London Press.

-- (1943) *The Countryman's College*. London: British Council.

-- (1944a) *Education in Transition*. London: Kegan Paul, Trench & Trubner.

-- (1944b) *The Education Bill, 1944*. London: University of London Press.

-- (1949a) *Secondary Education for All*. London: Routledge & Kegan Paul.

-- (1949b) *Part-time Education in Great Britain*. London: Turnstile.

Department for Education and Science (1965) *The School Building Survey 1962*. London: HMSO.

Donzelot, J. (1980) *The Policing of Families: Welfare versus the state*. London: Hutchinson.

Drake, B. (1984) *Women in Trades Unions*. London: Virago.

Dudley Edwards, O. (2007) *British Children's Fiction in the Second World War*. Edinburgh: Edinburgh University Press.

Dunn, J. (1988) *The Beginnings of Social Understanding*. Oxford: Blackwell.

Dyhouse, C. (1986) 'Mothers and daughters in the middle-class home *c*.1870–1914'. In J. Lewis (ed.) *Labour and Love: Women's experience of home and family 1850–1940*. Oxford: Basil Blackwell.

Fethney, M. (1990) *The Absurd and the Brave*. London: Book Guild.

Finch, J. (1984) *Education as Social Policy*. London: Longman.

Findlay, J.J. (1923) *The Children of England: A contribution to social history and to education*. London: Methuen.

Finn, D. (1987) *Training without Jobs: New deals and broken promises*. Basingstoke: Macmillan.

Fisher, H.A.L. (1917) 'Introduction of the 1917 Education Bill, Parliamentary debates, House of Commons, 10 August 1917'.

Reprinted in W. Van der Eyken (ed.) (1973) *Education, the Child and Society: A documentary history 1900–1973*. Harmondsworth: Penguin.

Ford, J. and Sinclair, R. (1987) *Sixty Years On: Women talk about old age*. London: Women's Press.

Franklin, B. (2002a) 'Introduction'. In B. Franklin (ed.) *New Handbook of Children's Rights*. London: Routledge.

-- (ed.) (2002b) *New Handbook of Children's Rights*. London: Routledge.

Freeman, A. (1914) *Boy Life and Labour: The manufacture of inefficiency*. London: King.

Freeman, K. (1965) *If Any Man Build: The History of the Save the Children Fund*. London: Hodder & Stoughton.

Freeman, M. (2002) 'Children's rights ten years after ratification'. In B. Franklin (ed.) *New Handbook of Children's Rights*. London: Routledge.

Frow, E. and Frow, R. (1970) *A Survey of the Half-time System in Education*. Manchester: Morten.

Gardiner, J. (2005) *Wartime Britain 1939–1945*. London: Headline.

Garnett, E. (1937) *The Family from One-End Street*. London: Penguin.

Garside, W.R. (1977) 'Juvenile unemployment and public policy between the wars'. *Economic History Review* 30(2), 322–39.

-- (1981) 'Unemployment and the school-leaving age in inter-war Britain'. *International Review of Social History* 26(2), 159–70.

Gilchrist, R., Jeffs, T. and Spence, J. (eds) (2001) *Essays in the History of Community and Youth Work*. Leicester: Youth Work Press.

Giles, T. (2002) *Not Evacuated*. Published privately by the author.

Gosden, P. (1976) *Education in the Second World War: A study in policy and administration*. London: Methuen.

Grant, I. and Maddren, N. (1975) *The Countryside at War*. London: Jupiter Books.

Graves, R. and Hodge, A. (1985) *The Long Weekend: A social history of Great Britain 1918–1939*. London: Hutchinson. First published 1940.

Green, B. (1994) 'Introduction'. In B. Green (ed.) *Britain at War*. Surrey: Colour Library.

Griggs, C. (1983) *The Trades Union Congress and the Struggle for Education 1868–1925*. Lewes: Falmer.

-- (2002) *The TUC and Education Reform, 1926–70*. London: Woburn Press.

Groves, R. (1949) *Sharpen the Sickle: The history of the Farm Workers' Union*. London: Porcupine.

Hall, G. Stanley (1920) *Adolescence: Its psychology and its relations to physiology, anthropology, sociology, sex, crime, religion and education*. New York and London: D. Appleton. First published 1904.

Hampton J. (2010) *How the Girl Guides Won the War*. London: Harper Press.

Hardyment, C. (1984) *Dream Babies: Child care from Locke to Spock*. Oxford: Oxford University Press.

Harris, B. (1995a) *The Health of the Schoolchild*. Buckingham: Open University Press.

-- (1995b) 'Responding to adversity: government–charity relations and the relief of unemployment in inter-war Britain'. *Contemporary Record* 9, 529–61.

Harvey, S. (2009) 'Children on the Home Front 1939–1945'. *Yours*, August.

Hattersley, R. (1983) *A Yorkshire Boyhood*. Harmondsworth: Penguin.

Heggie, M. and Riches, C. (2008) *History of* The Beano: *The story so far*. London: D.C. Thomson.

Hendrick, H. (1990) *Images of Youth: Age, class and the male youth problem, 1880–1920*. Oxford: Clarendon.

-- (1994) 'Constructions and reconstructions of British childhood: An interpretative survey: 1800 to the present'. In A. James and A.

Prout (eds) *Constructing and Reconstructing Childhood: Contemporary issues in the sociological study of childhood.* London: Falmer.

-- (2003) *Child Welfare: Historical dimensions, contemporary debate.* Bristol: Policy Press.

-- (2008) 'The child as social actor in historical sources: Problems of identification and interpretation'. In P. Christensen and A. James (eds) *Research with Children: Perspectives and problems.* Second edition. London: Routledge.

-- (2010) 'Late modernity's British childhood: Social investment and the disciplinary state'. In D. Bühler–Niederberger, J. Mierendorff and A. Lange (eds) *Kindheit zwischen fürsorglichem Zugriff und gesellschaftlicher Teilhabe. VS Verlag für Sozialwissenshaften.* Wiesbaden: Springer Fachmedien.

Heywood, J. (1959) (Second edition 1965) *Children in Care: The development of the service for the deprived child.* London: Routledge & Kegan Paul.

Hoare, J. (2007) Introductory notes to the film *Children at School.* In British Film Institute *Land of Promise: The British documentary movement 1930–1950* (booklet and DVD). London: BFI.

Hobbs, S. and McKechnie, J. (1997) *Child Employment in Britain: A social and psychological approach.* Edinburgh: Stationery Office.

Holdsworth, R. (2005) 'Taking young people seriously means giving them serious things to do'. In J. Mason and T. Fattore (eds) *Children Taken Seriously in Theory, Policy and Practice.* London: Jessica Kingsley.

Holman, B. (1995) *The Evacuation: A very British revolution.* Oxford: Lion.

-- (2001) *Champions for Children.* Bristol: Policy Press.

Holt, J. (1977) *Instead of Education.* Harmondsworth: Penguin.

Home Office (1933) 'Children and Young Persons Act 1933. Employment of children: memorandum and specimen forms of byelaws issued by the Home Office for the guidance of local authorities'. London: HMSO.

Horn, P. (1983) 'The employment of elementary school-children in agriculture, 1914–18'. *History of Education* 12(3), 203–15.

Horrell, S. and Humphries, J. (1999) 'Child labour and British industrialization'. In M. Lavalette (ed.) *A thing of the Past? Child labour in Britain in the nineteenth and twentieth centuries*. Liverpool: Liverpool University Press.

Howieson, C., McKechnie, J. and Semple, S. (2006) *The Nature and Implications of the Part-Time Employment of Secondary School Pupils: Final Report to the Scottish Executive Enterprise and Lifelong Learning Department* [SEELLD]. Edinburgh: SEELLD.

Howkins, A. (2003) *The Death of Rural England: A social history of the countryside since 1900*. London: Routledge.

Humphries, J. (2010) *Childhood and Child Labour in the British Industrial Revolution*. Cambridge: Cambridge University Press.

Humphries, S. (1981) *Hooligans or Rebels? An oral history of working class childhood and youth, 1889–1939*. Oxford: Blackwell.

Hunt, F. (1985) 'Social class and the grading of schools: Realities in girls secondary education 1880–1940'. In J. Purvis (ed.) *Education of Girls and Women*. Leicester: History of Education Society.

-- (1991) *Gender and Policy in English Education: Schooling for girls 1902–44*. London: Harvester Wheatsheaf.

Hurt, J.S. (1979) *Elementary Schooling and the Working Classes 1860–1918*.London: Routledge & Kegan Paul.

Hyde, R. (1952) 'School harvest camps'. *Agriculture* 58(10), 468–70.

Invernizzi, A. (2001) 'The work of children is not only work'. In M. Liebel, B. Overwien and A. Recknagel (eds) *Working Children's Protagonism: Social movements and empowerment in Latin America, Africa and India*. Frankfurt-am-Main: IKO: Verlag für Interkulturelle Kommunikation.

Invernizzi, A. and Williams, J. (eds) (2008) *Children and Citizenship*. London: Sage.

Isaacs, S. (1941) *The Cambridge Evacuation Survey*. London: Methuen.

-- (1961) *The Children We Teach*. London: University of London Press. First published 1932, reprinted 15 times by 1961.

-- (1965) *The Nursery Years*. London: Routledge & Kegan Paul. First published 1929, reprinted 11 times by 1965.

James, A.L. and James, A. (2001) 'Tightening the net: Children, community and control'. *British Journal of Sociology* 52(2), 211–28.

Jebb, E. (1929) *Save the Child! A posthumous essay*. London: Weardale Press.

Jeffs, T. (2002) 'Schooling, education and children's rights'. In B. Franklin (ed.) *New Handbook of Children's Rights*. London: Routledge.

Jenkins, C. (2000) 'New Education and its emancipatory interests (1920–1950)'. *History of Education* 29(2), 139–51.

Jenkinson, A.J. (1946) *What do Boys and Girls Read?* London: Methuen. First published 1940.

Jephcott, P. (1942) *Girls Growing Up*. London: Faber & Faber.

Jewkes, J. and Jewkes, S. (1938) *The Juvenile Labour Market*. London: Victor Gollancz.

Jewkes, J. and Winterbottom, A. (1933) *Juvenile Unemployment*. London: George Allen & Unwin.

Johnson, B.S. (ed.) (1968) *The Evacuees*. London: Gollancz.

Johnson, W. (1945) 'School harvest camps'. *Agriculture* 52, 18.

Jordanova, L.J. (1987) 'Conceptualizing childhood in the eighteenth century: The problem of child labour'. *British Journal for Eighteenth Century Studies* 10, 189–99.

-- (1989) 'Children in history: Concepts of nature and society'. In G. Scarre (ed.) *Children, Parents and Politics*. Cambridge: Cambridge University Press.

Joseph, S. (1946) *If Their Mothers Only Knew: An unofficial account of life in the Women's Land Army*. London: Faber & Faber.

Kean, H. (1990) *Challenging the State? The socialist and feminist educational experience 1900–1930*. London: Falmer.

Keeling, F. (1914) *Child Labour in the United Kingdom: A study of the law relating to the employment of children.* London: King.

Key, E. (1909) *The Century of the Child.* New York: Putman. First published 1900.

Kitchen, P.I. (1944) *From Learning to Earning.* London: Faber & Faber.

Klein, V. (1946) *The Feminine Character: History of an ideology.* London: Kegan Paul.

Koven, S. and Michel, S. (1993) 'Introduction: Mother worlds'. In S. Coven and S. Michel (eds) *Mothers of a New World: Maternalist politics and the origins of welfare states.* New York: Routledge.

Lavalette M. (ed.) (1999) *A Thing of the Past? Child labour in Britain in the nineteenth and twentieth centuries.* Liverpool: Liverpool University Press.

Lawn, M. (1987) 'What is the teacher's job? Work and welfare in elementary teaching, 1940–1945'. In M. Lawn and G. Grace (eds) *Teachers: The culture and politics of work.* London: Falmer.

Leonard, M. (1999) 'Child work in the UK, 1970–1998'. In M. Lavalette (ed.) *A Thing of the Past? Child labour in Britain in the nineteenth and twentieth centuries.* Liverpool: Liverpool University Press.

Lester-Smith, W.O. (1942) *To Whom do Schools Belong?* Oxford: Blackwell.

Levison, D. (2000) 'Children as economic agents'. *Feminist Economics* 6, 125–34.

Lewis, J. (1980) *The Politics of Motherhood: Child and maternal welfare in England, 1900–39.* Hemel Hempstead: Harvester Wheatsheaf.

-- (1986) 'Introduction: Reconstructing women's experience of home and family'. In J. Lewis (ed.) *Labour and Love: Women's experience of home and family 1850–1940.* Oxford: Basil Blackwell.

-- (1991) *Women and Social Action in Victorian and Edwardian England.* Aldershot: Gower Press.

Liddell, A. (1976) *Story of the Girl Guides 1938–1975: The official history of the Girl Guides Association.* London: Girl Guides Association.

Liddiard, M. (1954) *The Mothercraft Manual*. London: J.A. Churchill. First published 1923.

Lifton, B.J. (1988) *The King of Children: A biography of Janusz Korczak*. London: Chatto & Windus.

Lister, R. (2007) 'Inclusive citizenship: Realizing the potential'. *Citizenship Studies* 11(1), 49–61.

Lister, R., Smith, N., Middleton, S. and Cox, L. (2003) 'Young people talk about citizenship: Empirical perspectives on theoretical and political debates'. *Citizenship Studies* 7(2) 235–53.

Livingstone, R. (1941) *The Future in Education*. Cambridge: Cambridge University Press.

Lowndes, G.A.N. (1937) *The Silent Social Revolution: An account of the expansion of public education in England and Wales 1895–1965*. Oxford: Oxford University Press.

Macnicol, J. (1986) 'The evacuation of schoolchildren'. In H.L. Smith (ed.) *War and Social Change: British society in the Second World War*. Manchester: Manchester University Press.

Macalister Brew, J. (1943) *In the Service of Youth*. London: Faber & Faber.

-- (1957) *Youth and Youth Groups*. London: Faber & Faber.

Mackay, R. (2002) *Half the Battle: Civilian morale in Britain during the Second World War*. Manchester: Manchester University Press.

Mann, J. (2005) *Out of Harm's Way: The wartime evacuation of children from Britain*. London: Headline.

Mannheim, K. (1952) 'The problem of generations'. In K. Mannheim (ed.) *Essays on the Sociology of Knowledge*. London: Routledge & Kegan Paul. Paper first published 1928.

– – (1954) *Diagnosis of our Time: Wartime essays of a sociologist*. London: Routledge & Kegan Paul. Paper first published 1943.

Martin, J. (2005) 'Gender, the city and the politics of schooling: Towards a collective biography of women "doing good" as public moralists in Victorian London'. *Gender and Education* 17(2), 143–63.

-- (2010) 'Introduction: biography and history'. In J. Martin (ed.) *Making Socialists: Mary Bridge Adams and the fight for knowledge and power, 1855–1939.* Manchester: Manchester University Press.

Martin, J. and Goodman, J. (2004) *Women and Education 1800–1980.* London: Sage.

Mayall, B. (1989) 'Trumpets over the Range'. An unpublished paper on the history of adolescence. Thomas Coram Research Unit, Institute of Education, University of London.

-- (2002) *Towards a Sociology for Childhood: Thinking from children's lives.* Buckingham: Open University Press.

-- (2005) 'Childhood and generation study: End-of-project report to the Nuffield Foundation'. Unpublished paper. Social Science Research Unit, Institute of Education, University of London.

-- (2007) *Children's Lives Outside School and their Educational Impact* (Primary Review Research Surveys 8/1). Cambridge: Cambridge University Faculty of Education.

-- (2009) 'Generational relations at family level'. In J. Qvortrup, W.A. Corsaro and M.-S. Honig (eds) *The Palgrave Handbook of Childhood Studies.* London: Palgrave Macmillan.

Mayall, B., Bendelow, G., Barker, S., Storey, P. and Veltman, M. (1996) *Children's Health in Primary Schools.* London: Falmer.

McCulloch, G. (1989) *The Secondary Technical School: A usable past?* London: Faber.

-- (1991) *Philosophers and Kings: Education for leadership in modern England.* Cambridge: Cambridge University Press.

-- (1994) *Educational Reconstruction : The 1944 Education Act and the twenty-first century.* London: Woburn Press.

-- (2004) *Documentary Research in Education, History and the Social Sciences.* London: RoutledgeFalmer.

McFarlan, D.M. (1982) *First for Boys: The story of the Boys' Brigade 1883–1983.* London: Collins.

McGrath, M. (2009) *Hopping: The hidden lives of an East End hop-picking family*. London: Fourth Estate.

McLaine, I. (1979) *Ministry of Morale: Home front morale in World War II*. London: Allen & Unwin.

McMillan, M. (1911) *The Child and the State*. Manchester: National Labour Party Press Ltd.

-- (1930) *The Nursery School*. London: J.M. Dent.

Measures, J.V. (1943) 'Leicestershire school children help the farmers'. *Agriculture* 50, 84–8.

Miller, E. (1937) *The Growing Child and its Problems*. London: Kegan Paul, Trench & Trubner.

Ministry of Education (1945) *The Purpose and Content of the Youth Service: A report of the Youth Advisory Council appointed by the Minister of Education in 1943*. London: HMSO.

-- (1946) (reprinted 1959) *Youth's Opportunity: Further education in county colleges*. London: HMSO.

Ministry of Food (1941*) Food facts for the Kitchen Front: A book of wartime recipes and hints* (with a Foreword by Lord Woolton, Minister of Food). London: Collins.

Ministry of Information (1941) *You Can Help Your Country*. London: Ministry of Information.

-- (1945) *Land at War: The official story of British farming 1939–1945*. London: Ministry of Information.

Mizen, P., Pole, C. and Bolton, A. (eds) (2001) *Hidden Hands: International perspectives on children's work and labour*. London: RoutledgeFalmer.

Montagu, L.H. (1904) 'The girl in the background'. In E.J. Urwick (ed.) *Studies of Boy Life in our Cities: Written by various authors for the Toynbee Trust*. London: J.M. Dent.

Moore-Colyer, R. (2004) 'Kids in the corn: School harvest camps and farm labour supply in England, 1940–1950'. *Agricultural History Review* 25, 183–206.

-- (2006) 'Children's labour in the countryside during World War II: A further note'. *Agricultural History Review* 54, 331–4.

Morgan, A.E. (1943) *Young Citizen*. London: Penguin.

Morgan, K.O. (1975) *Keir Hardie: Radical and socialist*. London: Weidenfeld & Nicolson.

Morrow, V. (1992) 'A sociological study of the economic roles of children, with particular reference to Birmingham and Cambridgeshire'. Unpublished PhD thesis, University of Cambridge.

-- (1994) 'Responsible children? Aspects of children's work and employment outside school in contemporary UK'. In B. Mayall (ed.) *Children's Childhoods: Observed and experienced*. London: Falmer.

-- (1996) 'Rethinking childhood dependency: Children's contributions to the domestic economy'. *Sociological Review* 44(1), 58–77.

-- (2008) 'Responsible children and children's responsibilities? Sibling caretaking and babysitting by school-age children'. In J. Bridgeman, C. Lind and H. Keating (eds) *Responsibility, Law and the Family*. London: Ashgate.

Murray, K. (1955) *History of the Second World War: Agriculture*. London: Longman.

Musgrove, F. (1964) *Youth and the Social Order*. London: Routledge & Kegan Paul.

Nunn, P. (1920) *Education: Its data and first principles*. London: University of London Press.

Oakes, P. (1983) *From Middle England: A memory of the 1930s and 1940s*. Harmondsworth: Penguin.

Oldfield, C. (2001) 'The worst girl has at least 5 per cent good in her: The work of the Girl Guides and the YMCA with "difficult" girls during the inter-war period'. In R. Gilchrist, T. Jeffs and J. Spence (eds) *Essays in the History of Community and Youth Work*. Leicester: Youth Work Press.

Oldfield, S. (2006) *Doers of the Word: British women humanitarians 1900–1950*. London: Continuum.

Oldman, D. (1994) 'Childhood as a mode of production'. In B. Mayall (ed.) *Children's Childhoods: Observed and experienced*. London: Falmer.

Orellana, M., Thorne, B., Chee, A. and Lam, W. (2001) 'Transnational childhoods: The participation of children in processes of family migration'. *Social Problems* 48, 572–91.

Orwell, G. (1941) 'The lion and the unicorn'. Reprinted in W. Van der Eyken (ed.) (1973) *Education, the Child and Society: A documentary history 1900–1973*. Harmondsworth: Penguin. Paper first published 1941.

-- (1946) 'Boys' weeklies'. In G. Orwell, *Critical Essays*. London: Secker & Warburg. Paper first published 1939.

-- (1965) 'Notes on nationalism'. In G. Orwell, *Decline of the English Murder and other essays*. Harmondsworth: Penguin. Paper first published 1945.

Osler, A. and Starkey, H. (2005) *Changing Citizenship: Democracy and inclusion in education*. Buckingham: Open University Press.

Owen, D. (1964) *English Philanthropy 1660–1960*. Cambridge, MA: Harvard University Press.

Padley, R. (1940) 'Exodus'. In R. Padley and M. Cole (eds) *Evacuation Survey: A report to the Fabian Society*. London: Routledge.

Padley, R. and Cole, M. (1940) *Evacuation Survey: A report to the Fabian Society*. London: Routledge.

Pailthorpe, G. (1932) *Studies in the Psychology of Delinquency*. London: HMSO.

Parker, D. (1996) '"This gift from the gods?" Hertfordshire and the 1936 Education Act'. *History of Education* 25(2), 165–80.

Parsons, M. and Starns, P. (2000) *Evacuation: The true story*. Peterborough: DSM.

Pearse, I.H. and Crocker, L.H. (1943) *The Peckham Experiment: A study in the living structure of society*. London: George Allen & Unwin.

Pearson, G. (1983) *Hooligan: A history of respectable fears*. London: Macmillan.

Penn, H. (2004) 'Round and round the mulberry bush: The balance of public and private in early education and childcare in the twentieth century'. In R. Aldrich (ed.) *Public or Private Education: Lessons from History*. London: Woburn.

Pinchbeck, I. and Hewitt, M. (1969) and (1973) *Children in English Society*. Volumes 1 and 2. London: Routledge & Kegan Paul.

Pinson, H., Arnot, M. and Candappa, M. (2010) *Education, Asylum and the 'Non-citizen' Child: The politics of compassion and belonging*. London: Palgrave Macmillan.

Popular Memory Group (1982/1998) 'Popular memory, theory, politics, method'. In R. Perks and A. Thomson (eds) *The Oral History Reader*. London: Routledge.

Priestley, J.B. (1933) *An English Journey*. London: Heinemann/Gollancz.

Pringle, K. (1998) *Children and Social Welfare in Europe*. Buckingham: Open University Press.

Prochaska, F. (1988) *The Voluntary Impulse*. London: Faber & Faber.

Pye, V. (1943) *Half-term Holiday*. London: Faber.

Qvortrup, J. (1985) 'Placing children in the division of labour'. In P. Close and R. Collins (eds) *Family and Economy in Modern Society*. London: Macmillan.

-- (1987) 'Introduction'. *International Journal of Sociology* 17(3), 3–37.

-- (1991) 'Childhood as a social phenomenon: An introduction to a series of national reports'. Eurosocial Report 36. Vienna: European Centre for Social and Welfare Policy and Research.

Rathbone, E. (1924) *The Disinherited Family: A plea for the state endowment of the family*. London: Edward Arnold.

Reynolds, E.A. (1950) *The Scout Movement*. London: Oxford University Press.

Richmond, W.K. (1945) *Education in England*. Harmondsworth: Penguin.

Rose, N. (1985) *The Psychological Complex: Psychology, politics and society in England 1869–1939*. London: Routledge & Kegan Paul.

-- (1989) *Governing the Soul: The shaping of the private self.* London: Routledge.

Ross, E. (1986) 'Labour and love: Rediscovering London's working-class mothers, 1870–1918'. In J. Lewis (ed.) *Labour and Love: Women's experience of home and family 1850–1940.* Oxford: Basil Blackwell.

Rubenstein, D. (1969) *School Attendance in London 1870–1904: A social history.* Hull: University of Hull Press.

Russell, D. (1932) *In Defence of Children.* London: Hamish Hamilton.

Russell, P. (2007) Introductory note about the documentary film *The Children's Charter.* In British Film Institute *Land of Promise: The British documentary movement 1930–1950* (booklet and DVD). London: BFI.

Ryan, P. (1999) 'The embedding of apprenticeship in industrial relations: British engineering 1925–65'. In P. Ainley and H. Rainbird (eds) *Apprenticeship: Towards a new paradigm of learning.* London: Kogan Page.

St John, D. (1989) 'The guidance and influence of girls leaving school at fourteen: A study on the content, methods and contradictions in this process based on the girls' departments of the London County Council maintained elementary schools 1904–24'. Unpublished PhD thesis, Institute of Education, University of London.

Sanderson, M. (1994) *The Missing Stratum: Technical school education in England 1900–1990s.* London: Athlone Press.

Saunders, H.A. St George (1949) *The Left Handshake: The Boy Scout movement during the war 1939–1945.* London: Collins.

Scott-Davies, D. (2010) 'Being prepared'. *Best of British* April, 4–6.

Seaton, J. (2006) 'Little citizens: Children, the media and politics'. In J. Lloyd and J. Seaton (eds) *What Can Be done? Making the media and politics better.* Oxford: Blackwell.

Selleck, R.J.W. (1972) *English Primary Education and the Progressives 1914–1939.* London: Routledge & Kegan Paul.

Shamgar-Handelman, L. (1994) 'To whom does childhood belong?' In J. Qvortrup, M. Bardy, G. Sgritta and H. Wintersberger (eds) *Childhood Matters: Social theory, practice and politics*. Aldershot: Avebury Press.

Sherard, R. (1905) *The Child Slaves of Britain*. London: Hurst & Blackett.

Silver, H. (1980) *Education and the Social Condition*. London: Methuen.

Simon, B. (1965) *Education and the Labour Movement 1870–1918*. London: Lawrence & Wishart.

-- (1974) *The Politics of Education Reform 1920–1940*. London: Lawrence & Wishart.

-- (1986) 'The 1944 Education Act: A Conservative measure?' *History of Education* 15(1), 31–43.

Simon, E. and Hubback, E. (1935) *Training for Citizenship*. London: Association for Education in Citizenship.

Simon, J. (1989) 'Promoting educational reform on the home front: The *TES* and *The Times* 1940–1944'. *History of Education* 18(3), 195–211.

Simpson, J.H. (1936) *Sane Schooling: A record and a criticism of school life*. London: Faber & Faber.

Smith, D. (1987) *The Everyday World as Problematic: A feminist sociology*. Boston: Northeaster University Press.

Smith, L. (2008) *Young Voices: British children remember the Second World War*. Harmondsworth: Penguin/Imperial War Museum.

Smith, M. (1998) *Democracy in a Depression: Britain in the 1920s and 1930s*. Llandybie: University of Wales Press.

Somerville, M. (1945) 'School broadcasting'. *BBC Yearbook 1945*. London: BBC.

Song, M. (2001) 'Chinese children's work roles in immigrant adaptation'. In P. Mizen, C. Pole and A. Bolton (eds) *Hidden Hands: International perspectives on children's work and labour*. London: RoutledgeFalmer.

Spence, J. (2001) 'The impact of the First World War on the development of youth work: the case of the Sunderland Waifs Rescue Agency and Street Vendors Club'. In R. Gilchrist, T. Jeffs and J. Spence (eds) *Essays in the History of Community and Youth Work*. Leicester: Youth Work Press.

Spencer, F.H. (1941) *Education for the People*. London: Routledge.

Spring Rice, M. (1939) *Working Class Wives*. London: Pelican.

Springhall, J. (1977) *Youth, Empire and Society: British youth movements 1883–1940*. London: Croom Helm.

-- (1986) *Coming of Age: Adolescence in Britain 1860–1960*. Dublin: Gill & Macmillan.

Stacey, M. (1981) 'The division of labour revisited, or overcoming the two Adams'. In P. Abrams, R. Deem, J. Finch and P. Roch (eds) *Practice and Progress in British Sociology 1950–1980*. London: Allen & Unwin.

Stargardt, N. (2005) *Witnesses of War: Children's lives under the Nazis*. London: Jonathan Cape.

Starns, P.E. and Parsons, M.L. (2002) 'Against their will: The use and abuse of British children during the Second World War'. In J. Marten (ed.) *Children and War*. New York: New York University Press.

Stedman Jones, G. (1971) *Outcast London: A study in the relationship between social classes in Victorian society*. Oxford: Oxford University Press.

Steedman, C. (1990) *Childhood, Culture and Class in Britain: Margaret McMillan 1860–1931*. London: Virago.

Stewart, W.A.C. (1967) *Karl Mannheim on Education and Social Thought*. London: Institute of Education, University of London.

Stewart Brown, P. (1966) *The Big Test*. London: Girl Guides Association.

Stranack, D. (2005) *Schools at War: A study of education, evacuation and endurance in the Second World War*. Chichester: Phillimore.

Streatfeild, N. (1937) *Ballet Shoes*. London: Penguin.

-- (1941) *The Children of Primrose Lane*. London: J.M. Dent.

Street, A.G. (1943) *Hitler's Whistle*. London: Eyre & Spottiswoode.

Sutherland, G. (1984) *Ability, Merit and Mental Measurement: Mental testing and English Education 1880–1940*. Oxford: Clarendon Press.

-- (2000) 'Review of M. Lavalette (ed.) *A Thing of the Past? Child labour in Britain in the nineteenth and twentieth centuries*'. *Bulletin of the Social History Society* 25.

Swan, P. (1989) *The British Documentary Film Movement 1926–46*. Cambridge: Cambridge University Press.

Sylva, K., Melhuish, E., Sammons, P., Siraj-Blatchford, I., Taggart, B. and Eliot, K. (2003) *Effective Provision of Pre-school Education (EPPE) Project: Findings from the pre-school project* (Research Brief no. RBX15–03). London: Institute of Education, University of London.

Sylva, K., Melhuish, E., Sammons, P., Siraj-Blatchford, I. and Taggart, B. (2004) *The Final Report: Effective pre-school education*. London: Institute of Education, University of London.

Tanner, J.M. (1981) *A History of the Study of Human Growth*. Cambridge: Cambridge University Press.

Tawney, R.H. (1924) *Secondary Education for All*. London: Labour Party.

-- (1934) *The School Age and Juvenile Unemployment*. London: Workers' Educational Association.

-- (1936) *The School Age and Exemptions*. London: Workers' Educational Association.

-- (1973) 'Keep the workers' children in their place', *Daily News*, 14 February 1918, reprinted in W. Van der Eyken (ed.) *Education, the Child and Society: A documentary history 1900–1973*. Harmondsworth: Penguin.

-- (1981) 'Why Britain fights'. In R.H. Tawney, *The Attack and Other Papers*. Nottingham: Spokesman. Paper first published 1940.

Taylor, A.J.P. (1965) *English History 1914–1945*. Oxford: Oxford University Press.

Thane, P. (1993) 'Women in the British Labour Party and the construction of state welfare 1906–39'. In S. Koven and S. Michel (eds) *Mothers of a New World: Maternalist politics and the origins of welfare states.* New York and London: Routledge.

-- (2004) 'Girton graduates: Earning and learning 1920s–1980s'. *Women's History Review* 13(3), 347–61.

Thomas, J.M. (2005) 'The work of the Special Areas Commission: Schemes for social improvement 1934–9'. Unpublished PhD thesis, University of London.

Thorpe, A. (2008) *A History of the British Labour Party,* Third edition. London: Palgrave Macmillan.

Tinkler, P. (1987) 'Learning through leisure: Feminine ideology in girls magazines 1920–1950'. In F. Hunt (ed.) *Lessons for Life: The schooling of girls and women 1880–1950.* Oxford: Basil Blackwell.

Titmuss, R. (1966) 'War and social policy'. In R. Titmuss, *Essays on the Welfare State.* London: Unwin University Books.

-- (1976) *Problems of Social Policy.* London: HMSO. First published 1950.

Tizard, B. (2010) *Home is Where One Starts From: One woman's memoir.* Edinburgh: Word Power Books.

Tizard, B. and Hughes, M. (1984) *Young Children Learning: Talking and thinking at home and at school.* London: Fontana.

Todd, S. (2005) *Young Women, Work and Family in England 1918–1950.* Oxford: Oxford University Press.

Tomlinson, R.R. (1947) *Children as Artists.* London: King Penguin.

Trades Union Congress (TUC) Annual Reports for 1926, 1927, 1932, 1934, 1936, 1941, 1949. London: TUC.

Truby King, F. (1942) *Feeding and Care of Baby.* Christchurch, NZ: Whitcomb & Tombs, and London: Oxford University Press. First published 1913.

Turnbull, A. (2001) 'Gendering young people – work, leisure and girls clubs: The work of the Nation Organisation of Girls Clubs and its successors 1911–1961'. In R. Gilchrist, T. Jeffs and J. Spence (eds) *Essays in the History of Community and Youth Work*. Leicester: Youth Work Press.

Tyler, N. (1996) *They Fought in the Fields: The Women's Land Army – the story of a forgotten victory*. London: Sinclair-Stevenson.

United Nations (UN) (1989) *Convention on the Rights of the Child (UNCRC)*. New York: Office of the High Commissioner for Human Rights. <http://www2.ohchr.org/english/law/crc.htm> (accessed 12 January 2011).

Urwick, E.J. (ed.) (1904) *Studies of Boy Life in our Cities: Written by various authors for the Toynbee Trust*. London: J.M. Dent.

Van der Eyken, W. (ed.) (1973) *Education, the Child and Society: A documentary history 1900–1973*. Harmondsworth: Penguin.

Van der Eyken, W. and Turner, B. (1969) *Adventures in Education*. London: Allen Lane Penguin.

Wade, A. and Smart, C. (2005) 'Continuity and change in parent–child relations over three generations' (Award number ROOO 239523). Final report to the Economic and Social Research Council.

Wallman, S. (ed.) (1979) *Anthropology of Work*. London: Bedford Square Press.

Walvin, J. (1982) *A Child's World: A social history of English childhood 1800–1914*. Harmondsworth: Penguin.

Ward, C. (1990) *The Child in the City*. London: Bedford Square Press.

Ward, S. (1988) *War in the Countryside 1939–45*. London: Cameron Books.

Watson, J.B. (1928) *The Psychological Care of the Infant and Child*. London: Allen & Unwin.

Webster, C. (1983) 'The health of the school child during the Depression'. In N. Parry and D. McNair (eds) *The Fitness of the Nation: Physical and health education in the nineteenth and twentieth centuries*. Leicester: History of Education Society.

-- (1985) 'Health, welfare and unemployment during the Depression'. *Past and Present* 109, 204–30.

Wedgwood, J.C. (1973) 'Debate on the 1917 Education Bill. Parliamentary debates, House of Commons, 10 August 1917', reprinted in W. Van der Eyken (ed.) *Education, the Child and Society: A documentary history 1900–1973*. Harmondsworth: Penguin.

Weller, S. (2007) *Teenagers' Citizenship: Experiences and education*. London: Routledge.

Welshman, J. (2010) *Churchill's Children: The evacuee experience in wartime Britain*. Oxford: Oxford University Press.

Westall, R. (1985) *Children of the Blitz: Memories of wartime childhood*. London: Viking.

Whitney, B. (1999) 'Unenforced or unenforceable? A view from the professions'. In M. Lavalette (ed.) *A Thing of the Past? Child labour in Britain in the nineteenth and twentieth centuries*. Liverpool: Liverpool University Press.

Whitty, G. (1997) *Social Theory and Educational Policy: The legacy of Karl Mannheim*. London: Institute of Education, University of London.

Wicks, B. (1988) *No Time to Wave Goodbye*. London: Bloomsbury.

Williams, R. (1961) *Culture and Society 1780–1950*. Harmondsworth: Penguin.

Williams, S. (2000) *Ladies of Influence: Women of the elite in inter-war Britain*. Harmondsworth: Penguin.

-- (2004) 'Domestic science: The education of girls at home'. In R. Aldrich (ed.) *Public or Private Education: Lessons from history*. London: Woburn Press.

Williams, S., Ivin, P. and Morse, C. (2001) *The Children of London: Attendance and welfare at school 1870–1990*. London: Institute of Education, University of London.

Wilson, E. (1977) *Women and the Welfare State*. London: Tavistock.

Wisley, C. (ed.) (2009) *A Companion to Early Twentieth Century Britain*. Oxford: Wiley-Blackwell.

Wood, D. and Dempster, D. (1961) *The Narrow Margin: The Battle of Britain and the rise of air power 1930–1940*. London: Hutchinson.

Woodhead, E.W. (1943) *Education Handbook No. 1*. London: Jarrold.

-- (1944) *Education Handbook No. 2*. London: Jarrold.

Woolf, V. (1982). 'Introductory letter'. In M. Llewelyn Davies (ed.) *Life as We Have Known It: By Co-operative working women*. London: Virago. First published 1931.

Zelizer, V. (1985) *Pricing the Priceless Child: The changing social value of children*. New York: Basic Books.

-- (2005) 'The priceless child revisited'. In J. Qvortrup (ed.) *Studies in Modern Childhood: Society, agency, culture*. London: Palgrave Macmillan.

Page numbers in *italics* refer to illustrations